LETTERS TO
VIMY

ORLAND FRENCH

ARPress
ILLUMINATING IDEAS
EMPOWERING VOICES

ARPress
45 Dan Road Suite 5
Canton MA 02021

Hotline:	1(888) 821-0229
Fax:	1(508) 545-7580

Ordering Information:

Quantity sales. Special discounts are available on quantity purchases by corporations, associations, and others. For details, contact the publisher at the address above.

Printed in the United States of America.

ISBN-13:	Paperback	979-8-89356-457-0
	eBook	979-8-89356-456-3

Library of Congress Control Number: 2024904569

ABOUT THE AUTHOR

ORLAND FRENCH grew up in Waverley, Ontario, a couple of kilometres from the farm where his Uncle Oscar was raised. This little crossroads village near Georgian Bay is nestled in a valley among the glacial hills of northern Simcoe County. Orland worked in the newsrooms of *The Ottawa Citizen* and *The Globe and Mail* and was a regular *Globe* columnist covering provincial and national politics. Later he taught journalism at Loyalist College in Belleville, Ontario and developed an interest in local history. For a decade, he was president of the Hastings County Historical Society. His interest led to producing history and geology books on the counties of Prince Edward, Lennox & Addington, and Hastings. He also advised clients on developing their own local history books through the Friesens History Book Program. For his work as a volunteer in history-related projects, he was awarded the Queen Elizabeth II Diamond Jubilee medal in 2012 and the Governor-General's Caring Canadian Award in 2013. *Letters to Vimy* bridges the gap of a century between the years of the First World War and today. It serves as a teaching tool and learning mechanism for readers of the book. Mr. French is pleased that younger members of the family began to develop an interest in their great-great-Uncle Oscar as the author worked on this project.

Time, like an ever-rolling stream,
Bears all of us away;
We fly, forgotten, as a dream
Dies at the opening day.

From "O God Our Help in Ages Past", by Isaac Watts, 1719 (using modern inclusive language), often sung at Remembrance Day ceremonies. In our family visit to Nine Elms Military Cemetery, we sang this in a little graveside ceremony for Uncle Oscar.

Thanks to the Family of Uncle Oscar French

Writing a book often seems like a lonely, solitary exercise, but clearly it isn't. It is often inspired by circumstances. If Uncle Oscar hadn't written letters home to his mother, if my grandmother hadn't saved them, and my parents and my brother Gerald hadn't done likewise, if I had not developed an interest in history, I wouldn't have written this book. So, I want to acknowledge the lineage that led to the publication of *Letters to Vimy*:

My uncle, Pte. Oscar French, who took the loving care and precious time to write faithfully to his mother throughout his two-year experience with the Canadian Expeditionary Force;

My grandmother, Mrs. Samuel French (nee Emily Hodges), who saved Uncle Oscar's letters in a little flower-print box all her life;

My father, Oscar's favourite little brother Elmer, and my mother **Eunice (nee Grigg),** who saved the box in an old trunk full of family collectables in the family home in Waverley;

My brother, Gerald Oscar French, who saved the box in the same old trunk in his garage until his death in 2010;

My sister, Patricia Chernesky, and her husband Richard, who organized and directed our tour of Vimy Ridge in October 2013;

My brother, Warren French, and his wife Eileen, who provided financial assistance to publish this book;

My wife Sylvia who provided valuable proofreading and editorial services; and

My various nieces and nephews, who expressed genuine interest in learning about a long-dead great-uncle who died in a war almost totally buried in their sense of history.

Thanks also to Lt.-Col. Ian Sutherland (Ret'd), who read over my manuscript for errors and gaffes and misinterpretations relating to the military and political history of the First World War.

I was also inspired by author Susan Evans Shaw, who wrote the following in the preface of her book *Canadians at War*:

My grandfather, Captain James Lloyd Evans, died in battle on September 1, 1918.

When my grandmother died in 1969, my aunt Gwladys found an old suitcase full of letters Jim had written during the war. My aunt couldn't face the painful memories and gave them to my father. Some years later, Dad suggested I might like to have a look at them. Not only did I read every letter, but I set to work transcribing them for a family publication. The sad enormity of the loss of my grandfather became clear. A shadowy figure, about whom I had occasionally boasted as a child, now had flesh and personality. Jim Evans had been a loving husband, devoted father, and a soldier to the very core of his being.

I saw my grandfather's death as a pointless waste in a wasteful and pointless war.

(Used with permission)

I too set about reading all of Uncle Oscar's letters and transcribing them for a family publication. Then I got thinking about creating a fictional correspondence with him a hundred years later. I went to France and stood at his grave, and this book began to take shape.

Official portrait of Pte. Oscar French

Oscar's parents, Samuel and Emily French of
Waverley, Ontario.
French family archives

Oscar, child in centre, and his family, Samuel and Emily French and siblings. French family archives.

TABLE OF CONTENTS

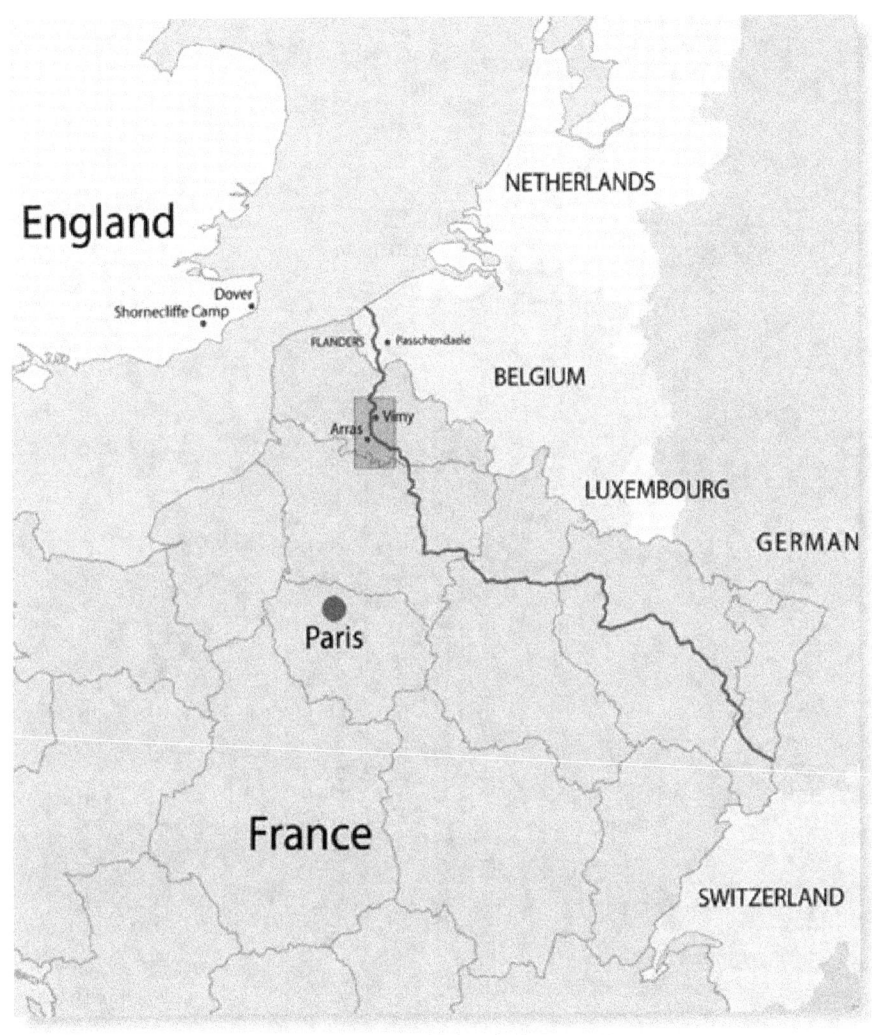

Vimy in northeastern France
on the front line of battle
Joe VanVeenen map

England

NETHERLANDS

Dover
Shorncliffe Camp

FLANDERS • Passchendaele

BELGIUM

Vimy
Arras

LUXEMBOURG

GERMAN

Paris

France

SWITZERLAND

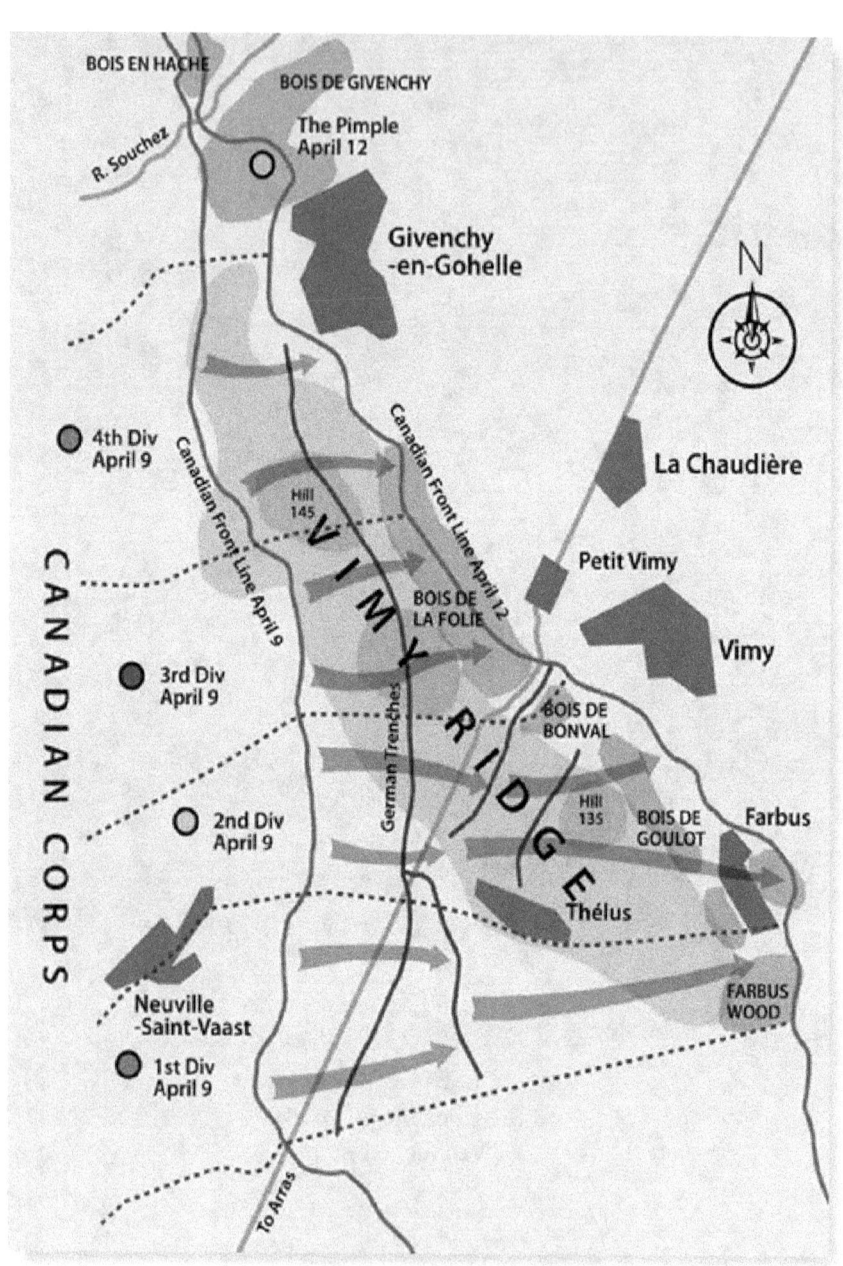

Details of the Vimy attack showing
locations of Canadian divisions
Joe VanVeenen map

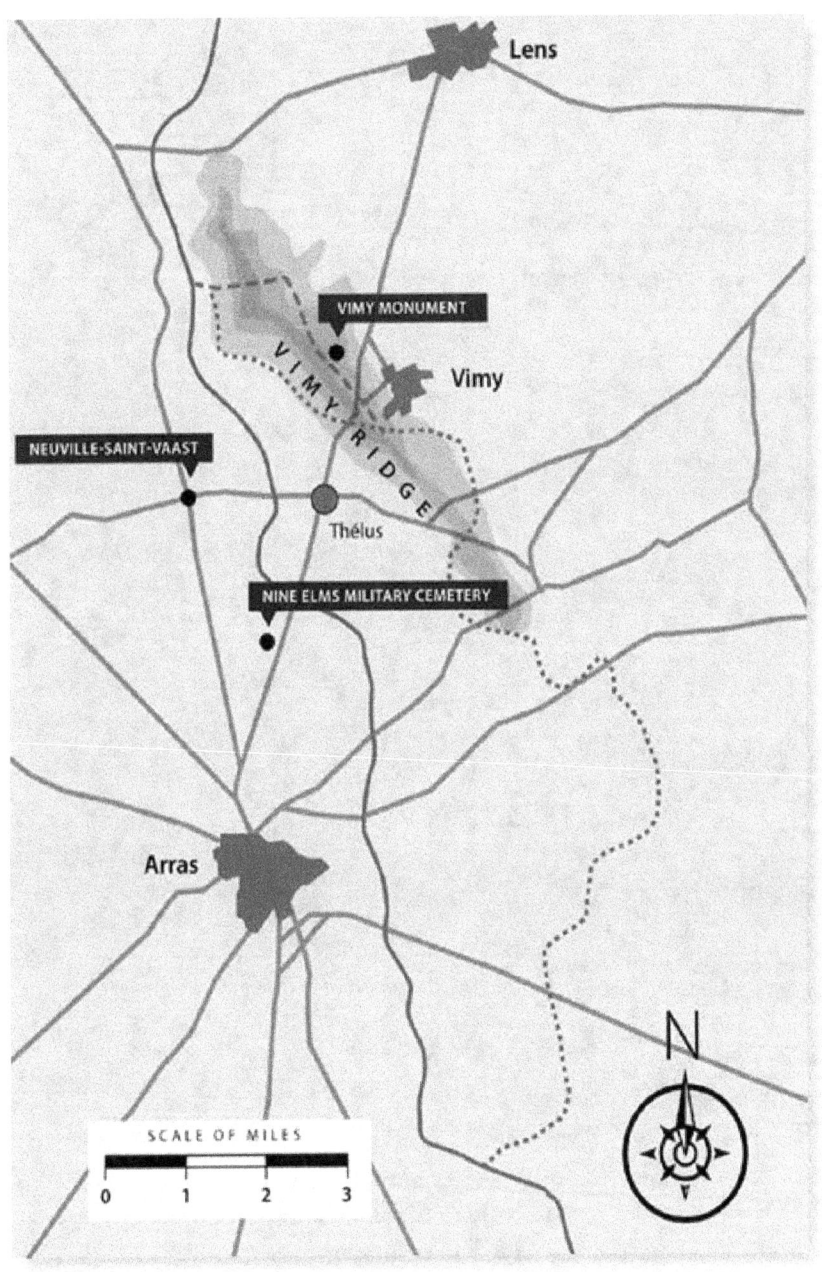

Locations of certain monuments
and cemeteries at Vimy
Joe VanVeenen map

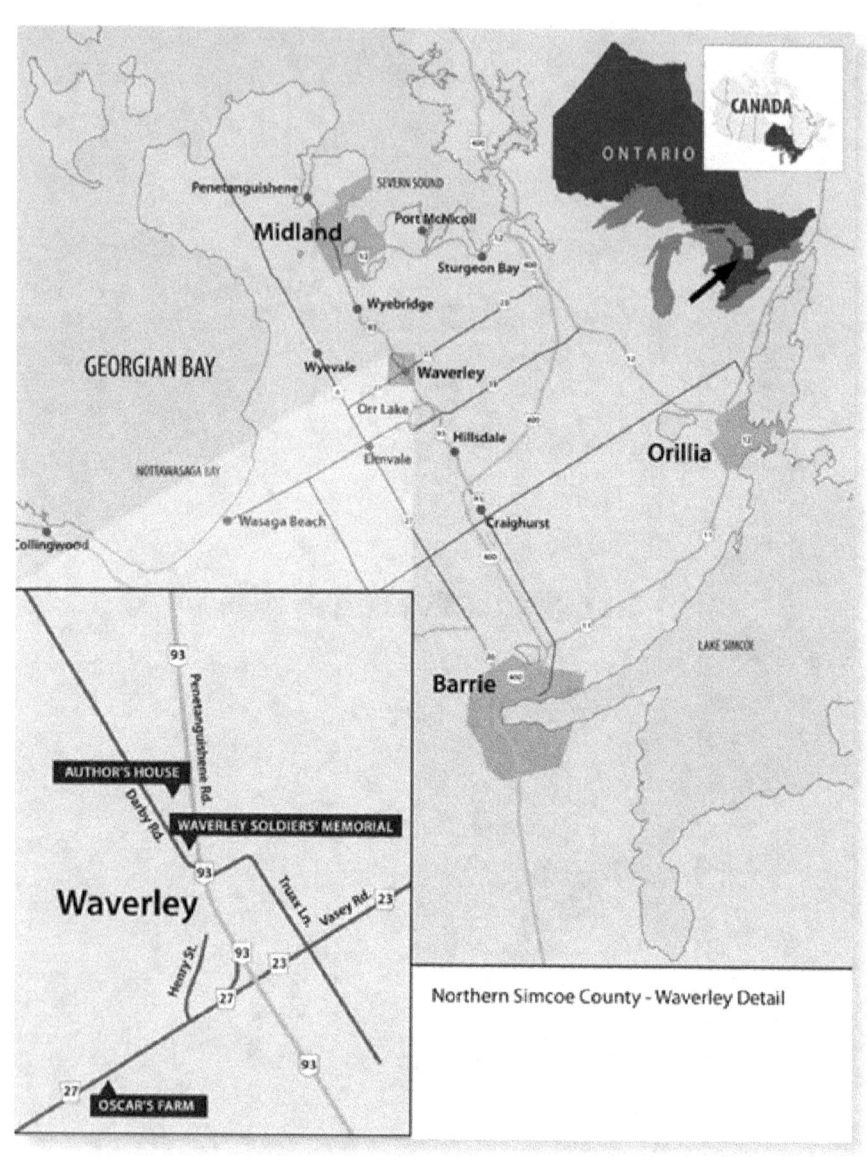

Location of Waverley and Oscar French's farm
in northern Simcoe County
Joe VanVeenen map

PART ONE: LETTERS TO
VIMY

Orland French, nephew of Oscar French, imagines what it would be like to exchange correspondence with his uncle a hundred years after his death at Vimy Ridge in 1917.

The Mail as a Weapon of Victory

GETTING THE MAIL to soldiers in the field, and the return of mail from them to their families in Canada, was very important for morale both at home and abroad in the First World War. Every effort was made to move the mail as expeditiously as possible. Given the millions of items handled, the speed with which the mail moved in wartime a century ago seems miraculous today. Details of the British and Canadian wartime postal systems are found in the chapter on Problems with the Mail.

INTRODUCTION: PTE. OSCAR FRENCH GOES TO WAR

BY THE EARLY SUMMER of 1915, the First World War was going badly for all sides. The whole world knew that the military struggle of European empires would be a long and bloody confrontation. The boys who had rushed to sign up the previous autumn lest the war end early, before Christmas, had become seasoned soldiers or dead men. Christmas 1914 had come and gone, Easter 1915 had come and gone, and nobody talked of getting home before Christmas 1915. It too would come and go, as would Christmas 1916, then Christmas 1917, and on and on, week by bloody week, before the war was halted just one month before Christmas 1918. The blood of thousands, and tens of thousands, and hundreds of thousands, would stain the soil of Europe before all the exhausted armies quit fighting in November 1918.

The first Canadian troops into France, the Princess Patricia's Canadian Light Infantry, arrived in December 1914. The 1st Canadian Division reached France in early February 1915. April brought the first green growth of spring and also a sample of the true horrors of modern warfare. The Germans introduced poison gas in an effort to drive the Allied forces from the Ypres Salient, a bulge in the line near the city of Ypres in Belgium. The Canadians fought valiantly and began to establish the Canadian reputation as a bunch of tough buggers. But in 48 hours of fighting, the Canadians suffered 6,035 casualties, including more than 2,000 dead.

The body counts, as we call them now, were reported in the papers.

And yet young men, well aware of the potential horrific consequences, continued to sign up for King and Country. Recruiting pressure was intense. Patriotism flowed like sticky molasses over the nation, and you'd better have a darned good reason for not signing up if you were young and able.

My uncle, Oscar French, was one of those susceptible young men. A teenager, actually. Only 18. High school age but old enough to go to war, to kill or be killed.

Oscar was a teenager off a farm in Waverley, Ontario; one of those young and able lads ready to serve as fodder in the trenches. Of course, nobody went to war intending to get killed. That would happen to some, of course, but the odds were in favour of you returning. Maybe wounded, maybe gassed, maybe mentally unhinged, but you'd likely come back and have a grand adventure to talk about. You would have sailed the Atlantic, seen Buckingham Palace, downed a pint in a British pub, dodged death and done a thousand things you could never expect to experience if you plodded through life ploughing the fields in Waverley.

Or you could be dead. But what an adventure-packed, short life you would have had, having seen London and all that first, before marching into a hailstorm of Hunnish bullets.

As he attended classes in Midland High School, perhaps Oscar wasn't paying too much attention to his lessons. He was no doubt musing on the possibility of signing up to go fight in Europe. His buddies from Waverley were joining up. George Reynolds and Oscar said farewell to their friends and family and shipped off to their training at Niagara Camp on the same day in April. They died on the same day in France and would share an eternity together under the sod in the same cemetery near Vimy Ridge. Billie Quinlan signed up and died in the battle for the Ypres Salient. Not only didn't he come back, they couldn't scrape together enough of him to give him a battlefield burial. His name is one of 55,000 entries carved into the Menin Gate in Ypres, commemorating men whose bodies were vaporized or shredded on bloody battlefields.

Luke Adamson had gone over the top, in a manner of speaking, by signing up. So had Billie Faragher. On June 5, 1915, Oscar succumbed to social pressure and his own emotions. He applied for enlistment. His application was approved at Niagara Camp on June 15. He was 18. (Official records vary on his date of birth. The birthdate on the family headstone in Waverley sets his birthdate as December 30, 1896, so we'll go with that. The family ought to know, but headstones have been known to be wrong.)

His regimental number was 408445. In military parlance, it was to become an integral part of his name.

I never learned much about Uncle Oscar from my relatives. My dad, Elmer, the youngest child in the family of 12, was only five when Oscar went to war. Although Dad was often mentioned in Oscar's letters as one of his favourites, my father didn't have much recollection of his sibling. To me, Oscar was an unknown young man who had marched away to a war, far distant in time and place, and gotten killed. Pretty much end of story.

Now that I want to know more about him, all of his contacts are long dead. But I came into possession of a series of letters he wrote home to his mother, who was my grandmother. From his letters, I have been able to glean hints of his interests and passions. He didn't tell his mother about the horrors and deprivations of the war; he was mostly her loving son telling her about the weather, some of the places he visited, and asking a lot of questions about the family's activities. Keeping in touch, sustaining his own morale. And hers. A handwriting expert told me that, in her opinion, not only was he aware that he was withholding the realities of war from his mother, he was denying them to himself.

As I read through his letters from France, which are reprinted in their entirety elsewhere in this book, I came to an odd realization: The only link I have with my family of that era is through letters written by a lonely soldier sitting in a tent or trench several thousand kilometers away a century ago.

There were little hints about life in Waverley as he commented on letters he had received from his mother. For instance, there must have been an arsonist on the loose in October 1915. Oscar wrote to his mother, "Billie Parker must be having quite a time of it, sitting up at nights now watching his store. Somebody around there must want a chance to see the Waverley fire brigade in action."

In my childhood, I had two visible links with Uncle Oscar: One was an official portrait in an elaborate oval frame that rested in the back of a closet of my family's home. The other was a portrait in stone of a soldier in First World War gear atop a monument at Waverley. The Waverley Soldiers' Memorial was donated by the Patriotic Ladies of Waverley in 1920 to commemorate the dead of the First World War. Later, stones were added to honour the dead of the Second World War. When I was a kid, the stone figure in First World War kit seemed that of an older man. Only when I was much older myself and interested in this project did I become aware that the figure was actually of a very young man, probably a teenager. About Oscar's age. I can see that now.

Most of what I know of Oscar is listed in his attestation papers in Library and Archives Canada. Here is what I gleaned from that document:

Oscar French, of Waverley, Ontario, born December 30, 1897 (as stated earlier, I believe he was born December 30, 1896), father named Samuel French, of Waverley, Ontario, a farmer, unmarried, Methodist, willing to be vaccinated, no experience in the militia or any other military force. Oscar answered "yes" to two critical questions, which would have seemed routine at the time: (a) Do you understand the nature and terms of your engagement? (b) Are you willing to be attested to serve in the Canadian Over-Seas Expeditionary Force? Well, of course he answered "yes" to both. To answer "no" would have meant rejection. Gaining acceptance was the whole point of enlistment, but the authorities took pains to ensure that he knew and approved the nature of the engagement. The attestation paper was further signed by a magistrate, who stated, "The Recruit above-named was cautioned by me that if he made any false answer to any of the above questions, he would be liable to be punished as provided in the Army Act.

"The above questions were then read to the Recruit in my presence.

"I have taken care that he understands each question, and that his answer to each question has been duly entered as replied to, and the said Recruit has made and signed the declaration and taken the oath before me, at Niagara, this 5th day of June 1915." The signature is illegible.

And what did Uncle Oscar agree to?

"I, Oscar French, do solemnly declare that the above answers made by me to the above questions are true, and that I am willing to fulfill the engagements by me now made, and I hereby engage and agree to serve in the Canadian Over-Seas Expeditionary Force, and to be attached to any arm of the service therein, for the term of one year, or during the war now existing between Great Britain and Germany should that war last longer than one year, and for six months after the termination of that war provided His Majesty should so long require my services, or until legally discharged."

Furthermore, Uncle Oscar took an oath of loyalty to the king and his heirs and successors.

"I, Oscar French, do make Oath, that I will be faithful and bear true allegiance to His Majesty King George the Fifth, His Heirs and Successors, and that I will as in duty bound honestly and faithfully defend His Majesty, His Heirs and Successors, in Person, Crown and Dignity, against all enemies, and will observe and obey all orders of His Majesty, His Heirs and Successors, and of all the Generals and Officers set over me. So help me God."

So swore an 18-year-old youth from Waverley, of complexion sallow, eyes hazel, hair brown, standing fearlessly before the magistrate and the recruiting officer, ready to don a uniform and head overseas, weapon in hand, to do battle with the Hun. He eventually became a master of one of the most efficient killing machines of the war: the machine gun. I like to think of him as a gentle man, like my father, who wouldn't hurt a sparrow. When in my teens I purchased a mail-order .22 rifle (from Eaton's for about $16), Dad warned me that I was not to go about shooting little birds. Groundhogs, maybe, but not birds.

I'd like to think Uncle Oscar was of that kindly nature. But I have no idea how many Germans he mowed down with his machine gun. (Since it took a crew of several men to operate a machine gun, he wasn't necessarily pulling the trigger. However, in his letters he makes mention of how proficient he was with both rifle and machine gun. He admired the fact that it could fire 500 rounds a minute. I can see him squatting or kneeling in the mud, finger holding the machine-gun trigger as 500 bullets a minute spewed out of the muzzle and scythed down the advancing enemy.)

Off he went to train with the 37th Battalion. The 37th Battalion was drawn from Northern Ontario, of which Waverley in northern Simcoe County was considered part. We didn't send raw recruits overseas. They received training in Canada, and then in Britain, all the time chafing to get to the front lines.

Oscar first buttoned up his uniform at Niagara-on-the-Lake in June 1915. On occasion he proudly signed himself as "Pte. O. French, Machine Gun Section, 37th Battalion, No. 408445." Usually it was "your loving son, Oscar."

Like his buddies, he itched to get on the train heading for Halifax and the trans-Atlantic crossing. He often mentioned his friends Billie Quinlan and George Reynolds, wondering what had become of them. They obviously both made it to France, for in the end, they share a public space with Uncle Oscar. Their names are also on the Waverley memorial to the dead. Billie Quinlan's is immediately above Oscar's.

The last letter Oscar wrote in Canada was on the train over the night of November 26-27, on the way to Halifax. His next letter, undated, was from Bramshott Camp, Liphook, Hants, England, around December 5. Liphook is southwest of London, near Portsmouth.

Bramshott has a reputation for being one of the most haunted villages in Britain. It claims to have 17 ghosts, including that of the silver screen master of horror, Boris Karloff, who lived in the village until his death. Mind you, that piece of trivia has nothing to do with Uncle Oscar's military career, since Karloff died in 1969, although some of the other 16 ghosts may have been hanging around the local pubs during Oscar's stint in Bramshott.

Training at Bramshott continued until February, when he was transferred to Shorncliffe, near Folkestone southeast of London, on the coast near Dover. It was almost within earshot of the cannons in France. On June 24, he wrote from Shorncliffe, saying he would be leaving next morning with 350 infantrymen and 40 machine gunners. His next letter, two days later, was datelined "somewhere in France" where the big issue seemed to be "trying to make the French shopkeepers understand when we want to buy anything."

It had been barely a year from the time of his recruitment until he reached the battle lines in France.

For security purposes, "somewhere in France" became his unspecific address until it changed permanently forever and ever to Nine Elms Military Cemetery, Thelus, France.

If Uncle Oscar had returned from the war and lived a healthy life, he might well have reached the 1970s or 1980s. He would have seen for himself the Second World War (who knows, he might have reenlisted to fight Hitler, wishing he had plugged the Chief Nazi in the First World War), the emergence of a vibrant post-war Ontario economy, travel by jet plane, and the first men to walk on the moon, via television.

In most of my letters, I have repeated the relevant excerpt from his correspondence at the beginning, so the reader will have a reference point. Uncle Oscar's letters are reprinted in their entirety in the second section of the book. Readers may notice differences in editing styles between Oscar's letters and my text. I did not amend his letters to conform with contemporary style.

For the reader, I hope I have written an entertaining and informative account of the First World War from an innovative perspective – a nephew and his uncle having a chat across a hundred years of history.

HELLO, I'M YOUR NEPHEW

January 2016
Canada

Dear Uncle Oscar:

Though you have been dead for many years – almost a century – I feel a strong desire to write to you. You have never heard of me for the very simple reason that I was born 27 years after you died. My name is Orland Clare French, and I am the third son of little Elmer, your kid brother you spoke of so fondly in your letters to your mother. I am your nephew.

Your mother, Emily, was my grandmother, whom you always addressed respectfully as "Dear Mother" and to whom you sent your letters addressed to "Mrs. Samuel French, Waverley, Ontario." You could not know this, but your dear mother saved the letters you wrote to her during your adventures with the Canadian Expeditionary Force in the First World War. Of course, you didn't call it the First World War, because you could not have known there would be another, arguably more horrendous, Second World War. You may have known your conflict as "The Great War" or the optimistically grandiose descriptive, "the war to end all wars," which we now know it wasn't.

I am writing to you from a hundred years hence, in your time. These letters to you have been prepared, in a general sense, on the one-hundredth anniversary of what we call the First World War, World War I, or WWI. I came into possession of your letters after my older brother, Gerald Oscar French, died in 2010. He was Elmer's first-born, and you can see he was named in honour of you. Elmer repaid your fondness for him. Your mother packed your letters tightly in a flower-print cardboard box, along with some other official papers and memorabilia I will describe in due time. They were placed in an old wooden chest along with other family mementoes, where they rested in the upstairs hall in the family home in Waverley for many decades.

That home was the stucco house just north of the Waverley memorial or cenotaph. Excuse me, you couldn't know about the cenotaph, of course. It wasn't built until after the war to commemorate all the men from the area who died in battle. On the singular column, it bears the names of you and your friends who didn't return from the war. There are 88 names in total. I wonder how many you knew.

The farm near Waverley, circa 1920s, where Oscar grew up.
French family archives

But back to the house. It was the one your parents moved to when your brother Owen took over the farm. I lived in the house from the time I was born until I went to college. My bedroom was the west one, with the arched window. The trunk with your letters, and other keepsakes of the time, sat in the hallway outside my parents' bedroom all the time I was growing up. It was rarely opened. When my mother died, the trunk and its box of letters were moved to Gerald's home in Barrie, where they continued to languish in storage, gaining antiquity with every passing year. When he died, I recovered them from the old trunk and began reading them.

I knew nothing about you, except that you were one of Dad's older brothers and that you enlisted with the army and were killed in the war. If there is an afterlife, I assume that is where you are, but I hope they have gotten you out of those muddy, lice-ridden uniforms and into some decent civvies. In the afterlife, do you have a memory of your previous life?

Do you remember that awful day on Vimy Ridge where you and your crew trained your machine gun on the enemy? Do you recall the choking smoke, the gritty dust, the ear-thumping noise of battle, the whine of bullets and the stuttering of machine-gun fire, the burst of shells, the cries and screams and moans of dying men? Do you recall the whistling approach of a shell with your name on it, just before oblivion?

Do you know you were one of about 65,000 Canadian soldiers who died on the battlefields of the First World War? That on the Easter Monday of April 9, 1917, you were one of 37 machine-gunners killed in the battle to secure a spine of shell-scarred farmland called Vimy Ridge?

You were most gracious and kind to your mother, keeping a pledge to write to her frequently. Your letters were always most reassuring, never hinting at the horrors of the battlefield right before your eyes. Other than asking for new boots, you never complained. I have the letter you wrote the day before you died, and there is not a hint in it that a horrific battle was looming. You wrote that you were having "a swell day" and that "the sun is shining, and it is warm as summer." Picnic weather. Some picnic. Your letter was brief; you said you were in "rather a poor place for writing." Perhaps sitting in a muddy trench or tunnel below Vimy Ridge, no doubt you were. The next day, Easter Monday, it was "over the top" at 5:30 a.m., onward and upward toward the heights of Vimy Ridge. You never made it. A shell got you as you tried to liberate the little village of Thelus on the southwest slope of the ridge.

Machine-gunners maintain their deadly weapons on Vimy Ridge. Machine-gun nests were grouped to protect each other and provide collective firepower.
Library and Archives Canada, MIKAN 3241489

You didn't die alone. Nearly 3,600 of your compatriots fell with you; another 7,000 were wounded. But if it's any consolation, the Canadian Corps drove off the Germans and took the ridge. That achievement, dislodging the Huns when the French and the British armies couldn't, is credited with giving Canada a sense of national identity. It is celebrated as a defining moment in the development of our nationhood. You were a part of that.

If you don't mind, I intend to publish your letters along with my responses. You have, still long after your death, something to contribute to the story of our country. I hope Canadians will find some interest in two lads from Waverley yakking about a long-ago war. I'll try to keep it lively.

Your nephew,
Orland

A FIVE-YEAR GUARANTEE

Exhibition Camp, Toronto
Spring 1915

I got a wristwatch with that money I was given. It is not a very fancy one, but I got a five-year guarantee with it and it has been running fine so far.

Dear Uncle Oscar:

In the *Elmvale Lance* of April 23, 1915, I read in the Waverley News that "George Reynolds and Oscar French of the 3rd Contingent made their last visit to parents and friends Sunday before leaving for Niagara." I hope you had a grand party. I assume you were given some money by your friends as a farewell gift when you left home. Sorry to tell you the brutal, honest truth, Uncle, but you won't be needing that five-year guarantee.

Your nephew,
Orland

THE HILLS OF WAVERLEY

Bramshott Camp
Liphook, Hants, England
November 1915

Well mother my first sight of England was certainly a grand one as I don't think I ever saw a more beautiful place than the harbour of Plymouth. The fields are quite green now and the high cliffs along the shore are covered with a reddish moss. The towns here look quaint to us and in the towns the streets are very narrow, and the houses are much more closer together than in Canadian towns. The fields in the country are laid out in all sorts of queer shapes and they are generally fenced with hedges.

Dear Uncle Oscar:

The first thing we have to do for our readers is set the scene. Few if any of them will recognize Waverley. It wasn't much more than a dot on the map when you were on the farm and, you know what? It's still a dot on the map. Originally, it bore the French family name and was known as "French's Corners," after farmland owned by our ancestors. The school property, and the Methodist church and cemetery too, were carved out of land owned by your grandfather, Thomas. After the rectangular layouts of farms in Canada, you would find the fields of England rather higgledy-piggledy. Roads the same, wandering over the landscape like a homeless pig or a drunken Englishman in search of a pub. Our roads run straight and true: square corners, square fields, square people.

Waverley among the hills. It's a pastoral setting. I can tell from your letters that you often longed to return to it, as soon as your job in Europe was done. Our home village of Waverley is a small cross-roads community lying in a bowl surrounded by gently rounded hills in Huronia, an area of north Simcoe County. To the north was Victoria Hill, to the south, Rowley's Hill, to the west, French's Hill, and to the east, Watt's Hill. The only way you could escape from Waverley without climbing a hill was to go north and skirt around the base of Victoria Hill.

If you peel back the layers of forestation and soil on the hills, you will find that they are nothing more than piles of sand and gravel, laid down by glaciers 13,000 years ago. The rolling hills are now pitted with holes where gravel has been removed, the farmers learning that the real wealth of their land lay beneath the soil, not in it. At least one construction company was born in Waverley, starting out with two men, two shovels, and a small truck.

The hills gave rise to an annual spring rite called "The Flood." The "Pond Field" on top of Victoria Hill would retain large amounts of water during the spring melt, until the pond broke through the snow retaining it and rushed down through the bush into a gravel pit next to our house, then on to a stream that flowed to Georgian Bay.

This little creek arose at the east side of Waverley, between the village and Watt's Hill, in a spring-fed pool (Bannister's Pond). The stream meandered northeast through a broadening valley towards Georgian Bay at Victoria Harbour. Over Rowley's Hill to the south lay Orr Lake, which was little more than a swamp flooded by a low dam at the west end. This mud-bottomed basin was our closest swimming hole, but returning home from it required a long bicycle climb up Rowley's Hill (usually we walked and pushed) that negated all the refreshing elements of the swim.

Out of Orr Lake flowed the Wye River, which rambled in a circuitous route through Elmvale to the west, before swinging north to Wyevale, then northeast through Wyebridge through the Wye Marsh into Midland Bay below Martyrs' Shrine. You may recall the story of Fathers Jean de Brebeuf and Gabriel Lalement martyred by Iroquois raiders in 1649. Martyrs' Shrine was built in 1925 to commemorate the murders, across from the location of a fort called Sainte-Marie among the Hurons.

From the top of French's Hill, a steep west-facing slope about a mile distant from the village, you could see the plain of the Wye. Below this hill spread out "Elmvale Flats," a legacy of the proglacial lake that formed with the retreat of the ice cap. In fact, when the glacier receded, the hills around Waverley appeared as an archipelago of islands in Lake Algonquin. From the top of the hill, you can easily see all the sweep of Nottawasaga Bay and the Blue Mountains across it and beyond. Your farm lay between Waverley and the hill.

Does this all sound nostalgically, achingly familiar?

In a larger context, Waverley was located north of Barrie, which was in turn north of Toronto. I don't know how long it took you to get to Toronto by train from Midland or Elmvale, but today a motorcar can easily make the trip in a little more than an hour. You wouldn't believe how wide and smooth our roads have become. It's just as well because there are no passenger trains in that part of Ontario. The automobile killed them. And sometimes our wide and smooth roads are so full of vehicles you could beat them with horses. The average speed in some cities is slower than in the days of horse-drawn carriages. 'Strue.

During all of your life on earth, and most of mine, Waverley was the crossroads intersection of the corners of four of Simcoe County's northern townships: Tiny, Tay, Flos, and Medonte. The first three, it was said, were named after the pet dogs of Lady Sarah Maitland, wife of Sir Peregrine Maitland, Lieutenant Governor of Upper Canada. I've sometimes wondered about that story. How do three townships wind up getting named after dogs? Maybe one day in exasperation Maitland said, "This country is going to the dogs!" and his wife said, "Okay, Perry-winkle. Let's name some townships after them."

Your dad's farm was in Flos Township. You remember the old Methodist Church in Waverley? I was very surprised to learn a few years ago that the church, now known as the United Church, had been preserved as a heritage building under the auspices of Tay Township. This seemed odd to me because it had always been in Flos Township. It turns out that in 1998, the township boundaries were realigned and all of Waverley was awarded to Tay Township. I don't know what Tay did to deserve this award, but they are very lucky fellows indeed!

It's a pretty part of the province, I think you'll agree. So sorry you never got back to it.

Your nephew,
Orland

BARROOM BRAWLERS FROM CANADA

June 13, 1915
Niagara-on-the-Lake

Billie Quinlan and George Reynolds left with the reinforcements last Wednesday and I guess they are well on their way across the ocean by now. I hated to see some of our fellows going and the rest of us staying behind.

Dear Uncle Oscar:

You are obviously anxious to get across the sea and into the fight. Well, that seems to be our nature. We like to display our loyalty to the Empire and show the world how tough we can be.

When you were a kid, about five or six years old, Canadian soldiers went off to Africa to fight in the Boer War (1899-1902). It was probably the first live war you were aware of, and perhaps it fueled a young boy's desire to someday become a soldier and a war hero.

In my day, at about the same age, in the 1950s, we had the Korean War, with lingering overtones of the Second World War. In the schoolyard – this would appall teachers today – we would form up regiments of juvenile snotty-nosed soldiers, arm ourselves with sticks, which became imaginary rifles in our hands, and engage in a firefight. We'd point the sticks at each other, go "ah-ah-ah-ah-ah" like a machine gun, and shout out, "I got you, Rick. You're dead." If Rick was co-operative, he would fall down dead, lie there for a few moments like a real body, then crawl back to his lines to recover miraculously and fight again. I don't remember any girls playing this game.

Our inventive minds confused history: The enemy soldiers were "Chinks" or "Gooks" (Korean War) wearing swastikas (Second World War Germans). These are unacceptable terms today, but PC – political correctness – hadn't been invented yet. We were Terry and the Pirates from the funny papers. Beyond all that were the mystical images from another war not yet faded into obscurity: those Germans who had gassed Uncle Verne and put a bullet through Uncle Oliver's mouth and sent you to your grave. We didn't know much about them, except we knew there was a captured German machine gun at the cenotaph. Sometimes we would creep up behind it, gently settle our knees into the knee sockets, and quietly go "ah-ah-ah-ah-ah." You didn't do it too loudly because that was somehow disrespectful of the dead, you guys listed on the obelisk at the cenotaph. Besides, we didn't know how to go "ah-ah-ah-ah-ah" in German.

So, our re-enactments of imaginary battles were fueled with images drawn from three wars. You, in turn, were influenced by Canadian exploits in the Boer War. It is regarded as the first overseas war in which Canadian troops participated. In fact, this was the largest military action undertaken by Canada since the country had been born in 1867. It was one more step on the road to Canada becoming a nation.

Some will object and say, "What about the Gordon Expedition to Khartoum?" Well, yes, Canadians guided the British boats up the Nile (apparently our expertise as wilderness canoeists was highly respected), but those lads were regarded as civilian employees. They did not wear uniforms.

You may remember that the Boer War, a.k.a. the South African War, was a dispute between Great Britain, a world military giant, and two small republics, Transvaal and Orange Free State, occupied by Boers who were descendants of Dutch immigrants. These two Afrikaner countries were surrounded by British territories and, considering they were up against the planet's strongest power, would seem to have been the underdogs.

The Boers posed no threat to Canada. It was highly unlikely they would come marching up the Penetanguishene Road from Barrie and lay siege to Waverley. Nevertheless, Britain's claim was popular in English Canada, and people were pestering the government of Sir Wilfrid Laurier to do something to help poor old Mother Britain. This attitude did not prevail in Quebec, or among recent immigrants to Canada, who wondered why on earth Canadians would want to run halfway around the globe to shoot at a bunch of Boer farmers who had never done a thing to them.

Ottawa and Pretoria are 13,000 kilometres (8,000 miles) apart. I saw a memorial stone in a cemetery on Amherst Island in Lake Ontario, near Kingston. The inscription reads, "To the memory of Corporal E.A. Filson, R.C.D. interred at Belfast, S.A. Nov. 7, 1900." I remember thinking it was a long way to go from an obscure island in Canada to an obscure battlefield in South Africa to find death. The RCDs (Royal Canadian Dragoons) spent 10 months in South Africa in 1900.

In the face of strong opposition in Quebec, Laurier reluctantly agreed to send a token force of 1,000 volunteer infantrymen. In time, more than 7,000 Canadians followed the sweet allure of gunsmoke to a different land in a different continent. One contingent, Strathcona's Horse, 500 mounted riflemen, was funded entirely by Lord Strathcona, the railway financier and high commissioner to the United Kingdom.

Of the Canadians sent to South Africa, 267 did not come home. That's a little less than four percent, somewhat less than the 10 percent who wound up under the sod or were blasted to bits in the First World War.

The thing about most British colonies was that if you wanted to go to war, you had to go overseas. Canadians could always pick a fight with our American neighbors next door, at our peril, but the Aussies and the Kiwis had to get in a boat to go find an enemy. The Aussies must have liked the warm climate of South Africa; about 20,000 showed up for the war. Around 500 died. New Zealanders put up a good show, sending more than 6,500 men and 8,000 horses, as well as doctors, nurses, and veterinarians.

The deaths of the soldiers were all their own doing, in a way. All the Canadians who clutched Mother Britain's apron strings in South Africa were volunteers. Nobody forced them to go. Laurier made sure of that; he didn't want to alienate his French-Canadian voters in Quebec. Those who went cited freedom, justice, and civilized behavior as reason enough to box the ears of the Boers. In reality, the fight was over control of lands that contained some of the world's richest gold and diamond mines. Did those poor sods from the colonies really think Britain would go to war with Boers over truth, justice, and orange groves? For individual participants, lofty ideals probably played second fiddle to their desire for adventure and a chance to see the world.

But why, given the might of Britain, the greatest military power in the world, did the Brits want help from its Empire? It was matter of testing allegiance. What's the point of having an empire if you can't draw on it in times of adversity? Britain could smell a major European conflict in the near future, particularly with Kaiser Bill building up a huge navy in Germany and treaties locking European nations into a pre-war dance step.

This feeling was captured in a couple of verses from "Marching on Pretoria," a popular song that emerged from the Boer War:

Hooraah! Hooraah! From hill and dale they come
Hooraah! Hooraah! They've made the business home
Round the world you heard that beat of Britain's ceaseless drum
When we went marching on Pretoria

Far from overseas our brothers flocked to join the flag
Joining us at British part was neither bluff nor brag
Foot to foot they stood with us beneath that dear old flag
When we went marching on Pretoria

In a larger war, Britain might need help from its colonies. And they responded, although they didn't have a lot of choice. Once Britain declared war, its dominions were automatically drawn in. The only option was to determine the depth of the commitment. For instance, Prime Minister Laurier vowed that Canada's volunteer force in South Africa was not a precedent for future conflicts, but it was. When Britain entered the First World War, so did Canada. We became automatic players on the world stage; because of our institutional, emotional, and historicties with Britain, we could not refuse. The *Statute of Westminster* in 1931 loosened the ties but still we responded. In every major international conflict in the last 70 years, we have played a role. Unlike our southern neighbour, we have never tried to be an isolationist country. Even where we have no direct interests at stake, it seems we can never turn down a barroom brawl. We kind of relish our reputation as a tough little kid.

Not that you would know anything about barroom brawls.

Your nephew, Orland, who has never once participated in a barroom brawl!

Your nephew,
Orland, who has never once participated in a barroom brawl!

FROM U-BOATS TO NUCLEAR BOMBS

Niagara Military Camp, August 22, 1915

...the German submarines have been very active this last week. I wonder if the sinking of the Arabic *will have any effect in drawing the United States into the war. I guess the Yankees will satisfy themselves by sending a few more friendly notes. I see there were two Americans drowned on the* Arabic...

Dear Uncle Oscar:

I note some impatience, in your recent letter, with American reluctance to enter the Great War. Well, they sure are an isolationist lot until their own comfort is threatened. When they finally get into a war, they usually come out on the winning side, and then they boast about saving the world.

The United States finally did enter your war, just before you died. Congress declared war on Germany on April 6, 1917, only three days before you were killed at Vimy Ridge. Maybe the shell got to you before the news.

Woodrow Wilson was U.S. president, you'll remember, and he had done his best to keep his country neutral. And, as you noted, even the occasional U-boat attack on shipping that killed Americans wasn't enough to draw the Yanks into the war. See, the Germans had special rules for the United States. They said they wouldn't attack American ships without warning, and if they did attack in error, they would try to help the passengers as much as possible. War brings out some strange logic.

Truth was, the Germans didn't have enough U-boats to command the seas. They were afraid that if the Americans came into the war, they'd be done like dinner. As it eventually turned out, they were right. But by early 1917, Germany had a huge fleet of U-boats and was ready to strut its stuff on the high seas. Altogether in the war they built 360 of them. (Speaking of strutting, you should have seen them goose-stepping their way across Europe in the 1930s and 1940s. They had this flag that looked like a pinwheel and an arm-stretching exercise where they shouted "Heil Hitler" to rouse support for their self-appointed human deity. Silly people. Silly but deadly.)

The Kaiser took the gloves off the torpedoes, as it were, and unleashed the underwater wolves of war. Any ship that could be construed as supplying aid to the allied forces was subject to puncturing by a German torpedo. The intent, as you are aware, was to prevent North American aid and armaments from reaching Britain and Europe.

Public sentiment in the U.S. was already turning strongly against Germany, especially after the publication of a diplomatic note called the Zimmerman Telegram. This was an astounding offer to Mexico to become Germany's ally. Here was the deal: Funded by Germany, Mexico would attack the United States on its southern border. When the war was over (assuming Germany would be victorious, of course), Mexico would be given Texas, New Mexico, and Arizona. These were former Mexican territories that had been lost to the United States in various military escapades. It was a no go. Mexico, preferring not to replace tacos with sauerkraut, rejected the deal. With increasing German attacks on American ships, Wilson had no choice but to seek permission to go to war. And away they went.

You would be interested to know that the pattern was repeated in the Second World War. That war, which was truly global, began with

German aggression in 1939, with all the goose-stepping I mentioned earlier. Germany soon overran all of continental Europe. Britain was on the verge of collapse, yet the Americans remained stubbornly out of the war. Then – remember I said they reacted when their own comfort was threatened? – Japan, allied with Germany, attacked the American naval base at Pearl Harbour and sank a large number of U.S. warships. It was like poking a wasp nest. Within days, the U.S. was at war with both Japan and Germany, and Italy too, the third member of the Axis.

Germany was defeated by the overwhelming military strength of its Allied enemies in May 1945. The Japanese surrendered in August after witnessing the brutal destruction of two of their cities by a pair of atomic bombs. That's right, one bomb, one city. Atomic bombs, hydrogen bombs – you have no idea what I'm talking about. All the explosives of Vimy Ridge and more wrapped up in one neat airborne package and delivered by a single airplane. Today, we can put them into radio-guided missiles and throw them anywhere around the world. With the push of a button, we can kill millions of people in one explosion.

Many of these missiles are stored in nuclear-powered submarines (modern-day U-boats) that can stay at sea, submerged, for weeks, even months, at a time. Because these weapons are so powerful, we have staved off nuclear war through a policy known as MAD – Mutually Assured Destruction. It was based on the assumption that any nuclear attack by one side would result in such a massive nuclear retaliation that both sides would be obliterated. Hence, Mutually Assured Destruction.

Mad, indeed. Oh, it's a wonderful world you've saved for us.

Your nephew,
Orland

A BUCK A DAY AND A DIME BONUS

Niagara Military Camp
A Company
37ᵗʰ Battalion, C.E.F.
Aug. 22, 1915

Well mother I was thinking of signing over about twenty dollars a month. They will send it home every month out of my wages and after we get moving around I won't have a very good place to keep it. It may come in useful and if you don't use it all dad can put it into the bank in his name and draw it for me when I come back.

Dear Uncle Oscar:

I'm wondering what you did with all the money you got paid in the battlefield. I hear privates were paid one dollar a day, plus 10 cents field allowance. Imagine a 10-cent bonus for the privilege of being shot at. Do you know what you can buy for a dollar today? Nothing. Well, almost nothing. You can't buy a newspaper or a cup of coffee. Or a chocolate bar. A cuppa java – that's slang for a cup of coffee – will cost at least $1.50. We've even figured out ways to make fancy coffees costing up to five dollars. That would be a week's pay for you. In case you're wondering, today's army pay schedule starts at around $100 a day.

Of course, we have to adjust your dollar for inflation. A dollar in 1917, adjusted for inflation, is worth about $18 today. Well, okay, you could buy lunch for two, barely, in a fast-food restaurant today for

$18. But you couldn't take a date to a movie for that. Oh, what's fast food? We have invented ways to prepare and cook food very quickly, so we can get a greasy hamburger and French fries in about two minutes. You don't even have to get out of your car. You just drive up to a post, tell it what you want, and then drive up to a window in the wall of the restaurant where a pair of hands will push out a bag of food and wish you a nice day. I'm not making this up. My dog loves to hear me talking to a post because it means a treat is coming his way.

That's a nice arrangement, sending $20 a month to your family. After all, what would you spend it on in France? Mademoiselles down in the village? If you are getting a dollar a day, this represents about two-thirds of your monthly army pay. In today's terms, accounting for inflation, that would be about $360. That would buy quite a few groceries. Milk today is more than a dollar a quart (nine cents in your day); a loaf of bread $2 or more (seven cents in 1915); and a gallon of gasoline nearly six bucks (eight cents in your day). And we measure it in something called metric, which I won't try to explain.

You might wonder how we carry around all the cash for our groceries. Well, we don't. The dollar bill and the two-dollar bill have gone the way of the dodo bird, replaced with coins. The penny became so incidental that it has been abolished. But mostly we carry credit cards. These are little plastic (hmm, do I have to explain plastic?) cards with electronic encryptions that allow ... this isn't easy. Never mind how they work. Let's put it this way: If we want real currency, we only have to stick one of these cards, smaller than a playing card, into a hole in a machine on a wall and out pops paper money. Let me correct that. We use plastic bills that you can see through instead of paper now. Well, that's a simplified way of describing it, but that's what happens. We can also stick plastic cards into parking meters to pay for parking. (Yes, they charge for a space to leave your car on the street.) We can drive up to a gasoline pump, stick a card in it, fill the tank, and drive away. We never speak to anyone. We just take the stuff, and they don't call the cops.

Where does the money come from? Out of our bank account, where it appears magically by remote electronic deposit from our employer. So we don't actually have to carry money except for small purchases.

You can use a card on a public phone, if you can find one. Not many around now since we all carry cell phones in our pockets. Cell phones are smaller than a cigarette pack and you can call anywhere in the world, instantly. If you had one on you, I could call you right now, unless the Huns have knocked out the cell phone tower. I could even send you a picture by phone because they're part camera, part movie screen.

Notice that I said we fill our cars with gasoline. Yup, just like you did in 1915. A hundred years later we have billions of automobiles, running on the same sort of internal combustion engine that you used. Sure, they have been much refined – you can hardly hear them – and so has the gasoline, but the system is the same. Drive down to the corner gas station and fill up with gasoline. Now that would be familiar to you, once you figured out how to use the credit card.

Your nephew,
Orland

Recruits underwent rigorous training at Niagara Camp.
These scenes from a postcard collection show various exercises.
(1) machine-gun training, (2) physical drill, (3) kit inspection.
French family archives

YOU CAN'T PRINT THAT!

Niagara Military Camp
A Company
37ᵗʰ Battalion, C.E.F.
Aug. 22, 1915

I see by the papers that the 35ᵗʰ, 37ᵗʰ, 38ᵗʰ, 74ᵗʰ, 75ᵗʰ, 76ᵗʰ and 94ᵗʰ battalions are going to Toronto for the winter. There is to be another reinforcement draft to be picked out before long, I think. Toronto would be a good place to winter but I would like to get to England.

Dear Uncle Oscar:

I used to wonder what persuaded you and tens of thousands of other young men to sign up for war. As you discovered, it's a dangerous business. Excitement? Adventure? Getting away from home? Peer pressure? These attractions seemed plausible in the early stages of The Great War, but less so as the war advanced. Thousands of men rushed to sign up in the first few months, hoping they would get to see something of Europe before the war ended. After all, the experts said the war would be over by Christmas.

You signed up in the spring of 1915. By that time, with Christmas long past, the cost of war was apparent. Thousands were dying, many thousands more wounded, with the war bogged down in the mud of Belgium and northern France. The machine gun, the cannon, and poison gases were horrific weapons against which no one seemed to have devised any reasonable defense. Officers on both sides were still sending in mounted cavalry.

In today's world, the carnage of the First World War would be splattered across our gory TV screens every evening. Our phone texts and Facebook pages would drip with blood. Public pressure would have ended the war in a week. Still, you signed up.

But the thing was, you couldn't know, could you? Extreme censorship blocked the paths of enlightenment. Reporters were banned from the Front. The British government wouldn't allow reporters anywhere near the battle lines. When a couple of American reporters sneaked in and wrote stories for the press back home, they were arrested and threatened with execution. Later in the war, some journalists were allowed near the Front, but only under tightly controlled conditions. Your hero Lord Kitchener detested them, referring to reporters as "drunken swabs." I'm not saying they weren't, mind you, but His Lordship's attitude showed a certain irreverent tone and a lack of respect for a noble profession.

The British went to extraordinary lengths to twist the facts to please the public. For example, newspapers using "facts" fed to them by the British military reported a fantastic victory by the British in the Battle of the Somme in the summer of 1916. Somehow the Brits neglected to mention that they had 20,000 killed and 40,000 wounded on the very first day. Had those facts been included, a curious and appalled public might well wonder how a battle could be so badly planned that the home side would lose 60,000 men in a single day. Over the next five months of that battle, both sides lost a total of more than a million men. A million! You can see how the war might have been ended sooner if people had only known what was going on.

But you were oblivious to the early losses of the war because your government kept you blind. In August 1914, less than three weeks after the war began, Parliament passed the *War Measures Act*. It didn't specifically apply to reporting, but it covered "censorship and control and suppression of publications, writings, maps, plans, photographs, communication and means of communication." This broad-ranging legislation was applicable wherever the government determined that the "security, defense, peace, order and welfare of Canada" was threatened. (*The War Measures Act* would be used decades later to back up police actions against suspected independence subversives in Quebec.)

The Act didn't seem to anticipate how ordinary press coverage of the war might affect morale at home. When Canada lost 6,500 wounded and dead soldiers in its first major battle of the war – Ypres in April and May 1915 – the government began to worry about how the public would react to the news. By that time, you were well along in your plans to join the Expeditionary Force. In June 1915, while you were at Niagara, the government of Robert Borden established the office of the Chief Press Censor. The censor's job was to ensure that stories criticizing military policy did not appear in the papers. He could also ban stories that he felt were aiding the enemy, including any that contained accounts of troop movements or embarrassed Allied troops.

Newspapers rather welcomed the appointment of Lieutenant-Colonel Ernest J. Chambers as chief censor. As the former editor of *The Calgary Herald,* he was one of their own. Generally, newspapers supported the war effort, although they felt forced through competition to carry reports and photographs that were not favourable to the cause. With the rules of censorship nailed to the newsroom wall, they all had a set of rules to follow.

Still, they were frustrated by the British government's refusal to allow reporters near the Front. Since Canadian troops were incorporated into British forces, there was no news on how things were going for them. The federal government appointed Max Aitken, later Lord Beaverbrook, as an "eye-witness" to the war. He was close to influential people in London, and he managed to deliver a dispatch in April 1915 reporting terrible casualties in the Second Battle of Ypres.

In spite of censorship, news of the real horrors of the war slowly began to leak out from returning wounded soldiers, letters (although censored) from soldiers at the Front, and American reporters who were not subject to the same censorship rules. The chief censor, in fact, had banned 250 publications, of which 225 originated in the U.S.

Eventually, Canadian publishers tired of dining on a diet of selective propaganda. Here's how the editor of Saturday Night magazine put it in an editorial in August 1917: "We have been fed too long on cocksure confidence and optimistic piffle. Wars are not won that way. If we cannot bear to hear the truth in our war news, to have it presented in unvarnished, truthful paragraphs, we are a poor lot and unworthy of success."

Perhaps the truth in all its unvarnished details would not have deterred a young man from Waverley from risking his life to defend King and Country. But it might have given him pause to reflect.

Your nephew,
Orland

LOCKING UP THE ENEMY

Exhibition Camp, Toronto, November 1915

I suppose you heard about the big powder factory up near Parry Sound being blown up yesterday. We got the news here last night and the 74th and 75th battalions received orders to be ready to go up there, but they did not go as there were plenty of soldiers much nearer than Toronto. I don't know as sending soldiers up there would be much good as it likely was the work of a single German spy. It seems funny that more of the Germans in Canada who are having just the same privileges as British shouldn't be in the pen.

Dear Uncle:

Well, yes, we've got to get those dirty Huns locked up before they blow away the country. In the emotional turmoil and paranoia of a wartime atmosphere, it's easy to imagine that a German spy could blow up a munitions factory and that all Germans should be locked up for the duration. In the 21st century, we would judge this action to be a horrible infringement on human rights but, in fact, that's what we did in Canada. Not only in the First World War, but in the Second as well.

As you know, by 1916 a lot of Germans and other undesirable Europeans were interned in Canada. I note by the wording of your letter that you want more Germans "in the pen." It would have been difficult to put them all in jail. As it was, special regulations under the *War Measures Act* compelled the registration of more than 80,000 "enemy aliens" – many of them Canadian citizens – to be placed under a careful government watch. And some were packed away for careful storage until the war's end.

They weren't placed in "the pen" or penitentiary, they were sent to concentration camps. Germans were the most hated and despised. During, and immediately after the war, we locked up 8,579 enemy aliens as prisoners of war, including more than 2,000 German immigrants. And not just Germans. Austro-Hungarians, Turks, and Bulgarians too. We locked up more than 4,000 Ukrainian men, along with some women and children, with Austro-Hungarian citizenship. Never mind that they may have left their homeland because they didn't want to be part of the Austro-Hungarian Empire. Foreign origin was all that counted. It was the fear, you see, that a German-born person, or even a Canadian-born citizen with German roots, would not only renew loyalties to the Old Country in Europe, but become an underground guerrilla force to disrupt Canada from within. In fact, few charges were laid and only a handful of internees were convicted of expressing "pro-German sentiments." That's a long way from blowing up a munitions factory. In peacetime these ideas seem unimaginable, but in wartime, when the Hun is mowing down thousands of Our Boys and the propaganda machines are running flat-out, these feelings become very real. They form all sorts of hot buttons that politicians love to push. We shouldn't be too quick to judge your feelings in the real time of war. Even at a hundred years distance, we have seen plenty of examples of racial intolerance materializing out of thin air because of a perceived atrocity by one ethnic group of extremists or another.

The *War Measures Act* disenfranchised all German-Canadians naturalized after 1902. German clubs were dissolved, German schools closed, and German newspapers suppressed. German-sounding town names were changed; Berlin, Ontario became Kitchener. German immigrants pretended they were Dutch, Scandinavian, or Russian to avoid persecution.

Those who were arrested were sent to special camps set up in remote places – and as you know, we have a lot of remoteness in Canada. Escape would be difficult. If the mosquitoes didn't get you, the swamps would. While usually only men were detained in these camps, sometimes their wives and children followed them because they had nowhere else to go. Only two camps, in Vernon and Spirit Lake, British Columbia, were set up to receive women and children. Internship was terribly costly to these families. Personal property was seized or destroyed and family life was ruined. Some of these camps were located in national parks. During the war, the parks budget was reduced, but the parks commissioner got permission to use enemy alien internees as cheap labour. Camps were opened at Banff, Jasper, Mount Revelstoke, and Yoho.

The War Measures Act, intended for use during the First World War, has become a large piece of our Canadian legacy. Its powers were actually extended after the war to meet the perceived threats of international socialism, as implied in the success of the Bolshevik revolution in Russia. It was used again in the Second World War to justify the internment of Japanese Canadians (we were at war with Japan), and again in 1970, this time internally. The federal Liberal government of Pierre Trudeau used it to suppress an "apprehended insurrection" in Quebec by nationalist Quebec terrorists.

Ukrainian-Canadians felt most aggrieved by the internment program. For years, they sought official acknowledgement of the historical wrong inflicted upon them. Through an aggressive campaign in the 1980s and 1990s, the Ukrainian-Canadian community slowly pressed the Canadian government into recognizing the injustice and establishing a fund to support commemorative and cultural activities to recall the internment program. A permanent exhibit of Canada's internment operations was opened in Banff National Park in 2013, nearly a century after the War Measures Act was first passed.

The guns of the Great War may have fallen silent in Europe in 1918, but repercussions of the war go on forever.

Your nephew,
Orland

SHOUTING INSULTS FROM
THE TRAIN WINDOW

Niagara, Sept. 26, 1915

We had two hours to spend in Toronto before our train left so had a look around and got my dinner in Eaton's. I lost my cap out of the train window somewhere between Bradford and Alandale and didn't get it until Friday morning. A section man found it and they sent it on up.

On the train to Halifax, Nov. 15, 1915

We passed through Levis, a town just across the river from Quebec about midnight last night and our first stop this morning was at a town named Riviere du Loup. The fellows had lots of fun with the Frenchmen there making fun of their town. Our train just passed another French town called Rimouski now. Every town we pass we stick our heads out of the window and yell till we can't see.

Dear Uncle Oscar:

I had hoped that after your letter of September 26 you would have been more cautious about sticking your head out the window of a moving train. Apparently not, according to your November 15 letter.

I'm sure you are aware that Canada has always been a divided nation, a situation not helped at all by young Protestant Orangemen from Ontario shouting insults from a train at Catholic Frenchmen in Quebec.

As a nation, we've had our growing pains over the past century, with the English and French warily respectful of each other as we gradually matured. English Canada has shed many of its British frocks and gowns in favour of a more international image, while a significant number of French-Canadians reached for a form of coat-tail independence.

You might wonder what has become of all the familiar symbols of colonial nationhood of your day. Well, we have our own flag, we have our own national anthem, and we have our own constitution. Old white men from England are no longer appointed as Governor General. Several women have served as GGs, including one of Chinese ancestry and another who was a black television journalist from Haiti. Don't try to figure it out. Just assume these developments reflect the changing nature of our society.

Now that I've piqued your interest, let me begin with the flag. I'd like to think that your action and your loss of life at Vimy played a role in Canada's desire to have its own flag. As I explain elsewhere, one of the first stirrings of Canadian national pride came after victory at Vimy.

I imagine you see the Union Jack flying everywhere. That would be the flag you enlisted under and are serving under, representing England and the British Empire. As a symbol of Canada, it has disappeared. (Oh, yeah, we no longer have the British Empire anymore either. Nowadays, it's the Commonwealth, and we've kicked a few members out of the club for unseemly behaviour.) We haven't used the Union Jack for more than a century. Our Maple Leaf flag replaced the Red Ensign in 1965. It has red bars at either end, with a red maple leaf mounted prominently on a white field in the middle. No crosses or diagonal slashes or having to remember which white slash went on top so you would know whether the flag was flying correctly or upside down, signaling distress. We can pretty much tell when a leaf is upside down.

We've had this flag since it was approved by Parliament under the government of a Liberal named Lester Pearson. Not everyone in Parliament approved; a former Conservative prime minister, John Diefenbaker, was said to have cried when the new flag was first raised on Parliament Hill on February 15, 1965. But he was such a good actor that no one could say whether the tears were genuine.

Being good Canadians, we didn't rush into this decision. We had been using the Union Jack a long time, and also its derivative, the Red Ensign. The ensign was a flag created in 1707 as the flag of the British Merchant Marine. You'll remember it as being red, with a Union Jack in the upper left corner. From about 1870 to 1904, it was commonly used on land and sea as Canada's flag. As various provinces entered Confederation, their coat of arms was added to the ensign, sort of like sticking gold stars on a record of attendance. In 1922, these symbols were replaced with the Canadian coat of arms, and the new version was authorized for official use on Canadian buildings abroad. After another world war, it was adopted for use on government buildings in Canada.

As I said, we didn't hurry into this decision. After the flag was codified in 1922, some serious talk began about getting a new flag for Canada. A committee of the Privy Council began to research new designs in 1925, but it didn't get anywhere. Canada's actions during the Second World War (1939-1945) strengthened the nation's self-identity, and after the war a renewed push began for our own flag. A select parliamentary committee called for submissions. And when it received more than 2,600 designs, did it marvel at the creative genius of Canada? It did not. It threw up its hands in despair and gave up.

In the lead-up to Canada's centenary in 1967, nationalist fervour grew and grew. Pearson proposed that the country adopt a new flag before its 100th anniversary in 1967. Out of a number of submissions, three were chosen – none of which was the final design. Our flag, like our politics, is a compromise. Pearson favoured three maple leaves on a single branch, on a white field edged with blue on either side, representing the seas to the east and west of us. (Should we have had blue across the top, representing the Arctic Ocean?) Another design offered a variation of the Red Ensign with the Union Jack (British Heritage) and the fleur-de-lis (French heritage). The red-on-white design won out, mostly because there was historical precedent. King George V had proclaimed red and white as Canada's colours in 1921.

So, 40 years after that first committee began to play around with the flag's design, we finally got a flag of our own. Naturally, there was some resistance to change – a few likened it to a logo on a sugar sack. People in Western Canada said, "Wot's a maple tree?" because they don't have any. But relatively quickly, the flag was adopted worldwide as a symbol of Canada. This acceptance was hastened immeasurably by prominent and lavish use of the flag during Expo 67, a world's fair held in Montreal on man-made islands in the St. Lawrence River, as if we didn't have enough land.

We have our own national anthem now. We no longer sing "God Save the King" (actually, we've had a queen for more than 60 years); we sing a little ditty called "O Canada." It goes something like this:

O Canada! We stand on guard for thee!
O Canada, the true north strong and free,
I think that I will never see,
A plant more glorious than a maple tree!
Oh-oh! Canada.

Actually, I'm paraphrasing. That may have come from an old satirical revue called *Spring Thaw*. "O Canada" was around when you went marching off to war, although there were a number of versions. One of them asked God to "defend our rights, forfend this nation's thrall." Forfending a thrall is really hard work, especially in mid-winter. Another promised, "At Britain's side, whate'er betide, unflinchingly we'll stand, with hearts we sing, 'God save the King'..." And there you are, standing by Britain's side, ready to take one for His Majesty.

And what happened to that stirring old favourite, "The Maple Leaf Forever"? If you'll recall, there was a line in it that didn't sit well with Quebec nationalists. Those were the Frenchmen you were hollering at out the window as your troop train rocketed through Quebec on the way to Halifax. You know the line:

> *In days of yore, from Britain's shore,*
> *Wolfe the dauntless hero came,*
> *and planted firm Britannia's flag,*
> *on Canada's fair domain.*
> *Here may it wave, our boast, our pride,*
> *and joined in love together,*
> *the thistle, shamrock, rose entwine,*
> *the Maple Leaf forever.*

Of course, the song suggests Wolfe the Dauntless (a.k.a. known as Wolfe the Dead, since he was killed on the Battle of the Plains of Abraham) planted firm Britannia's flag in the dead bodies of the defeated French forces. You can see why French Quebeckers might be upset by that vision. They've been harbouring a grudge over that for more than 250 years. At various times they call themselves separatists or sovereigntists or some other phrase that might win them a sort-of independent state within Canada. They have on occasion established a government in Quebec, and once even elected enough members of Parliament to form Her Majesty's Loyal Opposition. Since their brand of Loyal Opposition was dedicated to breaking up the country, this objective might seem a tad treasonous. Did we hang them, as some countries would? No, we awarded them a generous pay cheque and a nice parliamentary pension.

All because you and your buddies hollered out a train window. Sheesh! See what we had to patch up?

Your nephew,
Orland

The liner *Lapland* carried Oscar French and other Canadian troops from Halifax to England in November 1915. As the liner neared Europe, soldiers were ordered to sleep on deck, in the rain, in case of being torpedoed by a U-boat

PAWNS OF ROYAL INTRIGUE

Bramshott Camp
Lipshook, Hants, Eng.
Dec. 16th, 1915

The last day we were in London we went to the Tower of London that used to be the King's palace and a state prison. We were through the Bloody Tower where the two young princes were murdered way back in the time of Richard II and seen the narrow stone stairs where their bodies were found many years after they were murdered. The portcullis or gate that is raised and lowered and which was made at the time of William the Conqueror nearly one thousand years ago is still there.

Dear Uncle Oscar:

I'm glad you sampled some of Britain's history. I am about to lay on you a lengthy history lesson focusing on your demise on Vimy Ridge.

I have been trying to figure out who killed you. No, I don't mean the guy who fired the cannon that showered you with shell. I mean, I am trying to determine who bears the most responsibility for your death. And all I can say is that it came down to a bunch of power-mad European aristocrats who played war games with real flesh-and-blood soldiers. Today we might call it penis envy at an international level.

The dime novel explanation of the war is that it started with the assassination of Archduke Francis Ferdinand, heir apparent to the Austrian throne, by an extremist in Sarajevo, Serbia. So how did my

Uncle Oscar from Waverley and hundreds of thousands of other men wind up being slaughtered in northern France and Flanders because of a madman's bullet in Serbia?

What resulted was what we today call the domino effect. Knock over one domino and the whole line tumbles. Austria attacked Serbia; Russia rushed to the aid of Serbia to keep Austria from getting to a warm-water port. But behind the scenes, there were hidden links: Russia was allied with France and England in a Triple Entente; Germany was linked with Austria-Hungary and Italy through its Triple Alliance. Since France was an ally of Russia, Germany attacked France through Belgium, mostly just because it was there and in the way. Britain rushed in to help Belgium and France, and all the dominions of Britain – like Canada, Australia, and New Zealand – were sucked into the war.

And you, from a farm in Central Ontario, were drawn off to the blood-soaked soil of France.

Of course, it is not that simple. The alliances emerged from centuries of mistrust and aggression, twisted and warped by intermarriages of royal households. The roots of the conflict went back hundreds and hundreds of years. An essay called "The European Conflict and Conditions that Brought it About", in an atlas produced by Rand McNally at the start of the war, reached all the way back to the third century to recount the instability of the Balkan Peninsula, where this mess began. And it might have stayed there except for the alliances I outlined above. The rivalry among the powers of northern and central Europe, while also long rooted, were more immediate. France, having lost badly to Germany in the Franco-Prussian War in 1871, was anxious to regain the province of Alsace-Lorraine that had been claimed by the German federation as its spoils of war. Germany was flexing its naval muscles, determined to overcome the marine military advantage enjoyed by Britain. Britain was equally determined not to let this happen.

It was a family affair, of sorts. Kaiser Wilhelm II of Germany was the grandson of England's Queen Victoria and first cousin of King George V of England. The Czar of Russia, Nicholas II, was a first cousin of Wilhelm and of King George. In a famous photograph of the time, Czar Nicholas II and King George V look like identical twins.

The royal continental linkages were mostly Queen Victoria's doing. She and her Prince Consort, Albert, produced nine children out of their marriage bed and planted them like seeds throughout the royal households of Europe, mostly German. It was Queen Victoria's hope that by having royal family links with the crowned heads of the other major European powers, strong ties through blood relationships might forestall the spilling of blood on the battlefield. As some historians have noted, there are all kinds of examples to prove the weakness of this theory. All you do is introduce family jealousies into the already tenuous mix of international relationships.

You know, of course, that Victoria herself had found marital bliss and happiness in a German court. Her husband Albert, who died at a relatively young age and whom the queen mourned in black for the rest of her life, came from the House of Saxe-Coburg and Gotha. He was the son of Ernst, the Duke of Saxe-Coburg and Gotha. Victoria, like many modern married women of today, kept her maiden reference to the House of Hanover. Her son, Edward VII, succeeded her in 1901 as a member of the House of Saxe-Coburg and Gotha. Her grandson George V took the throne with the same name in 1910, but intense public opinion against Germany in the First World War forced him to change the family name to the House of Windsor in 1916. He and his British relatives gave up their German titles and names; Prince Louis of Battenberg became Louis Mountbatten, for example. (Just as an aside: Lord Mountbatten was killed in 1979 when the Irish Republican Army blew up his fishing boat in Ireland.)

Now, if you will bear with me, dear Uncle, I will lay out the details of Queen Victoria's seeding of Europe with her British progeny. Then I will speculate on how this may have contributed to one of the greatest misjudgments of the war and why you came to die at Vimy Ridge.

Here's how Victoria's family tree took root in Europe.

Her first-born, Edward (born 1841), married Alexandra, daughter of Christian IX of Denmark.

Alfred (born 1844), Duke of Edinburgh and of Saxe-Coburg and Gotha, married Marie of Russia.

Arthur (born 1850), Duke of Connaught, married Louise Margaret of Prussia.

Leopold (born 1853), Duke of Albany, married Helen of Waldeck-Pyrmont.

Victoria (born 1840), Princess Royal, married Friedrich III, German Emperor. Watch this one for further details.

Alice (born 1843) married Ludwig IV, Grand Duke of Hesse and by Rhine.

Helena (born 1846) married Christian of Schleswig-Holstein.

Louise (born 1848) married John Campbell, 9th Duke of Argyll.

Beatrice (born 1857) married Henry of Battenberg.

You see how this goes. First make a link with Denmark. Maybe this was compensation for stealing the entire Danish fleet in 1807. Then link to Russia, and then Prussia, and a bunch of German states. Keep in mind that there was no country called Germany at this time; there was Prussia and a string of related German provinces. The nation of Germany would form in 1871 out of victory in the Franco-Prussian war.

Now, why would all these states want ties to Britain through a family of British-born monarchs who were going to produce heirs to their various thrones? Because it was quite an honour. Britain was a superpower in the 19th century. Under Victoria's rule, the island nation had blossomed into a worldwide empire on which the sun never set. Through industrial growth, economic prosperity, and resources beyond measure in its global colonial empire, Britain was immensely powerful and wealthy. Being part of the empire, even if only through blood links with the monarch, had its benefits.

Of course, the Queen was not all-powerful. As the ruler in a constitutional monarchy, she was held in check by her government and parliament. Not so Wilhelm II of Germany, the Queen's grandson, who had risen to become Kaiser Bill during the First World War. He had powers that the King of England did not enjoy. He could name his own ministers, boss them about, and get almost any funding he wanted from the Reichstag.

Remember what I said about the dangers of planting family jealousies in the royal households of Europe? Let's take a look at the goals and aspirations of good old Kaiser Bill.

Wilhelm, sometimes known as William, was born to Prince Frederick William of Prussia (who became Emperor Frederick III) and Victoria, Princess Royal, the eldest daughter of Queen Victoria. Because of a traumatic breech birth, he had a withered left arm that was six inches shorter than his right. Throughout his life he made attempts to conceal his crippled arm; historians have speculated that the disability affected his emotional development. He has been described as vain, bombastic, and neurotic. He was unpredictable. As he grew into maturity, he leaned favourably to the Prussian-style manly expressions of steeliness and stolidness. He was almost always dressed in a uniform. If there was a softer side to him, he managed to conceal it.

His loyalties to his British ancestry were fragile, and he maintained a poor relationship with the English side of his family tree. However, he loved his grandmother Victoria, and he rushed to her side in 1901 during her fatal illness. However, he didn't get along well with his uncle, the Prince of Wales, later King Edward VII, who treated him like a malcontent nephew, not a German Kaiser. Nor did things go so well at home. His mother, Vicky, conveyed to him her impression that things German were inferior to things British, and this did not sit well with him. He became estranged from his parents. But still, he saw strategic value in retaining a good relationship with Britain, and at one point he even mused about forming an alliance with England. You take the seas, we'll take the land, and not a mouse in Europe would dare move. The overture was rejected.

Now we get to the jealousies. Britain ruled the waves, and Kaiser Bill made a decision to build up the German navy to equal that of Britain. Whether this was for strategic reasons or was fueled in part by a desire to be equal to his cousins is not entirely clear. For some reason, he thought the British wouldn't notice. Of course, they did, and they responded by expanding their own navy. Soon the countries were locked into an extremely expensive arms race (we have seen too much of that in our current century), and the British were convinced that Germany was hell-bent on invading their country. Why else would it spend so much money and time on building up its sea power? The two countries, once only slightly nervous about each other, became hostile, heavily armed camps.

Then comes the war. Dominos tumble all over Europe. Germany is backing Austria; Austria is at war with Serbia; the Russians, backing Serbia, go to war with Austria-Hungary; the Russians have an alliance with France, and here is Germany sitting in between. War with both France and Russia seems inevitable, yet Germany cannot afford to fight on two frontiers at once. It knows France will fight; it wants to recover the territory of Alsace-Lorraine it lost 40 years earlier. It is aware that

Britain has formed an entente with France, but the agreement is only recent, and everyone knows Britain and France have been enemies for centuries. If France were knocked out quickly, Britain would not likely come to its defense, especially if France had capitulated.

This is where the Victoria factor comes in. Victoria had planted all those British seeds throughout Europe, remember? This is just speculation, but is it possible that the Germans and the Kaiser were misled by the number of British monarchical links throughout the German/Prussian world? Perhaps they felt that Britain was actually soft on Germany because of those connections. They gambled that the British would not enter a conflict with them.

At any rate, in their back pockets the Germans had the Schlieffen Plan, designed to offset a two-front war against the French and the Russians. The Germans knew France would mass troops on its eastern frontier in an attempt to swarm into Germany and recover Alsace-Lorraine. The Schlieffen Plan was to advance quickly through Belgium, even though that little country was neutral, swing around the French armies in a northerly route, then swoop southerly and capture Paris, ending the war in 40 days. The Germans were very precise about that. They would set their clocks to arrive in Paris in exactly 40 days. The British wouldn't have time to react. Once France was subdued, the Germans would move their resources eastward and take on the Russians who, they assumed, would not even yet be pulling on their boots.

What they didn't take into account was the British resolve to guarantee the sovereignty of Belgium. When the Germans marched through Belgium on their way to France, Britain declared war on Germany. The Belgians resisted as best they could, putting up a stronger fight than the Germans expected. The British skedaddled over to the continent in a hurry and managed to slow the advance of Germany to a stop in Belgium and northern France. On the eastern front, the Russians showed a surprising ability to pull on their boots quickly, and the war was on, on both sides of Germany.

I should note that the Schlieffen Plan of outflanking the enemy was based on the success of Hannibal against the Romans many, many centuries earlier. Postwar analyses of the Schlieffen Plan was divided on its feasibility; some authorities felt it was outdated by technology and circumstances. Perhaps they shouldn't have used elephants. (That's a joke, Uncle. Hannibal used elephants to cross the Alps ... never mind.) In fact, many of the battle tactics practiced by both sides had been rendered impotent by advances in technology, in particular the machine gun and artillery shells. Elephants would have done no good.

At any rate, the advance stalled in northern France and Flanders; that's where you wound up. I suppose it is a bit of a stretch to blame Queen Victoria for your death at Vimy. After all, the old lady died 13 years before the war broke out. And anyway, if you hadn't died at Vimy, then you would probably have succumbed somewhere else. Unless Britain hadn't entered the war at all, which was quite unlikely in any event. In which case, you would have become a farmer in Ontario or followed your brothers to new opportunities out West. Ifs, ifs, ifs. Doesn't really matter. You're still dead, and so are Victoria, Nicholas II, George V, and Kaiser Bill.

As for why so many of your colleagues died in battle: It was a time when the quality of the individual soldier was secondary to the quantity of soldiers in the field. Last man standing would win the war of attrition, even if hundreds of thousands had to die to prove the point.

And what was the point? It was a clash of empires, a struggle of royal cousins and aristocrats to divvy up what was left of the unconquered world, a last gasp at supremacy of Europe. You might be interested to know, Uncle, that most of the instigators of this monstrous war were also crushed. Of the five empires that started the war, only one – Britain – survived. Germany and the Kaiser, the Russians, the Ottomans, the Austro-Hungarians – all collapsed after the First World War. We moved on into a democratic world. Adolf Hitler and a rejuvenated Germany tried again to restore world domination just two decades later, only to be crushed in another terrible war. The age of European empiricism was dead.

And so were you.

Lest you think that I have perhaps become maudlin as I view your war through the prism of a full century, let me quote from an essay in the *Rand McNally Atlas* I mentioned earlier, published in 1914:

> Thus, Europe resounds with the trade of millions of marching men, the rattle and clash of arms, and the wailing and weeping of children. One by one the nations leap to the struggle … everywhere the dark cloud of conflict spreads its terror and gloom over the land … men leave a plentiful harvest to reap a bloody one on the field of battle. The pawns of royal intrigue, they are forced to march to the field of slaughter, accompanied by the weeping of their women and children, and the thought of the misery to fall upon them.

It's an appropriate designation: The pawns of royal intrigue. You see, even in 1914, as early recruits were rushing eagerly off to war, wiser heads perceived that this would be a ruthless slaughter.

To close out this letter, I will tell you what became of the leaders of those empires. Wilhelm II, the last German emperor, died of a pulmonary embolism on June 3, 1941, at age 82. Czar Nicholas II of Russia was executed, along with his family, by Bolsheviks in July 1918. Russia and a number of other states were forged into the Union of Soviet Socialist Republics (USSR) by the Communists. Franz Josef I, who ruled Austria-Hungary for 68 years, died of pneumonia in 1916. The monarchy was dissolved in 1918 after Austria-Hungary was defeated, and the empire was broken into smaller countries such as Austria, Hungary, and Czechoslovakia. The Ottoman Empire was dissolved in favour of the Republic of Turkey in 1922, and the last sultan, Mehmed VI, left the country. The Third French Republic, under the leadership of President Raymond Poincare and Prime Minister Georges Clemenceau, demanded and won severe reparations against Germany. These punishments led to German discontent and the rise of the fascist regime of Adolf Hitler. The Republic lasted until the Germans occupied France in 1940 during the Second World War.

And what of the surviving empire, the British? King George V died of numerous health problems in 1936, to be succeeded by his son Edward VIII. Edward abdicated the throne for the love of an American woman, to be followed by his brother Albert known as King George VI. He ruled England through the difficult years of the Second World War (1939-1945) and died in 1952. His daughter Elizabeth rose to the throne and is still reigning, as of this writing, 64 years later. The heir apparent, Charles, Prince of Wales, is nearing 70 years old.

But the Empire has morphed, as we call it, into the British Commonwealth. Many of its former dominions, like Canada, are independent parliamentary democracies that no longer snap to attention at the sound of a British bugle.

And yet, we do feel warm and fuzzy whenever one of the Royals marries or pops up with a new baby. We still delight in the last vestiges of a once mighty empire, still pawns, in a way, of royal intrigue.

Your nephew,
Orland

TEXTBOOK TALES OF *NANCY*
AND THE BARRIE JAIL

Bramshott Camp, Dec. 30th, 1915

Elmer won't have far to go to school this winter. Give him the farthing and three penny piece for his bank.

Dear Uncle Oscar:

I have noticed in your letters that you are often asking about Elmer being in school. Since he had moved from the farm to Waverley in 1915, he didn't have to trudge so far to his classes. I guess he got about the same amount of education that most rural youngsters did in those days. You got a taste of high school in Midland, and I assume you were staying with your brother Roy. However, your little brother Elmer had a curious mind all his life, and I would say he was always striving to learn more. He was a constant reader of newspapers, particularly the *Toronto Star*, and he bought a Grolier encyclopedia so my sister Pat and I would have an improved source of general information in our home.

I must commend your teachers for teaching you clear, legible handwriting. Your penmanship is immaculate. Mine has always been a mess. Very rarely did I have to puzzle over a word as I transcribed your letters. Full marks, a great big A. Grammar, not so much. Pretty good, but with an occasional lapse here and there. Maybe a B-plus. I was amused to see some spellings that have changed with the times, such as your practice of writing today as to-day.

Good handwriting isn't much valued today. Some schools don't teach penmanship or cursive writing. Lots of young people write with their thumbs. They call it "texting" on their little hand-held electronic devices, and they push tiny buttons with their thumbs to create a text message that they send through the air to home, to the shopping mall, or around the world. It's really quite magical. I imagine in a few generations of evolution the thumbs will be larger than the fingers!

I have a textbook of yours, from high school. It is signed by you: "Oscar French, Midland High School, Midland Ontario." You guarded it jealously. In the back of the book there is a bit of doggerel threatening harm to anyone who might purloin your book:

> *Don't steal this book my young lad*
> *Or I will go and tell your dad*
> *And he will take you by the tail*
> *And drag you down to Barrie jail.*

That's fairly severe punishment for stealing a textbook. Did you realize they used to hang people in Barrie jail? Yep, four of them swung from the gallows. Is this poem original? I'd like to think so. It's the kind of thing I might have doodled in a textbook when I attended high school. By that time (1960), the school board had incorporated Penetang and the full school name was Midland-Penetanguishene District High School (MPDHS).

The textbook is the *Public-School History of England and Canada* (amended by someone's mischievous pen to read "Pengland and Oanada"), authorized by the Education Department of Ontario.

It seems to have become part of the Ontario curriculum in 1902, although it may have been published in the 1890s. Inside the cover you wrote a long list of names which were probably going to show up on a test: Samuel de Champlain, Laval, LaSalle, Talon, Frontenac, Montcalm, Wolfe, Sir Isaac Brock, Sir George Prevost, Sir James Yeo, William Lyon

Mackenzie, Papineau, Lord Durham, Joseph Howe, Sir Charles Tupper, Sir John A. MacDonald, Sir Wilfrid Laurier. You got Wilfrid right, but you bombed out on Macdonald. It's spelled with a small "d".

You had me on Sir James Yeo. Didn't recognize him. Turns out he was an officer of the Royal Navy who had been named Commodore of the Great Lakes British fleet in March 1813. His orders were to maintain British control of Lake Ontario during the War of 1812, subject to the direction of Sir George Prevost, Captain-General and Governor-in-Chief of British North America. Although Yeo had little experience in commanding ships, he came to be regarded as one of the heroes of the war. Yeo was on his way to take up his post on Lake Ontario when the Americans raided York (Toronto). No doubt this inspired him to take them seriously. After the war, he was placed in command of anti-slavery patrols off the west coast of Africa, a role he relished since he was an avowed abolitionist. The roles of Yeo and Prevost in Canadian history have faded from public view, but I suppose they must still have seemed important when you were in school.

Recently we marked the 200th anniversary of the War of 1812. I don't think your friend Yeo got much of a mention. In the interests of harmony between the U.S. and Canada, modern historians dispute whether either side won the War of 1812. It seems to me there is no question the British won. The American armies attempted to take Canada with the goal of pushing the British out of North America. They didn't. Therefore, they did not achieve their goal. Therefore, they lost, as I see it. Since the international boundary stayed much the same, one might argue that the British won the war, but didn't gain anything. However, on the broader scale of things, a ragtag band of breakaway colonies took on one of the greatest powers, if not the greatest power, on earth, and didn't come out of it badly. In fact, it set the tone for the rise in prominence of the United States of America. That accomplishment alone established the United States as a nation to be noticed and set it on its road to international superstardom (a word of modern excessiveness with which you are probably not familiar).

Cradled among the hills of northern Simcoe County, Waverley was well removed from the frontier action of the War of 1812. Naval battles were a different matter, and a couple of incidents on Georgian Bay brought the war closer to home. In September 1813, the British fleet on the Upper Great Lakes was reduced to a single supply ship, *Nancy*. This ship was chased into the Nottawasaga River about 15 miles west of your farm, Uncle. Under fire from American ships, the *Nancy*'s captain set his ship afire to prevent its capture. He and his crew rowed 360 miles northwest to Fort Mackinac. From there, they captured two American ships, the *Tigress* and *Scorpion*. After the war, the two ships were scuttled in Penetanguishene Bay under the terms of the Rush-Bagot Treaty that demilitarized the Great Lakes.

But their bones live on, as do those of the ship *Nancy*. The skeletal remains of the hulls of both *Tigress* and *Scorpion* have been raised and are on public display at the Penetanguishene Naval Museum. *Nancy* is similarly showing her old bones at Wasaga Beach. As sand and silt in the Nottawasaga River settled around the charred wreck of *Nancy*, an island gradually formed. In 1928, the remains of the hull were raised and put-on display in the *Nancy Museum*. The war was never far away, even from remote villages like Waverley. After the war, the Penetanguishene Road was opened to provide an overland route to Fort Penetanguishene, and the King's men came marching right through Waverley. Some of them camped in the area, and little Elmer, your favourite brother, found a couple of coins in his garden that may well have been lost by gambling troops. Well, it's a good story.

And I have discovered a direct connection between Waverley and *Nancy*. David Bannister, the first settler in Waverley, was a soldier who had been at Nottawasaga when *Nancy* was destroyed. After the war, he returned to England (he was raised in Leicestershire), married, and brought his bride back to Canada. He settled in Waverley in 1829, travelling there no doubt on the Penetanguishene Road. For a long time, before it became French's Corners, the cross-roads settlement on the hillside was known as Bannister's Corners. Bannisters lived there until, I don't know, the 1970s. The little waterhole to the east of the village, which serves as the headwaters of Hogg Creek, was always known as Bannister's Pond. When cattle were pastured in the field, it was little more than an undistinguished mud hole. Today it is a splendid decorative feature on the lawn of a comfortable country dwelling.

A couple of other settlers' names cropped up as well. Remember that long hill that sloped down to Orr Lake, always known as Rowley's Hill? That was named after John Rowley, a retired soldier who was the first settler in the area. Not so far away, across the road, another retired soldier named William Archer took up residence. The Archers were prominent even in my days at Waverley. Most of the settlement along the road took place between 1819 and 1830.

I attended public school, grades 1 to 8, at Waverley but not in the same building that you attended. Mine was constructed in 1926 and was a larger, three-classroom brick structure. Although it was last used as a school in the 1960s, it is a sturdy building and still exists as a craft shop and veterinary office. It fell victim to regionalization, the practice of closing small rural schools and scooping up children in yellow school buses to be transported to larger regional schools. I walked to elementary school every day, right past the cenotaph with your name on it. To reach high school in Midland, I had to do a bumpy daily commute on a large green bus operated by Howard Brandon out of Hillsdale.

Education has become much more accessible, with three of Elmer's four children advancing past high school into post-secondary institutions. The fourth, Gerald Oscar, the son named after you, being of a more entrepreneurial nature, made a pile of money in the ski business. That's right, skiing. Riding a pair of boards down a snowy hillside. People pay a lot of money to do that. I've done it myself.

Your slaloming nephew,
Orland

HE SHOOTS, HE SCORES,
HE PUTS MILLIONS IN THE BANK

Bramshott Camp, Dec. 30ᵗʰ, 1915
(Written on Oscar's 19th birthday)

What are they doing for sport around Waverley this winter. Has anybody started up a rink there. I haven't seen any ice or snow this winter yet but we get all the rain we want. Everything is as green as in summer here now.

Dear Uncle Oscar:

You will be pleased to learn that your little brother, Elmer, my father, carried on the sports tradition at the house in Waverley. For years, every winter, he and his buddies would build a skating rink outdoors on a piece of flat land just back of the house, where he later had a garden. He had levelled off a piece of land for the rink, and there was a building that served as a garage in my boyhood. In earlier years, it was a change room for the rink in winter and presumably a garage the rest of the year. It had thin boards that wouldn't support the weight of a car, so my dad put down some thick planks to drive on. One night I drove in, missed the planks, and broke through the floorboards. We had to jack out the car the next morning. Since I was only a teenager, I had a lot of explaining to do. The story was, and I'm sticking to it, that my sister Pat and I were backing the car into the garage to deliver a large Christmas present for Dad when I missed the planks. When he saw the present, a mechanical snow blower, he was somewhat mollified.

But let's get back to the rink. When I was a boy, my brother Warren built outdoor rinks – I helped too – on the backyard between the house and the garage. However, the yard was kind of lumpy and sloped a bit, so there was always a little hill at one end. Uncle Oliver Grigg, my mother's brother, used to set up a pipe from the well to a watering trough across the corner of the rink, so the thing was a bit lopsided. He brought his cows down from the farm on the hill for watering every morning because he didn't have a supply of water in winter.

I'm wondering if you played hockey. If so, what position did you play? Speaking of hockey, I'll tell you what's happened with professional hockey since you went off to France. When you departed in 1915, professional hockey in Canada was played in the National Hockey Association. Before that, in your lifetime, there had been the Amateur Hockey Association in Canada, formed in 1897, and then the Eastern Canada Amateur Hockey Association in 1905. When the ECAHA folded in 1909, two competing professional leagues emerged: the Canadian Hockey Association and the National Hockey Association.

Since the NHA was backed by wealthy businessmen with deep pockets, the CHA soon conceded centre ice and quietly retreated into the locker room of history. But men with deep pockets don't always get along. Three of the franchisees didn't see eye to eye with the owner of the Toronto Blueshirts, so they pulled out of the NHA and formed the National Hockey League. They were the Montreal Canadiens, Montreal Wanderers, and the Ottawa Senators, and a replacement team in Toronto, called the Arenas. You might be surprised to learn that a hundred years later, Les Canadiens are still around. There is still a team called the Ottawa Senators, although they are a relatively new incarnation of the old team. Curiously enough, the Senators logo is the head of a Roman centurion, which has nothing to do with the Senate. By 1926 there were 10 teams in Ontario, Quebec, and the northeastern United States. During the Depression of the 1930s and the Second World War, the league shrank to six teams which have become known as "the Original Six": Montreal Canadiens, Toronto Maple Leafs, New York Rangers, Boston Bruins, Chicago Blackhawks, and Detroit Red Wings. Now there are 30 NHL teams, and they lose money in hot spots like California, Florida, and Phoenix, where the best application of ice is in a tall cocktail glass.

Nevertheless, not one of the seven Canadian teams in the league managed to stumble into the NHL playoffs in 2016. While teams from vacation hotspots like Florida and California chased the puck to be named the best on ice, the boys from the ice-bound tundra of Canada were put on ice early.

There is still a team wearing blue shirts in Toronto. Named the grammatically challenged Maple Leafs, their goal in life seems to be to lose sufficient games at the end of the season to miss the playoffs. As of this writing – and I see no immediate reason why I am even bothering to qualify this comment – they last won the Stanley Cup in 1967. That's, let's see, almost half a century ago. Had you lived to a good old age, you would have seen them carrying the cup in victory laps around the ice.

The Leafs have a connection to the First World War through Conn Smythe, a famous Canadian sportsman. He purchased the Toronto St. Pats hockey team in the 1920s and re-established it as the Toronto Maple Leafs. Under his ownership, the Leafs won the Stanley Cup eight times. Earlier, during your war, he had served as an artillery officer in the Ypres Salient and the Somme. For an act of bravery, he received the Military Cross. In late 1917, he transferred to the Royal Flying Corps as an airborne observer. He was shot down and spent the rest of the war in a prison camp. Undeterred by this experience, he signed up again in the Second World War at age 45. He was badly wounded in a German attack on an ammunition depot, and for the rest of his life, he walked with a limp.

I doubt if the Stanley Cup was known as the Holy Grail of hockey in your day, as it is today. It was donated by Lord Stanley, Governor-General of Canada from 1888 to 1893, as something for the lads to shoot for as a championship trophy. It is still the top prize in North American hockey, although it has been usurped by the National Hockey League as its sole property. Nobody else can play for it. Franchises in the league are still owned by businessmen with deep pockets and sometimes shallow brains, who love to pay hundreds of millions of dollars for the bragging rights to how much money their team can lose. It's all tax write-off stuff, anyway. Oh, except the Toronto Maple Leafs. Richest team in the league. No matter how badly they play, the money just rolls in. Only thing is, they don't know how to spend it to build a winning team.

Girls of all ages play hockey in organized leagues, and women have formed two professional leagues in Canada. They play for the Clarkson Cup, named after another Governor-General, Adrienne Clarkson.

You want to know how much professional hockey players get paid now? Prepare to roll over in your grave. In your day, the big star was Newsy Lalonde, and he was paid $1,300 in 1917-18. In the 2015-16 hockey season, the top earner was a forward for the Pittsburg Penguins named Sidney Crosby. He was picking up $16.5 million a year, including endorsements. The league had a rule that no player could earn more than $12.86 million. The salary cap, that is, the total amount a team could pay to all its players, was $71.4 million in 2016. Recently, the Maple Leafs hired a coach for $50 million ($50 million, you read it right) in an attempt to fight their way back to respectability.

Where does the money come from to pay these guys? From the fans and from television rights, the rights to broadcast NHL hockey games on television. (Television is like radio with pictures.) Tickets cost in the hundreds of dollars. A hockey night out for a family of four can easily run more than $500. You might think only people with deep pockets can afford to go to a hockey game, and you might be right.

I don't recall any NHL stars out of Waverley, even from Elmer French's Outdoor Ice Centre.

Your nephew,
Orland

COUNT YOUR BLESSINGS

Bramshott Camp
Jan. 3rd, 1916

We are having a much easier time here than we had in Niagara. The hours for drill are much shorter and we have had no very long route marches yet but when we go on a march we have to take our full equipment that is take our blankets, great coat, mess tin, water bottle and haversack.

Dear Uncle Oscar:

Do you sing as you march? Are your songs patriotic rallying cries? You might be surprised to learn that World War I songs persist to this day. Generally, they are songs written to inspire pride and patriotic fervour among soldiers and civvies alike. Some songs longed for a lover, some songs shamed non-combatants into signing up, some were inspirational songs, such as "It's a Long Way to Tipperary." That one was written in 1914 to bolster the courage of British soldiers as they made a long and fateful journey to the Western Front. You no doubt know the popular marching song, "Pack Up Your Troubles In Your Old Kit-Bag."

Soldiers on a training route march.
French family archives

While most of the songs were, and still are, supportive of the war, there were dissenting voices even then. These came primarily from the United States, where pacifists anxiously watched the escalation of the European war. While anti-war protest songs came to the fore in the 1960s, out of the disastrous involvement of the United States in Vietnam (Cochinchina in your day), there were a few – but not many – protest tunes written during the First World War. One of them was "I Didn't Raise My Boy to be a Soldier." It's a song of a mother's lament for her son who is being recruited for war. The chorus echoes her plea:

I didn't raise my boy to be a soldier,
I brought him up to be my pride and joy.
Who dares to place a musket on his shoulder,
To shoot some other mother's darling boy?
Let nations arbitrate their future troubles,
It's time to lay the sword and gun away.
There'd be no war today, If mothers all would say,
"I didn't raise my boy to be a soldier."

This song reflected the anti-war stance of the American public before the United States entered the First World War in 1917. As the entry of the U.S. into the war became more likely, another protest song appeared in late 1916 or early 1917. Titled "Don't Take My Darling Boy Away," it began:

A mother was kneeling to pray
For loved ones at war far away
And there by her side, her one joy and pride,
knelt down with her that day

Then came a knock on the door
Your boy is commanded to war
"No, Captain, please, here on my knees,
I plead for one I adore"

Don't take my darling boy away from me,
Don't send him off to war
You took his father and brothers three,
Now you've come back for more.

It is quite evident that songwriters and singers of Empire countries were generally supportive of the war, while anti-war songs came from a country that was born in protest.

Australia, like Canada, played a bloody price in killed and wounded soldiers in the war. One of the better-known Australian anti-war songs with a First World War theme actually was written in 1971 ("And the Band Played Waltzing Matilda"). Although it purports to be the story of a swagman (bush wanderer) who loses his legs in The First World War, it was also seen as an indirect protest of Australia's involvement in the Vietnam War.

The Australians and New Zealanders took a pasting in the Battle of Gallipoli in The First World War. You may be sorry you were killed; this man was sorry he lived. A blast from a Turkish shell, not unlike the German shell that ended your life, allowed him to live but cost him his two legs. His days as a swagman "waltzing matilda" (roaming and camping in the bushland) were over.

"Never knew there were worse things than dying," he says. Cruel as it sounds, maybe you should count your blessings.

Your nephew,
Orland

THE NEWS STORY THAT LAID AN EGG

Bramshott Camp, Jan. 3, 1916

One of our boys got a letter from Canada to-day and he was showing us a slip of paper cut from a Canadian newspaper which gave an account of the time our battalion left Toronto and what a fine battalion it was. Of course, we don't take much stock of that as every battalion that leaves Canada gets a great write up in the papers. I am going to send you some English papers. I can't get used to them or read them like I read the Toronto papers. I wish you would send me a bunch of papers once in a while.

Somewhere in France July 7, 1916

I haven't got any letters from the West for some time but got a large bundle of papers from May just before leaving England. She sent me a lot of Orillia papers *and* Elmvale Lances *and a Western paper. Roy sends me papers every now and then and I certainly like to get them.*

Dear Uncle Oscar:

I'm very pleased that you miss your newspapers. I miss them too, in different ways. Many have shut down, and those that are left are pale imitations of themselves, with few exceptions. I have fond memories of the many years I worked as a newspaper reporter and columnist before I pitched myself into other word-related jobs. I wouldn't care to go back to the business in its present state. I was familiar with the newspapers you knew: the *Elmvale Lance*, the *Midland Free Press* (which your brother Roy would have sent you), even the *Barrie Examiner*. In your day, newspapers were the primary means of disseminating news.

I want to tell you about an amusing incident at the *Midland Free Press*. Maybe it piqued my curiosity in a newspaper career. When I was in grade nine, I took on a science project to raise young chicks. When they reached egg-laying age, one of them produced a three-yolk egg. While two-yolk eggs were uncommon but sometimes found, we had never seen a three-yolk egg. My mother insisted I take the yolks to Midland to show the editor of *The Free Press*. So I climbed onto a bus, and off I went to Midland. I was rather embarrassed by this because we had put the three yolks in a jar but they could have been any three yolks from anywhere. I walked around town for a while, feeling the yolks sloshing around in the jar in my pocket. I finally screwed up enough courage to walk in and see the editor. (Well, I dared not go home and report I had not seen the editor.) He was kind enough and asked to see the jar. I pulled it out of my pocket and, of course, by now all three yolks had merged together to form scrambled eggs.

He chuckled and I blushed, but he believed me. The next issue of *The Free Press* featured a hot little item about a shy student from Waverley whose high-school chicken had produced a newsworthy egg. I was delighted. All our neighbors commented on the story, and the high-school teachers loved it. It was just a funny little quirky story; the kind that always gets attention. Sure, later in my journalism career I would lay a few eggs on the editorial pages. The weirdness of that story also taught me to avoid strangers who wandered into the newsroom with potatoes that looked like Sir John A. Macdonald's nose (well, actually, most do!).

Today there are so many sources of news that newspapers can no longer compete and survive. Many have disappeared, including the *Midland Free Press* that folded in June 2013. It was founded in the year you were born: 1896. So, it survived 117 years. Like many, if not most newspapers, it had its heyday during the years of independent ownership. Its best years may have been under the direction of Herbert Cranston, a former *Toronto Star Weekly* editor. Cranston won a number of awards. The paper passed into corporate hands in 1965 when it was sold to Thomson Newspapers. From there it was traded from chain to chain like an orphan slave child–Thomson to Hollinger to Osprey to Quebecor and Sun Media–each of them stripping away a slice of the paper's resources, until it had nothing left to give. If I may mix my metaphors, it was then wrapped around a dead corporate fish and stuffed into a trashcan in the stinking back alley of big business.

My experience was with newspapers larger in circulation but maybe no more influential with their subscribers. After training at Ryerson journalism school in Toronto, I got my first job with the *Kingston Whig-Standard*, moving from there to the *Ottawa Citizen*, and later *The Globe and Mail*. *The Globe* calls itself Canada's national newspaper, but you wouldn't know it by that name. George Brown founded it in 1844 as *The Globe*. He was a major political player in the days of Prime Minister John A. Macdonald. In 1895, the year before you arrived on this planet, two papers called the *Toronto Mail* and the *Toronto Empire* merged to form the *Mail and Empire*. In 1936, the *M & E* joined forces with *The Globe* to take on the task of slaying the fiscal, social, and political dragons besetting the nation.

And so, I got into the business of slaying dragons out of journalism school. I eventually wound up with a daily dragon-slaying (or, perhaps at best, dragon-wounding) column in Canada's national newspaper. I've always regarded this as a significant accomplishment for a lad from Waverley, raised on the fodder of the *Free Press* and the *Elmvale Lance*. I tried to clarify issues but, even as I write this, it has been pointed out to me that the year I entered the world, 1944, was the year that the word "gobbledegook" made its first appearance in the English language. My detractors thought we made a team, apparently.

My dad favoured the *Toronto Star*, maybe because it reinforced his Liberal leanings. We picked up our subscription copies of the *Star* and the *Star Weekly* from Hornsby's Garage in Waverley, built on the southeast corner of the main village intersection. Another newspaper you might recall from Toronto was *The Telegram*, which was as Conservative as the *Star* was Liberal. It was founded in 1876 and lasted until 1971, when it collapsed. Out of the ashes came the *Toronto Sun*, a cheeky little tabloid designed and produced by former *Tely* employees for reading on the subway.

As a columnist with *The Globe and Mail*, I wrote for a while about provincial politics in Ontario. I don't know if you were aware of a character named E.C. Drury from Crown Hill, a little farming community not far from Waverley and east of Barrie. Drury founded the United Farmers of Ontario in 1913, and later became its head and Premier of Ontario after the UFO unexpectedly won power in 1919. One of the things he accomplished was the establishment of a forestry program to replant and restore massive wastelands that had been created by rapacious lumber barons. In your day, I imagine the sandy hills around Waverley and Orr Lake, which are now green with artificially planted pine, were little more than deserts. I have seen photos of the desolate hills that inspired Drury to get out the provincial shovel and start planting trees.

Well, Uncle, I started out telling you a chicken-and-egg story. I don't know if that little item alone propelled me into journalism, but it kind of pecked away at me, pardon the yolk.

Your nephew,
Orland

DRAWING LINES IN THE DESERT

Napier Barracks, Shorncliffe, Feb. 21, 1916

I suppose you have been reading of the great Russian victories over the Turks. It will help a lot to relieve the British forces in Mesopotamia. If the war ends this year, as a lot of people here think it will, the new battalions they are recruiting now will hardly see active service.

Dear Uncle Oscar:

Ah, Mesopotamia. If you knew what a mess the Brits made of Mesopotamia after the war, you might not cheer so hard for the Russians. The seeds of conflict in the Middle East were planted after the First World War, and we are still reaping their harvest a century later. History doesn't just happen and stay dormant. It is an ongoing, living creature. It is the cause of "cause and effect."

Few people of your day would recognize Mesopotamia today. You studied it in school, known then as the "cradle of civilization" of the Tigris-Euphrates river system. Today that area has been subdivided by arbitrary political decisions into Iraq, Kuwait, northeastern Syria, southeastern Turkey, and bits of Iran (Persia). Borders of these countries were decided by figuratively drawing lines in the sand, treating the inhabitants of these vast tracts of land like dirt.

And now the people of the dirt are rising up to challenge the white fellows who drew those lines, and we are all being drawn into the cauldron.

Canada went to war again. Just as you fellows found out, it wasn't over by Christmas. (And don't worry about those new battalions being disappointed by an early end to the war. They will be dying to get home in one piece.) I doubt if our new war will be over in my lifetime, even if I live to a great old age. And it's not even a war, in any sense that you might recognize. We don't declare war anymore; we just go and fight evil (as we perceive it) and hope we do the world some good.

You see, it's not against a recognized state. The enemy is not in uniform. We're battling a movement, an idea, with rockets and jet aircraft and shells. We're fighting something called the "Islamic State" in the Middle East. This is a self-defined terrorist gang that has taken control of swatches of Arab countries and is threatening Turkey. The group is called ISIS, standing for Islamic State of Iraq and the Levant. Their intent is to establish a caliphate (an Islamic state headed by a religious and political leader) by sheer force of intimidation and violence.

They rape women and shoot children, they murder anyone who disagrees with their beliefs, and they gain world-wide attention by beheading Westerners on camera and sending the pictures to the West. Like poking a hornet's nest with a sharp stick. Inevitably, the West responds with military action.

Actually, beheading is a traditional form of execution among some cultures, and we didn't take much notice of it until they began lopping off the heads of some of our boys. Then they got more inventive, dousing prisoners with gasoline and tossing a match onto the poor fellows.

So, Canada joined a coalition of 60-some nations who have pledged to take up arms against these extremely militant Islamic warriors. Since many of the nations are white, Western, and Christian, the whole affair seems to be a surrealistic echo of the Crusades.

This is somewhat unlike your war, which pitted Christian against Christian (in Europe), and the only difference in the end was the shape of the crosses in the cemeteries.

The current war is seen as a threat to the whole world. You might wonder, from your place in France, how a ragtag army of fanatics in the deserts of the Middle East could threaten Ottawa and Washington and London. War isn't what it used to be. It is very much a guerrilla war now. Suicidal fanatics even strap bombs to their bodies and blow themselves up in markets or in politically symbolic places. A couple of years ago, two extremists exploded bombs in Boston and disrupted the annual marathon (a road race for runners). Nineteen fanatics hijacked passenger aircraft in 2001 and rammed them into New York office towers and the U.S. military headquarters (called the Pentagon) in Washington. A fourth aircraft plunged into a field in Pennsylvania when passengers overpowered the terrorists. Periodically suicidal fanatics will explode bombs in highly vulnerable areas to terrorize civilians.

Fanaticism is found right here at home. A fanatic used his car to run down and kill a Canadian in uniform in Quebec. At the national war memorial in Ottawa, a fanatic gunned down an honour guard, then forced his way into the Parliament Buildings where he was shot dead by the Sergeant-at-Arms. That Sergeant was promoted to Ambassador to Ireland, where he got into a tussle with a protestor.

You might wonder what this has to do with your war in Europe. Well, there is a direct connection, even a century later. Actually, if you want a starting point to lay the blame for the friction between Muslims and Westerners, you might go back a thousand years, when the Pope and the Catholic Church started organizing crusades to send Christian soldiers marching as to war, to reclaim territories in the Holy Land.

So today, we are sending our armed forces off to the Middle East to fight the fanatics. It's not a Crusade, exactly, but damned close. And the source of this war can be traced to arbitrary decisions made after the end of the First World War. It is often said that the seeds of the Second World War, 20 years later, were planted by the punishments inflicted on Germany at the end of the First. It can also be plausibly argued that the seeds of our conflicts in the Middle East today were also planted at the end of the First World War.

Let me draw you a map. When you went to school, most of the Middle East was dominated by the Ottoman Empire, which we also know as Turkey. The Ottoman Empire was obliterated by the First World War. Its territories in the Middle East were arbitrarily divided into modern states such as Jordan, Syria, Lebanon, Saudi Arabia, Iran, and Iraq. The Arab leaders in most of these states had supported the allies in the war on the understanding that in the post-war world they would gain independence. However, after the war, the British and French made a pretence that the Arabs were not yet ready for self-government and established a number of countries as their protectorates. Needless to say, Uncle, that this did not sit well and another decade of unrest followed, where Arabs rose up in conflict against what they saw as their new colonial masters.

After the Second World War, the imposition of a Jewish state, Israel, on Palestine introduced further ethno-religious strains into the area. The famous Balfour Declaration during the First World War had introduced the concept of a homeland for Jews. In November 1917, Britain declared that it favoured the establishment of a home state for Jews in Palestine. Whatever the merits of this proposal, it was clearly timed to destabilize devotion to the Kaiser's cause among the large numbers of Jews in Germany. Nazi persecution of the Jews during the Second World War, resulting in the murders of millions, became known as the Holocaust. It was the prime reason for the creation of a Jewish homeland in Palestine post Second World War.

History never stays stagnant. It put the mess in Mesopotamia, dear Uncle, and continues to mess with the world decades later.

Your nephew,
Orland

SAM HUGHES, THE ROSS RIFLE, AND GETTING THE BOOT

Riseborough Barrack, Shorncliffe, March 13, 1916

We were up at five o'clock this morning and had our breakfast and were ready to leave for the ranges that are about five miles away at six o'clock. We got back at half-past one and had a good hot dinner. We fired five rounds apiece on the 100, 200, 300 and 400-yard ranges. Some of us have the Ross rifle and some the Lee-Enfield. I have a Ross and believe it is the better of the two. The Lee-Enfield that they are using now is very much shorter than the Ross but the bayonet is very long.

Somewhere in France, Aug. 19, 1916

Yesterday Sam Hughes was here and inspected the 6th Brigade. The King was over here last week but I don't think he visited the Canadian front.

Somewhere in France, Aug. 18, 1916

Say Mother if it is not too much trouble and you get a chance to buy them would you send me a pair of long boots. I don't know what they will cost or what it will take to send them but whatever it is I will make it right. I guess Dad would pick me out a pair sometime when he is in Midland. Size eight would be best so that I can wear a couple of pair of socks and get them with good high legs.

Dear Uncle Oscar:

Ha! I was wondering when you would get around to mentioning Sam Hughes, later Sir Sam Hughes (August 1915), and then the disgraced Sir Sam Hughes (forced to resign from cabinet, November 1916). I've been saving up these three letters so I could reply to them in one shot.

Our man Sam was one of the most controversial figures in Canadian military history. He was tenacious, he was egotistical, he was abrasive, and he was scrappy, uppity, self-absorbed, boastful, and impatient. In film clips from the era, he struts about as if he owns the army. In a way, he did. He was a legend in his own mind. He was also paranoid, seeing conspirators where there weren't any. Ultimately, because of his attitude and his actions, he didn't have to imagine them. They really did exist.

He has been pilloried by history, but as you will see, he did contribute something positive toward promoting our emerging nationalism.

To give him credit, he was the right man in the right place when war broke out in August 1914. The colonies had been given only a brief notice by Mother Britain in the summer that they should prepare for war. Although, if they had been reading the papers, they would have seen it coming. Suddenly Britain was fighting the Hun, and Canada was automatically engaged in the fight. Highly energetic, Hughes moved quickly in response.

Hughes had been Canada's Minister of Militia and Defence from 1911, so he had three years to dream up plans to build up troops and move into action quickly. When war broke out, he supplemented the regular force with militia, and he turned to the cadet corps to encourage military recruitment. Loyalty to the Empire, a longing for exotic action overseas, and a quick job with a pay cheque lured many young unemployed men into the Canadian Expeditionary Force. You, for example. They abandoned the plough and the axe and the wheelbarrow for a smashing new uniform and a dollar a day, plus 10 cents bonus for the privilege of being a Hun target.

Hughes's persuasive and overwhelming personality enabled the minuscule Canadian war machine to get up and running in a remarkably limited time. He started with a small pre-war peacetime force of 3,000 regulars; eventually more than 400,000 would serve overseas. From the outbreak of war in August 1914, he established Camp Valcartier as a training centre in Quebec in a matter of three weeks. Three weeks! It takes longer than that to write the memo today, in both official languages. Yes, it was chaotic, but it was there. From Valcartier, Hughes had troops ready to ship to Europe by October. He was very good off the mark at setting the machine in motion; it was how he conducted himself during the war that led to his downfall and dismissal from cabinet. But you could understand why a guy might take pride in raising an army from a somnolent summer pasture to the training fields of Britain in less than two months.

His detractors will say that the recruiting process was often bungled and the mobilization of the army was marred by the eccentric excesses of the enthusiastic Hughes. Furthermore, when the first troops arrived in Britain, they were poorly trained, even in the basics, and were often led by officers whose qualifications were more often determined by their links with business and Conservative ranks than with any useful military experience.

The location of Valcartier in Quebec was ironic because Hughes had exposed himself as an Anglo and Protestant bigot. Okay, "exposed" is a pejorative word; let's say he rather revelled in it. An Orangeman who expressed anti-Catholic sentiments, he sent English-Canadian officers to round up French-Canadian recruits, and he insisted that francophone volunteers (francophones, that's what we call them, now) speak English in training. Little wonder there was restrained enthusiasm in Quebec for the "British" war.

Hughes had one attribute that would have stood him in good stead among Canadian nationalists of later decades. His Canada-first policy. Hughes firmly believed in equipping Canadian troops with as much Canadian-made equipment as possible. Unfortunately, Canada seemed incapable of producing the quality of goods required for reliable performance in the battlefield. Here's the thing about Hughes: For all his grandiose visions of himself, he sent tens of thousands of men off to war with a rifle that jammed in battle and with boots that rotted and fell apart. Of the things that a man needs to survive on the battlefield, two of the most important are a reliable weapon and reliable boots. And Hughes provided neither. You could say with some justification that many a man died because of Hughes's obsession with a Canada-first policy.

Let's start with the rifle. The British government encouraged its colonial armies to adopt the Lee-Enfield as the soldier's weapon. However, it should also be noted that because of wartime demands, the Lee-Enfield rifle was not easily available to colonial troops and so they searched around for a substitute. The Lee-Enfield was a good rifle, but Hughes insisted on using a Canadian-produced weapon: The Ross Rifle. I know you preferred the Ross because it outperformed the Lee-Enfield on the firing range. And it's true, it did. But that's about the only place it did.

Part of the criticism of Hughes's insistence on using Canadian equipment was perhaps his closeness to some of his suppliers. Sir Charles Ross, developer of the Ross Rifle, is euphemistically described as being well connected with the Canadian political establishment – the establishment being the government in power that relied on contributions and assistance from the companies they were doing business with. Conflict of interest rules and full disclosure of political contributions were not nearly as transparent in those days as today. Let's face it: Patronage was rampant, as it often is in the realm of military purchases.

Here's a list of complaints compiled by detractors of the Ross rifle:
- It was too heavy for hauling easily across the battlefield, weighing 4.5 kilograms (9 lbs 14 oz).
- At 1.5 metres (60.5 inches), it was difficult to manoeuvre in the confined spaces of the trenches.

- If the bolt were not inserted properly, it could blow back into the face of the shooter. Or the rifle would misfire. The Royal North-West Mounted Police, which had been issued the rifle in 1905, were well aware of this problem. They recalled the rifle a year after it was issued.
- The magazine was badly designed, the bayonet often fell off, the safety catch could cut the thumb of the soldier using it, and a poor design made rapid fire difficult.
- Most importantly, on the battlefield where mud prevailed everywhere, the bolt would jam as soon as it saw a speck of dirt. At the Second Battle of Ypres, in May 1915, Canadians threw away their Rosses and picked up the Lee-Enfields of dead British soldiers. Despite modifications and improvements, the Ross had lost the confidence of the men in the field. In 1916, the Ross rifle was withdrawn from front-line service.

Small wonder you went into the machine-gun corps!

Hughes also preferred Canadian-made boots, but you know for yourself they were a miserable excuse for footwear. They leaked and fell apart. In fact, as noted above, you asked your mother to send you some decent boots. When a soldier on the front line has to write to his mother to ask for a pair of decent boots, you know his army has let him down. As I read in your later letters, your mother and father came through with a pair of boots for you. Presumably they served you well in the muck and mud. Among the collection of your letters, I found a clipping of an advertisement for boots made by a company in Penetanguishene, near your home, so I am guessing that your boots came from there.

But I have digressed. As you will know, the Prime Minister himself gave Sir Sam the boot. He kicked him out of cabinet. Despite his enthusiastic successes early in the war, Hughes wearied his superiors and his colleagues with his single-minded notion of how the war should be fought. His stubborn defence of the Ross Rifle stuck in the craw of Prime Minister Robert Borden. Criticism grew within cabinet and Hughes became politically isolated. Ultimately, he stepped over the line in assuming too much command of the Canadian overseas operation. Borden moved to limit Hughes' power. Hughes fought back, and Borden booted him out of cabinet in November 1916.

However, lost in all this abuse tossed upon the memory of poor Sammy is his pride in Canada, which ought not be forgotten. When Canadian soldiers first arrived in Britain, they were seen as colonial replacements to fill gaps in British formations. The Canadian government resisted this attitude, and Sam Hughes refused to let the Canadian units be split up. They trained in Britain together, they went to France together, and ultimately, they fought together at Vimy Ridge, four divisions side by side, shoulder to shoulder, sweeping the Germans off the hill and securing the heights for the Good Guys. That was you and thousands like you. You were there, you sacrificed your life, but your colleagues acting together achieved your goal and instilled pride in an emerging nation. To this day, we celebrate that victory and mark the spot with a massive monument atop Vimy Ridge. We take pride in that achievement, and rightfully so. In that crucible of Vimy Ridge, we say, we began to forge Canada as an independent nation.

Sam Hughes, that abrasive, insufferable, pompous, irascible, nationalistic old goat, had a lot to do with that.

Your nephew,
Orland

THE BIRTH OF CAMP BORDEN

Risboro' Barracks, Shorncliffe
June 12th, 1916

I got a letter from Roy last week and he said that they were forming a great camp near Barrie this summer at a place called Angus Plains and they expected that they would have about forty thousand men there training.

Dear Uncle Oscar:

The camp your brother Roy refers to still exists; it is called Camp Borden, or more properly, Canadian Forces Base Borden. Coincidentally it bears the name of the Prime Minister at the time it was created, Robert Borden. Although it covers 17,000 acres west of Barrie, there was no loss of prime farmland. You will remember those sandy hills south of Waverley, bereft of growth but littered with huge stumps of cut-away pines. The same was true at Borden, where lumber companies had grazed away towering pines and moved on.

The camp was built on a glacial moraine, which accounts for the sandy soil. It was not unlike the hills around Waverley. It was built in 1916 by the Barrie and Collingwood companies of the 157th Battalion, also known as the Simcoe Foresters and today as the Grey and Simcoe Foresters. The original intent was to use the base to train ground troops for the war in Europe, and initially it was occupied by 32,000 troops. But, as air power began flexing its wings, the base became the first flying station of the Royal Flying Corps Canada, later the Royal Canadian Air Force. An aerodrome was constructed, and the base was regarded as the finest military aviation camp in North America. In 1938, the base was expanded to include the Canadian Tank School. Nothing like ramming tanks across sandy fields and through pine forests! It hadn't been as ideal as an air-training base. The open sandy plains were known for local sandstorms, causing havoc for untrained pilots in planes with open cockpits. But keep in mind, this was a government project.

The base continues to be one of Canada's primary training centres for several branches of the Canadian Forces.

It's only 25 miles or so from Waverley. If you had trained at Borden, you could almost have gone home for lunch.

Your nephew,
Orland

SOMEONE'S IN THE BEDROOM
WITH KITCHENER

Riseborough Barracks, Shorncliffe, June 12, 1916

Wasn't that a corker about Lord Kitchener being lost. Nobody would believe it until they had seen a paper. They are having quite a time to determine on a man to take his place. I don't think that they will get anyone any better.

Dear Uncle Oscar:

Yes, wasn't that a corker about Lord Kitchener? Losing him to the Germans like that. A hero going down with his ship. Funny thing about history. Sometimes in retrospect you learn a lot more than you might want to. As they say in my generation, TMI – Too Much Information.

Let's have a go at this fellow's story. In your day, as far as you knew, he was an absolutely stalwart and stellar British military leader. For the record, he was Field Marshal Horatio Herbert Kitchener, 1ˢᵗ Earl Kitchener, KG, KP, GCB, OM, GCSI, GCMG, GCIE, ADC, PC. For those who want to figure out the alphabet soup, they can look it up elsewhere. GCMG, for instance, stands for the Most Distinguished Order of St. Michael and Saint George, for extraordinary non-military service in a foreign country. Our man Kitchener served his mother country in Western Palestine and Cyprus as a surveyor, then in Egypt, Sudan, Khartoum, South Africa, and India in a military capacity.

Kitchener, in name, in appearance, and in experience, was a model of British military bearing. With his plastered-down hair carefully parted in the centre, his brushed luxurious moustache, and a chestful of medals and braid sufficient to span the English Channel, he looked every bit the imposing military hero. He had a commanding image, used to effect on recruiting posters declaring "Your Country Needs You." His foreign record was impeccable, and he seemed the perfect man to organize Britain's battle with the Hun.

He was available at the right time. When the First World War began, Kitchener was appointed Secretary of State for War right away by British Prime Minister Herbert Asquith. This put him in the cabinet. Unlike many of his colleagues who viewed events through rose-coloured glasses, he did not believe the war would be over by Christmas. Kitchener began to prepare for the long haul. He figured on a war of at least three years (when you died, it was nearing three years in length, with another year and a half to go), costing hundreds of thousands of lives. He organized the largest volunteer army that Britain had ever seen, and he expanded materials production in preparation for the long and nasty fight. And he was right.

As it turned out, he also had a prolonged fight within the higher ranks of the military structure with Field Marshal John Denton Pinkstone French, 1st Earl of Ypres. We should perhaps digress from our discussion of Kitchy to examine the role of Field Marshal French. As far as I know, you and I are not related to French. Well, maybe through several dozen generations deferred, but he is of the landed gentry (related to the French/De Freyne family of Ireland, don't you know). You and I are products of the gentry who landed in Waverley, Ontario. I don't believe owning a farm in Simcoe County is quite the same thing. Anyway, he was a military officer of some importance, having distinguished himself during the Second Boer War and becoming Chief of the Imperial General Staff in 1912. Later he was known as The Viscount French. (Sometimes when I stared out the window during my lessons at Waverley public school, I was known as The Vacant French. That, again, is not quite the same thing.) Along the way, he picked up a knighthood and became Sir John.

Our namesake was the first Commander-in-Chief of the British Expeditionary Force in the First World War, but that was long before you showed up in France. French apparently got along with the French, I mean the ones who governed France, at least at first. As time went on, relations became strained over Sir John's strategies. Our man Kitchener was also unhappy with his performance, and so in late December 1915, after a period of backroom hemming and hawing about what to do with the leader in the field, Sir John French was called home to England where he became Commander-in-Chief of the British Home Forces. He was succeeded by Douglas Haig upon whom he would dump huge heaps of scorn.

Since "British Home" included Ireland, one of French's first duties was suppressing the Easter Rising of 1916. This coincided with rumours of a German invasion of Britain, an invasion that, according to French, was probably concocted in Kitchener's head. There was speculation about collaboration between the Irish and the Germans that French said he didn't believe for a moment. At any rate, he crushed the Irish Uprising. Although he had been demoted from his role in Europe, French was still in a position to take potshots at Haig for his conduct of the war. Over time, the tarnish was gradually polished off French's sullied reputation, and by the end of the war, he had been appointed Lord Lieutenant of Ireland where he was able to antagonize friend and foe alike with his fiery approach to life.

Now, I include this next bit so my wife can see that I possess a family trait, if indeed I have any connection to Sir John French.

Your British French has been described as a man of hot temper and mood swings. Okay, I plead guilty to that. He must have been short, for he apparently wore a long tunic to de-emphasize his diminutive stature. (I note from your attestation papers that you were five-foot-seven, which is not particularly tall, but tall enough not to require a long tunic for costume purposes.) Generally, French was well liked by the public and his men, an adoration not enjoyed by Haig.

Now, let's get back to Kitchener. When we left him several paragraphs ago, he was organizing a huge army and its supplies. However, by June 1915, he was drawing heavy political fire for not being able to arrange the provision of enough rifles and shells to keep up with demand. Given the rate of expenditure of tens of thousands of shells in any given attack, this is not surprising.

However, he did get credit for inventing "the Kitchener stitch" which was a technique for knitting socks with a seamless join of the toe. Until then, sock patterns included a seam in the toe that could be painfully annoying in a military boot. The Kitchener Stitch is still a recognized knitting term by yarn-knotters who probably have no idea that they are benefiting from a long-ago invention by a war hero.

They say a stitch in time saves nine, but it didn't save Lord Kitchener. On June 5, 1916, Kitchener boarded the armoured cruiser HMS *Hampshire* for a diplomatic mission to Russia. On the way, *Hampshire* ran into a mine laid by a German U-boat and sank with the loss of 643 lives, including Kitchener's. His body was never recovered.

As you said, "A corker, indeed." A distinguished career snuffed out in a few moments by a chance encounter with a mine.

Well, yes, but then the historians went to work. You can't believe how historians can savage a reputation. Over time, they delved into letters and dispatches and diaries and put together an unseemly personality profile of our beloved Kitchener. First off, there were some commentators, even at the time of his death, who were, shall we say, less than distressed at his loss. For all his brilliance at gearing up for the war, they suggested that he might have been losing his touch. C.P. Scott, editor of the *Manchester Guardian*, commented, "He could not have done better than to have gone down, as he was a great impediment lately." Hmm. That's a severe indictment. In other words, his death saved the British government the distasteful task of removing him from power. That sounds unkind, but this was war. What was the cost of one man's career given that the lives of hundreds of thousands depended on the questionable whims of his leadership?

And then, there were other less savoury revelations. Some biographers claim he was a latent or active homosexual, while others say he had a predilection for close and sometimes unwanted relationships with either sex. We needn't go into details here. Better we had closed the discussion of his career when *Hampshire* went down and let the *Guardian's* Scott have the last say.

Your nephew,
Orland

SHOOT FIRST AND SAVE THE WORLD

Somewhere in France
June 26ᵗʰ, 1916

I have reached France at last. I landed early this morning and had a nice little march up to our quarters. We are in tents for tonight and don't know when we will get a move from this camp. I had an uneventful voyage across the channel. We left Shorncliffe early on Sunday morning and did not get aboard our boat until four o'clock in the afternoon.

Dear Uncle Oscar:

Now that you're in France, keep your eyes open for the devil. You'll probably never have the chance but if you come across a certain German soldier, you would be forgiven for shooting him in cold blood. You will change history, and the world will thank you.

That German is Lance Corporal Adolf Hitler, who rose to power and led his country into a devastating Second World War that Germany ultimately lost. Millions died during that war, barely two decades after your war came to a halt, on the same battlefields that were so thoroughly raked over in the First World War. Unlike the First World War, where purposes were murky, the Second World War was good versus evil, a black-and-white division of morality and principle. Germany was clearly driven by the devil.

There is a persistent story that a British soldier actually had a wounded Hitler in his sights, but couldn't bring himself to kill a wounded man. Hitler later had a painting of the battle, and would point out the soldier in the painting and tell people, "That's the man who nearly shot me."

It would have been murder but, in the perspective of history, a murder that could have been justified.

Your bloodthirsty nephew,
Orland

THE FAMILY TREE BRANCHES OUT

Somewhere in France
July 11ᵗʰ 1916

I suppose Goldie is with Owen and Jennie this summer again. Tell Dora to keep on writing to me if I don't write to her very often as I like to get her letters. I suppose that you will all be taking in the 12th of July walk this year. Write and let me know where they held it. I suppose Roy is getting plenty of work this summer at the planing mill. I suppose Annie will be with you for a visit sometime this summer.

Dear Uncle Oscar:

Let's take a break from the war and bring you up to date on what happened to your brothers and sisters in the years after your death in 1917. Most of them lived a good long adult life, with the exception of the three little fellows who died as infants or young children (Albert Earl, Eddie, and a second Albert Earl).

Roy, the eldest of the family and with whom you lived for a short time in Midland, did well in the marine business. His full name was Thomas William Royal French. Now here was an anomaly. While many of your family opted to stay with farming, Roy got into the boat building and servicing business. He operated a rather grand-sounding firm called Great Lakes Boat and Machine Co. in Midland Bay, repairing, building, and servicing recreational boats and yachts sailing on Georgian Bay. He called it simply "The Shop."

Stories about Roy, known as Uncle Roy to me, are legendary. Like a cat, he seemed to have nine lives. Whether he was being pushed down the railway sideways by a locomotive, having the wheels drop off his car, or hanging upside down from an extension ladder, he seemed immune to the laws of accidental death or dismemberment. His annual family outings aboard one of his charter yachts turned into adventures recounted with glee and horror. "Remember the time he ordered the captain to pull into a private dock just as a storm hit?" It was one of the family legends – the boat jumped out of gear, drifted onto a shoal, and all the men had to get out and stand on the high side to keep the boat upright. Or the time he said he was departing Beausoleil Island Park at 7 o'clock and he meant it. As two older women, late, hustled down the dock toward the yacht he untied the bow. While the bow of the boat started to drift out, the women scrambled over the railing as he untied the stern line.

Roy could be an impatient man. Maybe that's where I got my impatience gene. His daughter Helen once purchased a flashy Plymouth Fury, a high-finned Chrysler product of the late 1950s packed with power. No matter how fast she drove, and she was not known for submitting to the arbitrary rule of speed limits at any time, he'd say, "Can't you go faster?" Roy died in 1966 of natural causes.

You'll remember the three children from the marriage of Roy to Agnes MacNeill: Alden, Florence, and Helen. Alden was born in 1908, only three years after my father, Elmer, his uncle. Because of the closeness of their ages, Alden and Elmer grew up more like brothers than uncle and nephew, and this held true through their adult lives. They attended meetings of the Masonic Lodge together.

Your sister Annie Elizabeth, next in line, married Silas Brown in Penetanguishene (Penetang to us) in 1903. Maybe you went to the wedding. They farmed in Tiny Township and had one son, David, who was born in 1914 before you went overseas. Annie died in 1948.

May Lecetta, your next sister, spent her married life farming on the wheat fields near Kindersley, Saskatchewan. She married William John Smith in 1911, and off they went to the wild blue yonder of the Canadian West. My western relatives (May, Goldie, Erne, Verne) were the mysterious branch of your family. During my childhood of the 1940s and '50s, they occupied a far-off part of Canada that was usually visible only through railway travel brochures and ads in the weekend magazines. Western aunts and uncles would pop up occasionally and do something memorable. Like the time May came "down" to Ontario and made bread for my dad. She must have thought she was baking for a threshing crew. We had loaves lined up on the kitchen counter, in drawers, in the fridge, maybe even on a sales table outside along the highway. She sure could bake bread. May and Bill had a son, Lorne. May died in 1969.

Owen was your brother that I probably knew best because he lived the closest and visited often. He inherited your family farm and later he and Jennie (married 1915, when you were getting ready for service) built a small frame retirement house in Waverley. Jenny seemed to spend much of her time in Drinkle's general store waiting for the mail, always a good time to review, renew, and repackage the village gossip. Once she caught a gang of young gaffers (me included) trying to cash in some soft drink bottles we had liberated from Hornsby's gas station across the road. Life lesson learned: We didn't do that again. And I don't think she told Mom, or I would have heard more about it. Owen and Jennie tooled about in a shiny black Pontiac fastback, circa 1950. Well, they didn't travel very far, but wherever they went, they rode in elegance. A fastback was a body style that sloped from roofline to rear bumper and is still admired by antique car buffs.

In later life, Owen became hard of hearing. Today we have "hearing aids," small electronic devices that fit snugly into the ear. His family was encouraging him to get a hearing aid because he was having trouble hearing much of anything, especially from Jenny. He once retorted, "I hear what I want to hear."

Owen and Jennie had two sons, Edward and Donald. Don took over the farm, but after a while, he felt he would rather sow seeds of faith from the pulpit and went into the Anglican ministry. Owen died in 1977.

Ernest (Uncle Erne to me) married Mabel Drummond and was one of the western French clan. I was always confusing May and Mabel. Dad used to talk about going out West on a "harvest excursion." Young men from eastern Canada would head west on trains in the fall to help bring in the grain harvest. I believe he went to help Uncle Erne. Dad told me one time he and the rest of the crew decided to walk over to visit a neighbouring harvest crew during their lunch break. They clearly had no idea of the vastness of the Prairie. "We walked and we walked, and after half an hour, we didn't seem to be any closer, so we turned around and went back," Dad said. Ernest died about 1963.

Your sister Laura Ethel married Fred Adamson, you'll recall, in 1913. They farmed near Beaverton on the east side of Lake Simcoe. We'd visit them once or twice a year; usually Dad would say suddenly, "Let's go visit Laura and Fred." It was an hour or so drive. It struck me odd that it seemed to be raining whenever we visited Aunt Laura. The ground was always wet and mushy. It didn't occur to me for a very long time that since Dad was a house painter, he couldn't work outdoors on rainy days, so we'd go visit Aunt Laura. It was no coincidence. Uncle Fred couldn't work the fields on rainy days either, so it was a good time to visit. Fred and Laura had five children: Douglas, Phyllis, Mildred, Betty, and Frances. Laura died in 1967.

Laverne, or as we knew him, Verne, born in 1894, went off to the Great War, just like you. However, he survived, although he was a victim of a gas attack and occasionally suffered from it all his life.

He married a delightful girl named Carrie, and they farmed near Carrot River in Saskatchewan. When they retired, they returned to

Ontario. For a while he worked as night watchman at Uncle Roy's machine shop. He also lived on Easy Street in Midland, a dream of most of us. Later, he and Carrie lived near Hespeler (now part of Cambridge). Verne resembled Dad, and one time on a visit to Waverley he went for a stroll wearing short pants. Shorts were not all that fashionable among men at the time (1950s), and a neighbourhood boy reported to his mother that he had just seen Elmer wearing shorts. His mother said it was highly unlikely that Elmer would be wearing short pants. She was right.

After Verne died in 1956, Carrie moved to Vancouver. She was, in my mind, a remarkably adventurous lady. One night, unannounced, she got off the bus outside our house in Waverley after travelling across the country from Vancouver. When we asked her what she would have done if we had not been home, she replied nonchalantly, "Oh, I know where the key is." One day, years later, when I was a travelling columnist for *The Globe and Mail*, I thought I would repay her with a surprise visit in Vancouver. As I approached her apartment building, I found her walking slowly along the street, carrying two grocery bags. I stepped up smartly and said, "Hello, Aunt Carrie." She glanced at me and said, "Oh, hello Orland. Well, come on in, and we'll make tea." She was as casual as if I had dropped by every day.

On another occasion, my wife Sylvia and I were on holiday in British Columbia, driving a borrowed sports car. Aunt Carrie navigated from the front passenger seat. She took great delight in that touring episode, boasting about getting reduced or free seniors' admission to almost everything, thanks to the generous Social Credit government of the day.

This is where you came into the family, born in 1896, two years after Verne. Your parents must have been an amorous couple for only 10 months after you were born, your sister Goldie Marion popped into the world.

Aunt Goldie was another of those glamourous, mysterious Westerners. She became an optometrist, one of the first female optometrists in the West. She loved Western Canada and was always promoting it. One Christmas, she sent me a book about a young boy riding horses and doing all the ranching things that people do in the West. I kept the book for years and re-read it several times. Once she sent Dad a stalk of wheat that she had picked out of an unusual place: the grill of her car. For some reason she had dropped off the road and unexpectedly taken a detour through a wheat field. I found this fascinating, that she could survive a terrible accident and laugh about it. I imagined her car bouncing through a ditch, ripping out a wire fence, skidding around in a wheat field, and coming to rest mired to the hubcaps in western clay. It was only years later, when I saw wheat fields in Saskatchewan, that I realized they were not separated from the roads with ditches and page-wire fences, as they are in Ontario. You could drive off the road almost anywhere, take a wild ride through a wheat field, and get back onto the pavement without doing any damage, except to the wheat.

A traffic accident eventually cost Aunt Goldie her life in 1975.

Your sister Dora Irene married Arthur Elijah Field on September 16, 1924. Art, as he was called, was born to Frank and Lottie Field and was raised on a farm on the Seventh Line of Flos, near Elmvale. Art left home around the age of 16 or 17 to seek his fortune in Toronto. He worked for various companies such as Canada Dry and Canada Wire and Cable. After their marriage, Art and Dora lived in a house in a Toronto suburb called Leaside. They had no children. In 1943, Dora suddenly died of a heart attack or stroke at the relatively young age of 43. Art remarried, to Anne Spiers McCall Dick, an immigrant from Scotland. They had one child, William, who became a banker. Art took over a grocery store and in 1956 moved to his old home territory of Elmvale and established Field's Fine Foods. Art and Anne purchased a magnificent old home on Queen Street, the main street of Elmvale, from a doctor named Corcoran. In recent years, in my lifetime, it became an elegant restaurant until it burned in 2010. Dr. Corcoran's son was my dentist in Midland. He must have known his stuff because later in my life other dentists would marvel at his work and say, "He was a hero. A lot of dentists would have pulled those teeth."

Art and my dad Elmer were good friends. Elmer was born in 1905, so he was only 10 when you went off to war. He married Eunice Edna Grigg of Waverley. Maybe you knew Eunice; she would have been nine years old when you went to training camp in 1915. She was one of five children of Eli and Elizabeth Grigg who farmed on top of Victoria Hill north of Waverley. It had a great view of the village. Her brother Oliver also served in the First World War and survived a close call with death. I used to wonder why he had a permanent dimple in one of his cheeks until Mother told me that was where the machine-gun bullet went through and took out all his teeth on one side of his mouth. You might say he survived by the skin of his teeth. That made him a genuine war hero to me. Doc Corcoran couldn't have done much for his teeth.

Mother and Dad had four children and occupied the house in Waverley, where your parents had lived, until they passed on. Gerald, the oldest, was named Gerald Oscar after you. Next in line was Warren Neil, then me, Orland Clare, and finally our young sister, Patricia Louise. Gerald was a hydro operator who became an entrepreneur and built Medonte Mountain Ski Resort north of Barrie, near Craighurst. It's part of Horseshoe Resort today. Warren earned his doctorate and became a civil servant in the Food and Drug Administration of the federal government. Pat became a "physio," short for physiotherapist. She moved out West, like some of her aunts and uncles, married an Alberta dentist, and lives in Calgary. I became a journalist and writer, working for newspapers such as the *Kingston Whig-Standard, the Ottawa Citizen, and The Globe and Mail.*

Dad died of heart failure at home in Waverley in 1973. I have often thought his occupation as house painter and decorator, working with lead-based paints, may have contributed to his early death. Mother lived alone in the house for nearly 20 years before she moved to a seniors' residence in Midland for a few years before her death. Gerald was reluctant to sell the Waverley property for a while until one day I had to shovel the snow off the roof of the vacant house. That was it. I said finally, "Sell it." So we did. Gerald died at his home in Barrie on April 1, 2010.

His son David just had another son, a fifth child, and Gerald's other son Greg is raising a family in China, so you can see the French line is still healthy and productive.

Your nephew,
Orland

SEX AND THE SINGLE SOLDIER
MARRIED ONES TOO

Somewhere in France, November 6, 1916

We are out of the line again and back in our billets for a short while. We have a pretty good place to stop in when we are out here. We are in an old house that has been fixed up and bunks put in and there is a couple of fireplaces, so we are able to have a fire when it is cold and wet. We have been issued with our winter clothes, got a leather jacket to-day and it is well lined so ought to be pretty warm. We are able to get a bath quite regular now and that is certainly a great help.

Dear Uncle Oscar:

Frequently your letters refer to being "out of the line" and "back in our billets." I assume this means you have been rotated out of your tour of duty in the trenches and sent back behind the lines for a rest. You haven't provided much detail about what you do during your rest periods, but I'm wondering if you are familiar with this little ditty:

Mademoiselle from Armentieres, parley-voo?
Mademoiselle from Armentieres, parley-voo?
She never could hold the love of man
'Cause she took her baths in a talcum can
Hinky, dinky, parley-voo.

There are many variations on this song, most of which I would blush to enclose in a letter even to someone who has faced the rigours of the front line. But I'm curious: Where do you get your baths "quite regular" now? From Mademoiselle Bernadette? Denise? Simone? I'm teasing you, Uncle. Even if you were getting your baths from Marie or Madeleine, you wouldn't tell your mother. It's like that time you wrote enthusiastically about your first visit to London. You told her about going to Buckingham Palace and the British Museum and other tourist attractions that would, naturally, be first on the list of any young man in uniform hitting the big city. I didn't notice any mention of enjoying visits to pubs like The Cock and Bull or The Whistling Pig.

Getting back to France, you know what I'm talking about. In any place where there are concentrations of men, particularly young virile men with raging hormones, women of a certain virtue are bound to show up, offering services such as bathing, beds, and beyond. You could call them ladies of the night, soothers of the soul, working girls, prostitutes, whores, or hookers, and so on down the list of steadily demeaning terms, depending on what you thought of them. In our world, they call themselves "sex workers," like it's a real job with union benefits (and may well be some day). Since the brothels behind the lines in northern France were legal, inspected, and regulated by the French government, it might come as a surprise to you to learn that a hundred years later brothels are still illegal in Canada. In fact, the role of the legal bordello in the First World War was not so distant from the goal of "sex workers" today who seek to have a legitimate place in the bedrooms of today's society.

They provide a service, just as women did in France during the First World War. It was good for business in a community busted by the war, and it was good for the morale of men who might be dead in a day or two.

I'm not saying you know from personal experience, for it is hard to imagine a young, teenage farm lad from Waverley, smothered within the confining arms of the Methodist Church, visiting such places. I'm just thinking you might have picked up some reports "from the front", if you catch my drift, from some of your buddies who were perhaps less restrictive – dare I say looser? – in their moral attitudes. Or maybe you went down to the village to take a look. That's okay. I'm not making judgments.

But then, as today, people's views were all over the map. The purists were opposed, the men were in favour, and the army dealt with prostitution as a fact of life that wasn't ever going to go away and could be beneficial, as long as it was regulated.

The French tolerated bordellos, but then the French are French, right? They even licensed them, and by 1917, there were 137 legalized brothels in 35 towns in northern France. Same on the German side. But ah, those British, where it seemed the only thing stiff they admitted to was the upper lip. The British did not encourage the purchase of sexual favours. Still, the class system was at work. Many people believed that enlisted men were incapable of controlling their sexual urges, unlike officers, made of sterner stuff, who came from middle-class and upper-class stock. Honest, that's what they believed, at least officially.

Your hero, Lord Kitchener, believed a self-controlled soldier was a superior soldier. He wrote an advice pamphlet for his soldiers in India, and later in France, in which he said: "Every man can by self-control restrain the indulgence of those imprudent and reckless impulses that so often lead men astray, and he who thus resists is a better soldier and a better man than the man of weak will who allows his bodily appetites to rule him and has not the strength of character to resist temptation and to refuse to follow any bad example he may see before him." All very Victorian in language and style and widely ridiculed by officers and men alike. Given what we learned later about Kitchener, as I wrote in another letter, the advice about controlling one's "imprudent and reckless impulses" seems a tad hypocritical.

They don't put much in the war history books about sex. You have to weasel out the facts from various postwar studies of letters and memoirs of veterans who returned. Not many of them would mention it, for fear of offending wives or girlfriends. And, as in any personal retelling of sexual adventures, you have to filter out a certain amount of braggadocio. Still, from what I've read, I've been able to put together a list of rules and conventions to be followed if one wishes to take advantage of the local pleasure sanctuary.

1. Know what you're getting into. Hard to believe, but there are examples of naive young men who had only a vague idea of what went on inside a brothel or a bordello. Maybe they went to play pinochle. You are going there to share sexual experiences with a stranger in exchange for money. In the crude vernacular of today, you are going there to pay to get laid. A woman will take off her clothes, and you will pay her to have sex with you. But be careful, you're dealing with a foreign language here. Make sure you know what you're looking for. A legal bordello is called a *maison toleree,* while a *maison de fous* is a lunatic asylum. Don't worry; you'll be able to pick out a brothel by the lustful line-up of smirking soldiers outside the door.

2. Do not panic and run. Young men who have gone over the top against German bullets and shells and shrapnel have panicked at the sight of naked women in a whorehouse. One soldier recalled that a group of his colleagues freaked out when they visited a brothel. "When five naked girls came dashing down the corridor we turned and ran."

3. Know your place. The "red lamp" houses are for enlisted men; the "blue lamp" houses are for officers. You do not want to share a woman with your commanding officer, nor do you want to meet your commanding officer coming in while you are leaving. "Evening, sir. Monique the redhead is available now. I believe she is your favourite."

Officers do not wish to share their women with the ranks. Later in the war, when the lines finally shift and the Allies move forward, officers will prefer to patronize German officer bordellos rather than mingle with their own men. Red Lamp brothels provided simple necessities: a cot, a thin sheet, a generous woman. One soldier reported that the experience was "like wanking but you had someone to talk to." At the Blue Lamps, an officer might get champagne and even eggs and bacon for breakfast.

4. Nothing's free. The madam of the house will collect a franc at the bottom of the stairs, and you will pay a franc or more to the companion of your choice upstairs, depending on how she has satisfied your cravings. You are lucky you are a Canadian. Apparently British soldiers often had to do without while their Empire buddies were sweating in the bed sheets, because they weren't paid as well and couldn't afford the action.

5. Dress for the occasion. You know, use prophylactics. We call these things French safes or condoms. You want to stay healthy so you can die in battle. Shot by a doc or shot by a Hun, your choice. Syphilis or gonorrhea could be a reasonable alternative to a shell burst. If you picked up the clap or something, you'd be guaranteed at least a month in a hospital. In fact, 150,000 men in the British army were admitted to hospital with venereal infections picked up in France. A month off the line could be comparable to buying yourself another month of life. It is also a much more pleasant way to become hors de combat than shooting yourself in the foot. Of course, there are risks to long-term health, but given the likelihood that you were going to die in the short term anyway, who cares? Maybe it is just soldier talk, but there are stories of men seeking out infected prostitutes and paying them extra just to pick up a disease. They would not dress for the occasion. You have to take your own prophylactics to a Red Lamp house. Blue Lamps, being of a higher quality, provide condoms for officers.

6. It's guilt-free sex. If a married guy did this back home, he'd be cheating on his wife. Not in France. There are different rules on the battlefield. It is forgiven under military convention. Brigade chaplains advise that such behaviour is excused under the abnormal conditions of wartime. A married man, used to having sex regularly at home, might lose his fighting spirit if he didn't have a sexual outlet at the Front. It is generally recognized that married men are used to regular sex and require it to keep them on an even temperament. Unmarried soldiers, not so much. However, in a blatant contradiction, it is also recognized that regular sex is required to maintain a man's physical health. Without using a whorehouse, your choices are limited to dating yourself or one of the other guys in the trench. Or you might find an unlicensed, unregulated, uninspected street vamp who could be infected with anything.

There you go. Enjoy the charms of Isabelle or Suzanne and slip off to dreamland, well away from the mud and the horrors of the battlefield. You might never come this way again.

Your nephew,
Orland

PS: I shouldn't tease you about your report from London. Here's what I wrote to my mother on my first visit to London in July 1967: "Took a bus tour of old London – saw the parliament buildings, Big Ben, Westminster Abbey, the Tower of London, London Bridge, etc. One night I walked down and stood on a bridge over the Thames while Big Ben struck the hour. Just like any other tourist, I suppose.

"Also went to the wax museum at Madame Tussaud's and the London Planetarium next door. Visited the famous market on Petticoat Lane Sunday morning. What a crowd there was there! In that area also, buildings are still in ruins after the bombing of World War II.

But what I did most in London was walk – one night I thought I'd never be able to walk again – but next morning I did some more."

See? I didn't mention women or pubs either. But I certainly noticed English women. The mini skirt was in full fashion in London, but the fad had not yet spread to North America. What I noticed was an incredible acreage of leggy female flesh in full public view, sometimes exposed as much as eight inches above the knee. Upon returning to my job at *The Kingston Whig-Standard,* I wrote a travel fashion article which opened along these lines: "I was in London three days before I noticed British girls had faces." Yes, in today's terms, that was terribly sexist and politically incorrect. It got by the editor then, but it wouldn't today.

OTHER WOMEN OF THE WAR

Dear Uncle Oscar:

In case I shocked you with my last letter, I want to assure you that there were other types of women who were fully engaged in the war effort.

Have you ever heard of Nellie McClung? She was a Western Canadian writer and political activist who published some tangy criticism of the war from a woman's point of view. I wonder if you ever read any of her comments. I don't imagine they made popular reading in the trenches.

Nellie Letitia McClung was one of Canada's earliest and most effective feminists. That is, someone promoting women's causes. In your day your mother could not vote. Nor could your sisters, unless they owned property. But wait a minute, neither could you, nor could most of the young men who were slaughtered on the battlefields of Europe. You had to be 21 to vote, and you had been a teenager when you signed on, and only 20 when you died.

Only mature men could vote and endorse the actions of a government that led its nation into war. McClung thought that might change if women, i.e. "the people," could have the right to vote.

Women were first granted the right to mark an X at a ballot box in Manitoba in 1916, thanks to pressures from people like Nellie McClung. The federal government capitulated in 1918, various Maritime provinces stumbled into acceptance through the 1920s, and the last hold-out was Quebec. It withheld women's right to vote until the 1940s.

What does this have to do with your death? Nothing, directly, except that the war changed social attitudes. When you and your young buddies went away to war, who do you think filled your jobs back home? Women. With hard-working men like you out of the country, women took your jobs. And, surprisingly, at least to the men left at home, they did a rather good job of it.

It opened the eyes of a lot of people: Women could do more than raise children, cook meals, clean floors, make beds, and wash windows. They were more than dainty creatures. They could do real work in a man's world.

McClung was convinced that empowered women could make the world a more civil place. Women hated to see their sons and fathers and husbands and lovers going off to war. They might modify the public lust for battle. On the other hand, men loved war, she thought, and the male-written histories of war tended to glorify military actions.

In Times Like These, a book she published just after the commencement of the First World War, McClung wrote, "History, romance, legend and tradition having been written by men, have shown the masculine aspect of war and have surrounded it with a false glory and have sought to throw the veil of glamour over its hideous face. Our histories have followed the wars. Invasions, conquests, battles, sieges make up the subject-matter of our histories." And losers don't write histories.

This was her view of how wars began: "Some glorious soul, looking out upon his neighbours, saw some country that he thought he could use and so he levied a heavy tax on the people, and with the money fitted out a splendid army. Men were called from their honest work to go out and fight other honest men who had never done them any harm; harvest fields were trampled by their horses' feet, villages burned, women and children fled in terror, and perished of starvation, streets ran blood and the Glorious Soul came home victorious with captives chained to his chariot wheel. When he drove through the streets of his own hometown, all the people cheered, that is, all who had not been killed, of course."

And in the same passage, she included a reference which brought to mind your own demise, as you will see: "We have all wondered what would happen if the people someday decided that they would no longer be the tools of the man higher up, what would happen if the men who make the quarrel had to fight it out. How glorious it would have been if this war could have been settled by somebody taking the Kaiser out behind the barn! There would seem to be some show of justice in a hand-to-hand encounter, where the best man wins, but modern warfare has not even the faintest glimmering of fair play. The exploding shell blows to pieces the strong, the brave, the daring, just as readily as it does the cowardly, weak, or base."

No matter how strong, brave, and daring you were, the anonymous exploding shell took your life. I place you among the strong, the brave, the daring, for how else could you force yourself to be in that place the day the Canadians took Vimy Ridge?

But you know what? Women vote like men. They also vote FOR men, even when they have a chance to increase the female component of parliament. Women have had the vote for almost a century, and still we have wars and military actions determined by male-dominated governments and parliaments.

McClung was one of those early Western Canadian populists who eventually founded social democratic parties like the Co-operative Commonwealth Federation (CCF). These parties promote policies that the care-giving side of our society, our mothers and sisters and aunts and daughters, naturally favour. These parties pushed for women's rights, and medicare, and fairer labour laws, and many other social improvements, which have been adopted for Canadians. They got elected as governing parties in some of the provinces, but they have yet to crack the national nut. No socialist government has yet held power in Ottawa.

Given the right to vote, Canadian women still vote for Liberal or Conservative national governments. In recent years, the New Democratic Party, successor to the CCF, was sniffing power from its base as the Official Opposition. But this position doesn't mean much. We've had a separatist party sit as Official Opposition too, but they have disappeared.

We have just come through a prolonged political exercise that I would call a bejeepers pre-election campaign. The ruling Conservatives tried to scare the bejeepers out of everyone with anti-terrorist legislation and tough-on-crime bills that promise to make Canada a safer place for all. And, oh yes, we had some of our aircraft over in the Middle East bombing the baddies. I'd love to see what Nellie McClung might have written about this lot.

As it turned out, the Tories were turfed out by the surging Liberals. The New Democrats were relegated to their familiar third-party status, where they could propose progressive programs to be adopted by the other two parties. And for the first time, the new Prime Minister created a cabinet composed equally of men and women.

Nellie McClung ought to have been pleased.

Your nephew in an evolving world,
Orland

REAPING THE IRON HARVEST

France, Nov 27th, 1916

We had quite a heavy rain yesterday and getting around in the mud to-day is like trying to learn how to roller skate it is so slippery. I was out for rations to-night and coming in after dark I had two or three nice headers. The fellow who was with me thought that was great fun but I got the laugh back on him when he took a dive into a shell hole which was filled with water.

Dear Uncle Oscar:

When you and your buddies were blowing up Europe with bombs and shells and mines, did you ever wonder how those churned-up masses of mud could be restored? Or did you think the land was ruined forever, paid as the price of waging a war for some obscure purpose? Could it ever again be as green and pastoral as those lovely rolling hills around Waverley?

I can imagine it would seem to have been ravaged in perpetuity, rich farmland reduced to muddy shell holes and trenches filled with festering bodies and rotting horseflesh.

Well, you know what? It's pretty much back the way it was. Whole villages, such as Passchendaele in Belgium, were rebuilt. Ypres, too.

And Arras, near Vimy Ridge in France. The trenches were filled in, so were the craters, and the farmer's life went on. When I visited Vimy and Flanders in the fall of 2013, I was amazed at how verdant and productive the farmland was. My head was filled with greyish images of muddy craters and tumbled-in trenches, but here was corn and kale and cabbage, all of monstrous healthy proportions, ready to be carted to market. Just down the road from where you are buried, a mountain of potatoes awaited trucks to haul them away to the *patates frites* factory. In the village of Passchendaele, by the cathedral, a huge tracked vehicle came rumbling up the road, reminiscent of a tank, but it was a four-row potato picker. The European farmer is highly mechanized. No more horses. In the village square, a dozen male cyclists lolled in the sun at their lunch. They were not battlefield riders, ready to be dispatched with a message from the Front. They were on holiday from Britain. The scene was all very normal and not at all warlike.

Shell holes and craters still pockmark the slope of Vimy Ridge.
The area is off-limits to visitors because of unexploded munitions.
Grass is trimmed by flocks of sheep.
Orland French photo

And yet a hundred years later, the war never really ends. People are still dying or are injured from munitions fired by the combatants in your war. As many as one in three artillery shells fired during the war were duds. They burrowed into the mud, only to rise to the surface decades later as something the locals call the "iron harvest."

You'll remember how the "frost action" of winter would heave stones to the surface of the fields. You'd have a field cleared of rocks but next year your harrow or plough would strike stones again as the frost action of winter pushed them to the surface. The same thing happens to artillery shells, bullets, and grenades. In fact, to any kind of foreign object. Even buttons. There's a military souvenir shop in Ypres where hundreds of brass military buttons are displayed in glass jars. They pop to the surface and are sold to tourists.

The iron harvest is exactly that. Farmers pick up unexploded munitions – shells, grenades, and the like – and carefully deposit them at the roadside where munitions experts collect them and take them away for disposal. They used to just dump them into the sea, but sanity and safer environmental laws stopped that practice. In fact, at the end of the war, millions of rounds of unused shells were dumped into the sea off Belgium and Holland, first by the British jettisoning their own supplies and later by the Belgians, who were getting rid of German munitions. Many of these contained mustard gas, which is still a dangerous hazard once it is released from its canister.

Shells recovered from the fields are exploded under careful supervision. Dig in the earth anywhere, and you're likely to hit something. With luck, it won't explode. Construction excavations, road construction, and similar activities expose unexploded munitions. The French Department of Mine Clearance (Departement du Deminage) carts away 900 tons of explosives every year. This is dangerous work. Stories abound of explosives experts blasted into dust by the detonation of a shell or bomb. Since the department was created after the Second World War, it has lost more than 600 staffers to exploding munitions.

Given the numbers of rounds fired during the war, the extent of lost munitions is not surprising. On the Western Front, it has been estimated that a ton of explosives was fired for every square metre of contested land. In some attacks, there was an artillery gun assigned to every 18 or 20 feet of front; sometimes they were almost hub-to-hub. Gunnery crews would fire, reload, fire, reload, fire for hours and days on end. In the Ypres Salient alone, British and German forces fired an estimated 300 million projectiles. If only 10 per cent did not explode – and that is a conservative estimate – then 30 million unexploded shells lie dormant in the soil beneath the rutabagas, Brussels sprouts, and corn.

Another significant danger area is around Verdun. During 1916, the Allies and the Germans hurled more than 60 million shells at each other, killing more than 305,000 men outright and disabling another 400,000. It is estimated that 12 million unexploded shells are sprinkled through the hills above Verdun.

Year after year, decade after decade, the danger continues. About 260 people have died and 535 have been injured around the Ypres area alone. As the shells rust in the ground, they become unstable. Even more hazardous are the gas shells, which will eventually corrode through their casings and release their deadly contents. This is the great danger of shells dumped into the sea.

In spite of the hazards, most of the farmland that had been destroyed by shelling and mining has been restored to its original flatness and is being cultivated. Around the Vimy Monument atop the ridge, and at other selected memorial sites such as Beaumont-Hamel, visitors can still see the tortured turmoil of the landscape as it was at war's end. Trenches, shell holes, and mine craters are clearly visible, although overgrown with grass and trees. "Keep out" warning signs are prominently placed. Flocks of sheep, which are apparently judged to be expendable, keep the grass mowed to a reasonable length. The tour guides insist none has been lost. Maybe the sheep stomp gently on the land.

Next to these preserved areas, just over the fence, the land has been returned to agricultural productivity, at great risk.

The super hazards of your long-ago war are the unexploded mines. You may have worked on these projects or at least been familiar with them. Miners and sappers would tunnel under German lines, pack the tunnels full of explosives, and blow them up. The intent was to kill as many Germans as possible, then rush forward and seize the crater before the enemy had a chance to react. They did the same to us.

One of the biggest attacks of this type was the mining of the Messines Ridge near Ypres in Belgium. More than a million pounds of explosives were packed into tunnels under the Germans on the ridge. At a signal, 19 mines were detonated simultaneously on June 7, 1917. The explosion was heard in London, 220 kilometres (138 miles) away, and seismographs in Switzerland 500 kilometres (310 miles) distant recorded a small earthquake. Six thousand Germans died in one big bang. Ka-BOOM!!

The danger is that there were 25 tunnels. One of them was filled with 50,000 pounds of bombs, which did not explode. It is live to this day, sitting under a farm, ready to blow. It probably won't, but still, it might. I wouldn't buy that farm in case I would buy the farm, if you know what I mean. The farmer knows it is there and has come to rationalize away its presence. It has been there so long, why would it explode now? But it might. There is a precedent. Another did, in 1955, apparently ignited by a lightning strike.

As I said, dear Uncle, the war goes on forever.

Your nephew,
Orland

SLAUGHTER OF THE HORSES

France, Dec. 31, 1916

What is Owen doing to exercise his horses this winter? I suppose that there is no bush work now. Is Dad keeping a horse out home now?

Dear Uncle Oscar:

I would imagine you had plenty of experience on the farm with horses. They pulled your ploughs, pulled your wagons and carriages, and did a lot of real and useful work. During the war I'm sure you appreciated the essential role that horses played in moving supplies to the Front. Today when we think of the loss of life on the Front, we think mostly of the men who died. Not enough credit is given to horses. They were so valuable that it was said, later in the war, the loss of a horse was more significant than the loss of a soldier. Horses had become more difficult to replace than humans. Before the attack on Vimy Ridge, more than 50,000 horses were toiling to support Canadian troops on the slopes southwest of Vimy.

This letter will become, dear Uncle, a little essay on what has become of the horse in North America since you died. Few of them do any real agricultural drudgework anymore. Most have gone into show business. And that's good for the horses. As a writer named C.W. Anderson said, "Many people have sighed for the 'good old days' and regretted the 'passing of the horse,' but today, when only those who like horses own them, it is a far better time for horses."

That wasn't true during the Great War. Let's try to imagine your experience with horses in wartime.

When the war began, all the combatants were equipped with cavalry units that were regarded at the time as essential ingredients of a contemporary military force. But on the battlefield, flesh-and-blood horses were extremely vulnerable to machine-gun fire, artillery, and gas attacks. Nor could they negotiate their way through the complexities of trenches or maneuver through coils and fences of barbed wire. And still, British cavalry units remained intact. This reflects a common anomaly of warfare: technical minds bust themselves to invent new and more effective ways for us to kill each other, but stubborn military minds cling to old, outmoded concepts. On the Western Front, where machine-gun bullets buzzed around like blowflies on a corpse, the British on occasion used cavalry charges throughout the war. You would know from experience what your machine gun could do to a horse. On the Eastern Front, where technology was not as advanced (nor was the observance of battlefield conventions) cavalry charges had more effect.

Cavalry charges aside, the Germans, the French, and the British – and the Americans when they finally showed up in 1917 – primarily relegated horses to the grunt work of hauling supplies and guns. The beasts tugged artillery, ambulances, and ammo wagons along treacherous muddy roads and across rough terrain, performing tasks that were impossible for primitive mechanical machines that easily bogged down in the mud.

These duties didn't protect horses from death and injury, by any means. They were as likely to get shredded by shellfire or mangled by machine-gun bullets as their human bosses. But unlike their human companions, and I say this with a grim dose of irony, they had no idea why they were there. I can't imagine how terrified they must have been by the screaming shells, the explosions of bombs, the stinging of a bullet strike. No solace for them that they were fighting for God and King and Country and Flag against the demonic excesses of the satanic Hun.

For someone from the farm, concerned about horses getting enough exercise in winter, the sights of dying horses must have been difficult to stomach. Here's a quote I came across from a cavalryman at Vimy: "I saw one troop receive a shell right amongst them; and for a moment they were lost in smoke. When the smoke cleared away, I saw a mass of mangled men and horses. I have grown accustomed to the sight of blood, and of men with limbs blown off, but a badly wounded horse is one of the most revolting sights I know."

Lieutenant Alan Thomas, 6th Queen's Own (Royal West Kent Regiment), wrote in his memoirs: "The sight that greeted me was so horrible that I almost lost my head. Heaped on top of one another and blocking up the roadway for as far as one could see lay bodies of our men and their horses. These bodies, torn and gaping, had stiffened into fantastic attitudes. All the hollows of the road were filled with blood. This was our cavalry. As I learnt afterwards, when our horsemen had gathered in Monchy, the Germans had put down a box barrage around the place – the four sides of the barrage gradually drawing inwards. The result of this shooting lay before me. Nothing that I had seen before in the way of horrors could be even faintly compared with what I saw around me now. Death in every imaginable shape was there for the examining. I walked up the hill, picking my way as best I could and often slipping in the pools of blood, so that my boots and the lower parts of puttees were dripping with blood by the time I reached the top. Nor I discovered on my way up, were all the men and animals quite dead. Now and then a groan would strike the air – the groan of a man who was praying for release. Sometimes the twitch of a horse's leg would shift the pattern of the heaped-up bodies."

Monchy is east of Arras, not far from your grave near Vimy.

As you will appreciate, the presence of horses was a morale booster. You farm boys liked having a familiar animal about. But they were messy too, pooping and peeing all over the place and polluting camps and battlefields with their bloated, disease-ridden carcasses. And when you think about the logistics of it all: horses not only had to haul enough food to the Front to feed tens of thousands of soldiers, they also had to haul enough feed for themselves. The care and maintenance of horses must have required thousands of human handlers.

Unlike humans, horses couldn't earn a "blighty", a recoverable wound that would earn them a trip back to an English hospital and a ticket out of the war. If they couldn't work, they were shot and dumped by the roadside. Handlers would encourage their exhausted charges to stay on their feet, because if they dropped from weariness, they were likely to be executed.

Canada was one of the major suppliers of horses for the war effort. Eight thousand sailed with the first contingent of Canadian troops in the fall of 1914. The British and the French relied on a supply of Canadian horses to keep their own troops mobile. By the end of the war, Canada had contributed about 130,000, or more than 10 per cent of the horses used on the Western Front. Work it out, and that's more than a million horses used by all armies. That's a lot of horse poop. About a quarter died in battle every year. That's a pile of dead horseflesh.

At the end of the war, did the uninjured horses come home? No, not many. A few favourites were saved, but most of them would have been as surplus back in Canada as they were in Europe. And so, many wound up in the butcher shops of France and Belgium. That's quite a reward for military service.

You see, dear Uncle, horses were falling from favour. The internal combustion engine, the noisy, stinking mechanical motor that propelled your lorries and tanks and aircraft, took over the world. The horse no longer provided the pulling power of industry. Oh, horses still work, all right, but they are not pulling ploughs or hay wagons. As I said, they're mostly in the entertainment business.

The heavy animals that you knew, the Clydesdales and Percherons, the Belgians and Shires, are kept around for show purposes, but they do little sweat work on the farm. They do things like stand under the hot lights indoors in arenas while judges measure their girths and cleanliness and the line of their backs. And we will often see a magnificent team in its polished leather and brass harness pulling a wagonload of giggling kids in a Santa Claus parade. Or they pull beer wagons in television commercials. We still have almost a million horses in Canada, with very few of them doing what you would recognize as real work. Of the three-quarters of a million mature horses who earn their oats at some kind of employment, about 18 per cent are involved in sports (racing, equestrian events), 18 per cent take owners and dude ranch riders on pleasure jaunts, and about 18 per cent are breeding stock. Not a bad life, considering the alternative that you witnessed.

The role of the horse in your war has become celebrated on stage and film. War Horse was a recent film, based on a book, which followed the twists and turns of the life of Joey, a farm horse sold into military service. From his agrarian life in England, he is transported to the horrors of the Somme and back again to Britain after hostilities ceased. The film revealed to modern moviegoers the terrors faced by horses in The Great War.

Probably the peak horse population in Canada was reached in 1921, when horses on Canadian soil numbered around 3.5 million. In the Canadian West, the farm horse outnumbered the population. Saskatchewan had a million horses, almost as many horses in 1921 as it has people today. But by that time the demise of the horse was already written on the stable door. In 1918, the federal government bought 1,000 light two-plough Ford tractors and offered them to Canadian farmers at cost, about $800. Dobbin was heading out to pasture.

Well, Uncle, you know that horses have reasonably long lives. They live, on average with good treatment, 25-30 years. They don't die off overnight. So a horse born in, say 1920, could reasonably expect to live until 1945.

But a couple of momentous world-shaking events happened in those 25 years. First, the realms of agriculture and transportation, where horses had previously found full employment, became mechanized. Cars spooked horses off the roads, tractors chased horses from the fields. Equine unemployment was rampant. And then along came another world war. But the Second World War, unlike yours, was highly mechanized and horses were not in as high demand.

Horses continued grazing on the Prairies and eating up a lot of valuable grasses better used for raising cattle and sheep. Farmers despaired that they couldn't sell their horses, and they were reluctant to slaughter them for nothing. Then the war ended and guess what? There was a market in Europe for horsemeat. Europeans were starving, they had no aversion to horsemeat, and another exodus of Canadian horses was shipped across the Atlantic. Yes, to a slaughter of a different kind, to wind up in the butcher shops of Belgium and the brasseries of Boulogne. By 1952, we had shipped almost a quarter million horses to Europe for food. That was almost as many as we shipped to Europe in the First World War as work animals.

Horsemeat has never become popular on the tables of English Canada, but it is still a tasty dish in parts of Quebec and in some high-end (that is, expensive) restaurants. But we still export a lot of horsemeat to Europe and Asia; most Canadians are amazed and possibly shocked to learn that Canada ranks as the third largest horsemeat exporter in the world, after Argentina and Belgium.

That's probably all you want to know about the future of horses, from your perspective. That's all I want to write, anyway. I'm sure your brother Owen's farm horses got plenty of exercise.

Your nephew,
Orland

PROBLEMS WITH THE MAIL

France, Mar. 20th, 1917

I don't know what is the matter with the mail coming from Canada now as I haven't had a letter from you for over a month and have only had your parcel and a letter from Verne and Tina since before I went to the hospital and that is a month ago. Most of the boys are saying that they haven't been getting any so I guess some of these fine days we will be getting a bunch of it.

France, March 29th, 1917

Mail has been very irregular in coming lately. I don't know whether you are getting my mail regularly or not, hope so anyway. We have just got our rations and the mail in for to-day. I got a letter from Owen written on March 8th.

Dear Uncle Oscar:

Well, well. You're sitting in a trench in wartime France, and you're unhappy that it takes a letter three weeks to get across the Atlantic, past German U-boats and ocean storms and snipers who would like nothing better than to pick off a courier on a bicycle bringing your letters and teacakes from Mom to your front-line dugout.

We are such creatures of habit. Once we get used to the mail, we want it every day and on time. Don't you know there's a war on? Fact is, mail was delivered to the Front so efficiently during the war that you came to depend on it, like waiting for old Joe the mailman at home to stuff letters in your mailbox at the end of the lane every day.

Making sure the mail got through was a high priority for wartime authorities. It was one of the best weapons of the war. Maintaining morale by getting letters to the front line was as important as the pounding of trenches by artillery and the raking of no man's land by machine guns. For all the heart-pounding periods of action at the front, there were often many more hours and days of sheer boredom. A letter from home was a welcome distraction. In return, the boys at the front would send home letters with souvenirs such as enemy uniform buttons, matchboxes and other small items, even silk cards from France. People at home loved hearing from their sons, husbands, and lovers. Just getting a letter – even a pre-printed postcard with check-off boxes – meant they were still alive. And, they might get a little insight into the war that they might not pick up from the papers.

But, as you know, you were restricted in what you could say about your work. You could describe your location simply as "somewhere in France" and everything else was subject to censorship. I don't recall a single thing in your letters home to your mother that would be unduly distressing. Except, maybe, your account of the murder at Bramshott Camp in England, which had nothing to do with you. I've wondered why you included that.

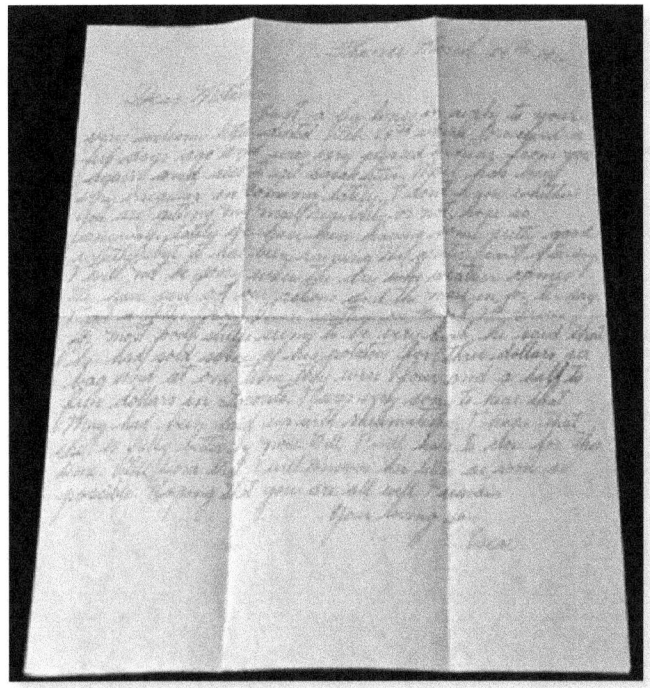

**A typical letter from Uncle Oscar, showing his very neat penmanship.
French family archives**

You must have seen some horrible sights in battle but you never reported any of them. That made sense. Authorities didn't want you sending information that would upset the home crowd. They didn't want to jeopardize public support for the war.

The numbers of pieces of mail delivered across the English Channel were astounding. The British set up a sorting depot at Regent's Park, from which mail was delivered by rail and ship to Le Havre, Boulogne, or Calais. As many as 12 million pieces of mail a week – *a week!* – were delivered through this system. Mail would be delivered in two days from England, meaning that Mom could write a letter on Wednesday, and Billy would be reading it in his bunk by Friday. By the end of the war, the Royal Engineers Postal Section had 4,000 employees. They had handled a total of two billion letters and 114 million packages. Of these, about 125 million were letters received from Canada and nearly 70 million being sent home from Canadian troops. Plus millions of parcels, newspapers, and other mailings. At war's end, the Canadian Postal Corps contingent overseas consisted of 31 Canadian post offices staffed by four officers, 44 NCOs, and 108 men (156 in all).

From the very beginning of the war in August 1914, the Canadian Postal Corps had been involved in providing special services for the Canadian Expeditionary Force. Field post offices were established at the various training bases including, of course, the main base at Valcartier, Quebec.

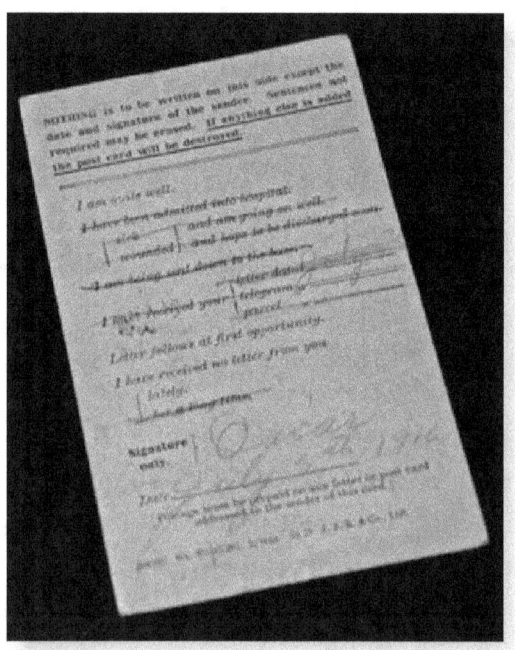

Quick messages to home could be filed on preprinted postcards.
No written material other than the address could be added to these cards.
French family archives

When 30,621 troops of the First Division departed Valcartier on September 30, 1914, the CPC was on board. Thousands of letters, newspapers, and parcels had been taken on board the *Franconia* before she sailed and were feverishly sorted overnight. Next day, they were sent to land by fast launch at Gaspe Bay for distribution to the homes of departing soldiers.

The efficiency continued in England. Upon arriving at Salisbury Plain in Wiltshire on October 14, the First Division set up camp and went into training. Postal workers moved quickly and were delivering mail on the second day after arrival. Would that the mail could move so expeditiously today! When the first Canadian units went to the battlefields of France and Flanders in February 1915, the CPC commander and 13 postal clerks went with them.

This envelope, typical of the many sent home by Oscar, contained the last letter he ever wrote. It is postmarked Toronto, April 27 and Waverley, April 28. In it he assures his mother he is "quite well". His mother received the letter almost three weeks after he died. French family archives

At the front line, a red and white CPC flag outside a tent was a welcome sight. It meant the mail was coming! Authorities tried to have mail delivered before dinner. This was great timing for morale, even if food went cold and uneaten while the men devoured the news from home.

Even from the perspective of a hundred years later, historical accounts of the day indicate that the mail service was incredibly efficient, given the circumstances. There was a war on, you know. But it was every private's right to grumble, so I guess your gripes about the missing mail are understandable.

Your nephew,
Orland

Oscar's letters tightly filled this flower print box.
French family archives

The neat and legible signature of Oscar French

MISSING THE PRIME MINISTER

France, Mar. 10, 1917
Dear Mother –

I am very much afraid that you will be thinking that I am getting very neglectful as regards writing as it has been some time since I wrote last but I have been feeling rather tough this last week or so. I was admitted into the field hospital nearly two weeks ago with bronchitis but expect to be out soon now. There was three or four days that I was feeling pretty blue but I am just about all O.K. again now.

Your loving son
Oscar

Dear Uncle Oscar:

Sorry to hear you were laid up with bronchitis. I don't wonder, given the conditions you are living under. While you have been convalescing, you missed meeting a Very Important Bigwig. The Prime Minister, or Premier as you would call him in your day, came to visit you and the boys at the Front.

Here's what I found in the War Diary of the 6th Brigade Canadian Machine Gun Company, for March 9, 1917:

Weather dull and cold. The Coy joined the Brigade on Parade Ground about W10b S.E. of MAISNIL BOUCHIE and was inspected by SIR ROBERT BORDEN accompanied by the HON ROBERT ROGERS and the HON J.D. HAZEN. Company paraded at 10.15 a.m. and marched

off to Review Ground at 10.20 a.m. The O.C. and 2ⁿᵈ in Command
attended Conference of CO's and adjutants at Brigade Hdqrs.

Sir Robert Borden? The Canadian Prime Minister? Yes, indeed. Two of his cabinet ministers, Rogers and Hazen, were with him. Had you been present, you might have heard an inspiring speech. (Maybe, in fact, he came to visit your hospital, but I don't know that.)

I had not realized that our Canadian Prime Minister was touring the European battle zone during the war. Apparently such visits were more common than I had imagined. King George V and his wife Queen Mary made a number of visits. I suppose there was no real danger, other than from the presence of U-boats in the Channel in getting to France, as long as they stayed well back from the action. As you well know, the Front didn't move very far, being a fixed line of trenches from Switzerland to the North Sea that rarely wavered more than a few miles.

During our military excursion in Afghanistan in the early part of the 21ˢᵗ century, then Prime Minister Stephen Harper visited our troops four or five times. That's easy today, when he can just hop on a plane and fly over from Canada in a few hours. No ploughing across the ocean for a week. That probably seems incomprehensible to you. It is probably equally incomprehensible that we would be fighting a war in those dusty, dirty deserts of Afghanistan.

Too bad you missed Borden. You would probably have been closer to a Canadian prime minister in France than you would ever be back in Waverley.

A report filed from the Front, and carried in the Huntingdon, Quebec, *Gleaner*, conveyed the sense of the moment. Written in the flowery language of the time, it portrays a national leader "deeply stirred" by all that he had seen.

Here's what it said:

Canada's confidence in the valour of her sons who represent her in the war for her own security and for the maintenance of the British Empire, with unimpaired strength for safeguarding civilization against the assault of the latter-day barbarians, was the keynote of the last remarks made by Premier Borden at the Canadian front. Sir Robert was deeply stirred by the sights of the day. He had seen many thousands of men inured to life in the trenches, hardened veterans, while yet for the most part, lads or young men. He had bidden a Nova Scotia Battalion, of which he is an honourary colonel, Godspeed. He had observed Battalion practice in which great attacking waves were being sent against trenches, and having seen other evidence of the evolution of the weapons of destruction to the point of terrible effectiveness, the premier was in a position to more fully understand the resolution of the men who, at their country's call go out into the open against them.

Among his hearers were many young university men of Toronto and McGill, members of the University Battalion through which from first to last, almost five thousand men have passed. They listened with eager attention, and gave Sir Robert three cheers and a tiger. Honorable J.D. Hazen was absent in the north during these latter visits on a pilgrimage to the cemetery where his son, who was killed at the Ypres salient, is buried.

Now, Uncle, I am perplexed by the phrase "three cheers and a tiger." The three cheers I understand, as in "hip, hip, hooray! hip, hip, hooray! hip, hip, hooray!" But the tiger? I saw an old film clip showing your boss, or ex-boss, Sam Hughes, standing in his official car leading "three cheers and a tiger." The best explanation I could find was that the "tiger" was a loud growl from the crowd that followed the three cheers. It's obviously an old expression, maybe a holdover from the Empire's days in India, which has been lost in time. We still do three cheers, although it seems a bit antiquated.

Let's get back to the report in the *Huntingdon Gleaner*:

Another brigade with the troops drawn up, was addressed by Sir Robert, who spoke briefly on Canada's part in the war. He said the Canadian people were represented in the field because they were utterly opposed to German ideas, as represented in the ravaging of Belgium, the destruction of the *Lusitania*, the murder of Nurse Cavell and Captain Fryatt and they fought for the right of individuals and free peoples. Sir Robert said he felt honoured in having an opportunity to speak to them. They had done glorious service in the past, and if the occasion should arise again, he knew they would not be content to rest upon the glory of the past. When they returned to Canada a warm welcome awaited them from the home folks.

You probably know about Edith Cavell. She was a British nurse working in Belgium who was convicted by the Germans of treason for helping allied soldiers escape from German-occupied Belgium to Britain. She made no attempt to defend herself and admitted information that strengthened the German case. Perhaps she didn't believe that even the dastardly Huns would execute women. But, in spite of intense international pressure to back off, they did. She was shot at dawn by a firing squad of eight soldiers. All men, I assume. Her death was highly exploited by British propagandists, and she became the most famous female casualty in the First World War. The world was outraged, and her name lives on today around the globe in the names of hospitals, memorials, and streets from Belleville, Ontario, to Dunedin, New Zealand, and Mumbai, India. (You would have known Mumbai as Bombay.)

It's amazing how long we can hold a grudge. The Edith Cavell Nursing School in Belleville was not founded until 1968, half a century and a couple of wars after the German atrocity. I suppose it is a little like recognizing the heroic exploits of Florence Nightingale during the Crimean War in the 1850s. But Nightingale was not executed for her work. She died peacefully in her sleep at the age of 90. The Cavell Building in Belleville was torn down in 2013.

Fryatt is not so well known today. Captain Charles Fryatt was a brave seafarer in the merchant marine who attempted to ram a German submarine, *U-33*. It seemed only fair. The German navy had been trying to sink his ship, the Great Eastern Railway steamer *Brussels*, operating between Rotterdam and Britain. He was hailed as a hero for his action, praised in Parliament and rewarded by the British government with a gold watch. Such was the emotion of wartime, even though he had failed to sink the sub. His public recognition nettled the Germans. On a subsequent voyage, the testy Huns captured him, convicted him of conducting a *franc-tireur* action and executed him on July 27, 1916. *Franc-tireur* was a form of guerilla activity. I suppose because he was in the merchant marine, not the British navy, his action fit the German interpretation of the phrase. Their official explanation of his conviction ran along the lines that if one merchant sea captain went unpunished for attempting to ram a U-boat, they would all want to do it. Never mind that the U-boats had been indiscriminately picking off merchant ships, like shooting groundhogs, without any warning or consideration that they were not part of the British navy. Such is the logic of war.

I don't know what became of Captain Fryatt's gold watch. Maybe it is in some German trophy case. At any rate, his execution was used to inflame public opinion against Germany, although you will not see Fryatt monuments sprinkled all over the world.

I'm sure the Prime Minister could have told you all this, had he come to your hospital bed.

Your nephew,
Orland

UP IN THE AIR,
THE HUN WAS IN COMMAND

Excerpts from the War Diary of 1917, 6th Brigade, Canadian Machine Gun Company

Feb. 27, 1917

Weather fine turning dull towards night. Guns on air-craft duty fired 750 rounds on German planes at 7.30 a.m. and 4 p.m. turning one plane back at 7.30 a.m.

March 25, 1917

Weather fine and warm. 500 rounds fired at low-flying planes.

April 18, 1917

Weather showery. 2000 rounds fired at low-flying planes.

April 19, 1917

Weather showery. 3000 rounds (fired) at low-flying planes.

April 20, 1917

Weather showery. 2500 rounds fired at low-flying planes.

April 21, 1927

Weather fine. 200 rounds fired at low-flying planes.

Dear Uncle Oscar:

I noticed in the Canadian Machine Gun Corps War Diary that the Huns were harassing you before breakfast with their lethal aircraft. They must have been up before dawn to get over your lines by 7:30. Maybe they were farm boys like you, up by five. Today's to-do list: Milk the cows, machine-gun the enemy.

If you were wondering why they were suddenly showing up over your trenches in the spring of 1917, it was because over the winter the Germans had received new aerial weapons. During the late winter and spring of 1917, the air war took a dramatic turn in favour of the Germans. According to War Diary excerpts which I have cited above, German planes appeared regularly over your front lines and were fired upon by Canadian troops. Did you manage to hit any with your machine gun?

Suddenly the edge in air power that had been enjoyed by the Allies disappeared behind a big Hunnish cloud. Using their new Albatros biplane fighter aircraft, the Germans were beating the bejeepers out of the Royal Flying Corps. Manfred von Richthofen, Ernst Udet, Erich Lowenhardt, and other German aces were cutting British planes to pieces. Their Albatroses, with superior maneuverability and rate of climb, made mincemeat of reconnaissance and scout aircraft of the Royal Flying Corps. In response, the British bumped up their air strength in the Arras sector to support operations. More planes, but not necessarily better. In April, the British lost 151 aircraft to the Germans' 119, with the consequent loss of 316 dead or missing airmen. Aircrews in British observation aircraft could expect to last two to three months before being knocked out of the skies.

The most celebrated German air ace was Manfred Von Richtofen, known as the "Red Baron" who led a group of red-coloured German aircraft known as Richtofen's flying circus. You must have heard of him. He was credited with 80 air combat victories. He knocked down 22 aircraft in a single month, nicknamed "Bloody April" (1917) by the British, including four in one day. He was a real menace in the skies, but he was not immortal. The Red Baron died on April 21, 1918, shot down over Morlancourt Ridge near the Somme River. Although the kill has been credited to Captain Roy Brown, a Canadian, there is some conjecture that the bullet which pierced Richtofen's upper torso was fired from a Vickers machine gun on the ground. Richtofen was pursuing another Canadian pilot, Wilfrid "Wop" May, uncharacteristically at a very low altitude, when he was hit. Although he managed to land his aircraft, he died soon after. He was flying a trademark red triplane, the Fokker Dr.1. Years later, Richtofen was celebrated in popular culture, including regular appearances in an American comic strip called Peanuts where a dog named Snoopy fantasized about doing a deadly doggy dance in the sky with the Red Baron. I imagine that sounds rather ridiculous to you, but that's our modern culture for you.

Did you ever wonder about becoming a pilot? You'd be up in the sky, out of the mud, the gore, the trenches, and the rats. Zipping about the sky, rat-a-tat-tatting at the Hun in his little airplane or observation balloon, you'd be far above the carnage on the ground. Oh, it was dangerous work all right, but if the end came, it came quickly. And when your day's work was done, you cruised back to the aerodrome for a cup of tea or a shot of rum, a bath and a clean bed.

Well, that's the way Billy Bishop saw it. He was our top Canadian aerial war ace, credited with 72 enemy aircraft kills. That's almost as good as Richtofen's 80. Bishop was a lad from Owen Sound who, like you, signed up for service on the ground. And, like you, he excelled on the firing range. He was reputed to be able to take out the eyes of a snake at a hundred yards. But when he got his boots dirty in France, he wanted no part of the hellish life in the trenches. One day he watched a Royal Flying Corps airplane land. He suddenly said, "It's clean up there! I'll bet you don't get any mud or horse shit on you up there. If you die, at least it would be a clean death."

Maybe you met him, although not likely. He was flying with 60 Squadron near Arras, France, in March 1917. That was your area, near Vimy Ridge. As I said, the Germans were having great fun in the sky. They were shooting down British aircraft at a rate of five to one, and the average life expectancy of an Allied pilot in that sector was only 11 days. Bishop got off to a bad start; he crashed a couple of aircraft and was ordered back to training school. But he didn't go; he soon established himself as an ace, knocking down 12 aircraft in April 1917. Once he crash-landed in No Man's Land and ran like hell for the Allied trenches, German bullets zipping all around him. For his exploits he won the Military Cross, the Distinguished Service Order, and the Victoria Cross, all without a trace of mud on his boots. However, there may have been streaks of horse shit, for historians dispute his total of kills, claiming it was actually far lower than he is given credit for. But Bishop had become a Canadian hero. He was a great propaganda icon for the war effort, and if he said he had shot down a plane or two or three, his superiors believed him. It was good for propaganda. Eventually he became so valuable to the war effort that he was pulled out of the front line in case he got himself killed.

In the Second World War, Bishop was promoted to the rank of Air Marshal of the Royal Canadian Air Force. He was deeply involved in establishing and developing the British Commonwealth Air Training Plan, which trained and produced 167,000 airmen from all over the Commonwealth. His name also lives on in Billy Bishop Toronto City Airport, located on the Toronto Islands near the Canadian National Exhibition grounds where you received some training.

I hate to say this, but if you had returned alive from the war, you probably wouldn't have received much of a hero's welcome. The guys in the skies were the darlings of the war. The grunts on the ground rarely got much public accolade. Well, yes, in Waverley, they would have thrown a party for you. And, I should mention this, almost a hundred years later the Town of Midland named a lane after you. French Lane.

Wop May, who escaped the Red Baron, knocked down several enemy aircraft during the war and retired, in one piece, after receiving the Distinguished Flying Cross. He came home to Canada to take up a career as a bush pilot, formed his own successful airline company, and eventually became immortalized in a song by Canada's folk story singer, Stompin' Tom Connors. Captain Arthur Roy Brown is still remembered as the pilot who shot down the Red Baron, even though the facts are under review. He was distinguished in his own right for having never lost a pilot in his flight during combat because he insisted that new pilots sit out dogfights and observe how they worked. After the war, he returned to Canada where he became an accountant and started a small airline. He tried to enlist for the Second World War but was refused.

Flying has become a tremendous business worldwide. Ordinary guys like Bishop and May and Brown who survived the war were the pioneers. Having learned how to fly their aerial kites, they came home and capitalized on their knowledge. Not for them the furrow or the forest. Their future was in flying. Today pilots coming out of the air force can often find a job with private airlines or commercial operators, but civil aviation was only getting its start in the 1920s. If an aviator wanted to cash in on his wartime flying experience, he'd have to create his own job.

Many of them became something called barnstormers. War-surplus airplanes were cheap, maybe only a few hundred dollars, so they'd buy a plane and become a barnstormer. They'd sell airplane rides, operating from a farmer's field, which is where the word barnstormer comes from. It was a great way to meet young women! Or they'd take their planes up and perform a series of aerobatic tricks: rolls, loops, dives, spins. In their twin-seaters, they'd soar into the blue with daredevils who would step out onto the wings to dance, walk the wing, or even step from plane to plane. Groups of barnstormers would form "flying circuses" which were better organized and maybe paid better. Others found employment as "bush pilots," flying small planes into isolated locations in Canada's vast wilderness areas. And those who wanted adventure on the shady side flouted the law by flying dodgy missions involving illicit cargo.

Airplanes were invented before the First World War but, like so many inventions, they come into their own during military conflicts. Airplanes have continued to play a major role in all wars since the First World War. However, the spin-off effect for civilian travel has been enormous.

Right now, as I write this letter in early 2014, a computerized tracking service tells me – let me look again – there are 7,685 aircraft airborne somewhere around the world. They are carrying more than half a million people, sitting in comfortable chairs, whizzing through the upper atmosphere in giant jet-propelled tubes called airliners.

That's an awesome figure, even from my perspective. I can't imagine what it means to you.

Your nephew,
Orland

HOW THE WAR ENDED

Dear Uncle Oscar:

No doubt you have been wondering how your war will end, or if it ever will. Well, yes, it did. Not with a bang, but a whimper, from Germany and her supporters. On November 11, 1918, Germany capitulated.

A few months earlier, this did not seem a likely outcome. After three years of sitting through a bloody stalemate, Germany finally made a gigantic move on the chessboard of Europe in the spring of 1918. As you know, the Western frontier wavered back and forth only slightly through 1915 and 1916, and even through most of 1917. Men fell and were replaced, only to fall themselves and be replaced, in an endless cycle of attrition.

And then the balance of power appeared to shift. As I noted earlier, the Americans joined the war in April 1917. However, they didn't arrive in any significant show of force until the summer of 1918. Meanwhile, through 1917 they had been supplying equipment, supplies, and money to the Allies.

The Germans took advantage of the delay. Things had turned in Germany's favour, or so the Huns thought. The Communists had routed the monarchy in Russia in the fall of 1917, murdering Czar Nicholas, his wife, and his children. Then the Communists signed a peace agreement with the Germans. This meant Germany could redirect its eastern forces to the Western frontier. Since France and Britain, and all their allied forces, had been unable to budge Germany in three years, the Germans decided it was time for the Big Push.

They would grab as much of France as they could, while the grabbing was good. Away they went. The Spring Offensive was launched on March 21. French and British forces reeled under the onslaught, and the Germans got within 50 miles of Paris. And then the tide turned.

In the underbelly of Europe, Germany became exposed to attack. Bulgaria collapsed and Austria-Hungary, Germany's major partner in this war, was teetering. The Allies could soon be gnawing at Germany from the south.

With the arrival of American forces and their resources in the summer of 1918, the Allies launched a major offensive and drove the Germans back, recovering all the land lost in the Spring Offensive. It became clear the Germans could not win.

In the German heartland, civil discord was rampant. Revolution was sweeping the country. The German navy mutinied, refusing further orders. It was clear the nation wanted no more of the war. Strong forces pressured the Imperial government to cave in. On November 9, 1918, Kaiser Bill abdicated and skedaddled into the neutral Netherlands. What remained of the German government sued for peace and signed an Armistice with the Allies two days later on November 11, 1918. Guns fell silent and church bells rang out. The war formally ended with the Treaty of Versailles on June 28, 1919.

In Britain, the cessation of hostilities occurred at the 11th hour of the 11th day of the 11th month, a moment we still commemorate nearly a century later.

In the last hours of the war, the futility of the conflict became more readily apparent. For the sake of neatness and synchronization, the agreed-upon hour of the ceasefire was set at noon Berlin time. Some troops knew the war was over but not all. It is estimated that as many as 10,000 lives were lost in that final morning.

Overall, the war killed about ten million soldiers and seven million civilians.

For many, the final moment of life came down to luckless timing. Ask George Lawrence Price about his fate if you meet him in the hereafter. Price was the last Canadian soldier to lose his life in the war. He was shot by a German sniper as he and his buddies pushed forward through the village of Mons on the morning of November 11. He died two minutes before the ceasefire.

It seemed a pointless death but then, weren't they all?

Your nephew
Orland

TIME TO SAY GOODBYE

France, April 8th, 1917

Well Mother I am in rather a poor place for writing now but will write soon again. With best love to all I remain,

Your loving son
Oscar

War Diary of the 6th Canadian Machine Gun Corps, April 8-9, 1917: No casualties occurred while moving but shortly afterward No. 2 Section had Ptes French and Defayette killed and 4 men wounded by shell fire...

Dear Uncle Oscar:

And so it's time to say goodbye, dear Uncle. We have reached the end of your life. The day after you wrote this letter, promising to "write soon again", you were killed by shellfire in the initial morning attack on Vimy Ridge. You never wrote another line.

But I have so much more to tell you! I want to tell you about finding your grave in Nine Elms Military Cemetery and visiting the monument at Vimy Ridge, plus relate the story of my joke on the German tourist and the history of Arras and, well, so much more.

So, here's what I propose to do. I have prepared a series of post mortem letters that will portray some post-war scenes of the Vimy area. Most of them are observations made by me on a tour there in

144

October 2013. Four of us visited your grave: my sister Patricia and her husband, Richard Chernesky of Calgary, and my wife Sylvia and myself. We flew to Amsterdam and approached Vimy along what we jokingly called "the German route," which approached Flanders and northern France from the east. It was roughly the route followed by the Germans as they crossed Belgium and invaded France.

ARRAS THE RESILIENT

Dear Uncle Oscar:

In our quest for your burial place, we stayed for a few days in the city of Arras. This city lent its name to the major British offensive in 1917, the Battle of Arras, in which the struggle for Vimy Ridge was a part. Your burial spot is only six or seven kilometres north of the modern town, along the Lens-Arras highway. Of course, you weren't trying to defend Arras. You were trying to drive the Germans out of Thelus, a village north of Arras, on the southwest slope towards the southern end of Vimy Ridge.

The war treated Arras very badly. Wartime photos show the city virtually destroyed. Just as it was picking itself up, the Second World War flattened it again.

And yet, we had a pleasant autumn holiday there, for Arras is a delightfully resilient town. Arras appears today to be a thriving city of 43,000 people. With a history dating back thousands of years, the town wasn't about to give up its life to a gang of Huns. Yes, I mean literally tens of thousands of years. Archaeologists have found evidence of stonework by forerunners of humans in the Scarpe Valley dating back 170,000 years. The town was founded by a Belgic tribe and was later an important Roman garrison town named Nemetacum/Artrebatum.

Arras has a long history of violence. It was invaded and destroyed by the Germains (sic) in 406 and 407 A.D. and by the Vikings in the 9th century. During the middle ages, a pageantry of feudal lords and fiefs disputed ownership of the town. Joan of Arc was imprisoned there. The Habsburgs and the French and the Spanish fought over it, with the French eventually prevailing. That wasn't the end of it. Death and destruction continued. The Reign of Terror after the French Revolution resulted in 400 executions and the destruction of several religious monuments.

Religion played a major role in the town's development. After the Abbey of St. Vaast developed into a wealthy Benedictine monument, the modern town spread around the abbey as a grain market. This drew the wrath of the Vikings in the 9th century. In the 10th and 11th centuries, the town became an important banking and trading centre and developed a reputation for the quality of its wool. From there, it became renowned for its fine tapestries to the point that in English and Italian, the word "Arras" became a generic term for tapestries.

I'm telling you all this so that you wouldn't think you were fighting over some desolate, insignificant chunk of French farmland. Given the paucity of history in the Waverley area, this would have seemed like very rich stuff indeed.

And so, on to the modern record. The First World War broke out on August 14, 1914. On September 6, only three weeks later, the Huns were barracked within the city and the Arras Citadel. The French counter-attacked and partly repelled the Germans, and the destruction of Arras was on. City hall was burned, so was the Arras Cathedral. In the prelude to the Battle of Arras (April 9 to May 16, 1917), the industrious New Zealand Tunnelling Company greatly expanded an intricate system of medieval tunnels in the chalky subsoil beneath the city, which were used by the British to hold the town. Overall, in the Arras region including Vimy Ridge, four tunneling teams of 500 men each worked around the clock for two months to construct 20 kilometres of tunnels. Upon completion, the caverns were capable of concealing 24,000 men.

The British offensive at Arras was to break through the German lines and end the war in short order. British forces augmented by Canadian, New Zealand, and Australian troops attacked the Germans on a front from Vimy to the northeast to Bullecourt south of the town. As a machine-gunner, you were probably aware that the attack employed heavy use of machine guns; eighty to a brigade. In human terms, it was a very expensive engagement: 160,000 casualties on the British side and 125,000 on the German.

Three-quarters of Arras was destroyed. But you know what? At great expense and effort, it was rebuilt to look almost exactly what it had been like before the war. So when our Expeditionary Force arrived in the fall of 2013, fine wine was flowing freely at a hundred patio restaurants on the grand plazas and everyone was having a great time.

Thank you for helping save it.

Your imbibing nephew,
Orland

DEPTHS OF SORROW
ON THE HEIGHTS OF VIMY

Dear Uncle Oscar:

After the war ended, monuments and cenotaphs sprang up like concrete mushrooms in every little town and village across Canada. It was pretty standard practice at the time to erect a monument in a town park, bearing the names of all who had died in The Great War. Your name is on the Waverley Soldiers' Memorial just south of your parents' home.

The Canadian government decided to do something on a grand scale to recognize the contributions all you fellows made during The Great War. It built a massive monument atop Vimy Ridge.

**The Vimy Monument gleams in the morning
sun above fog-shrouded slopes of the Ridge.
George Hutchison photo, courtesy Vimy Foundation**

If you could see the Canadian monument at Vimy, you might feel humbled and honoured that your country had erected such an immense memorial to you and the thousands of men who were slain fighting for Canada in the First World War. It is such an impressive work that even Adolf Hitler, the German rogue warmonger who terrorized the world during the Second World War, visited it in 1940 and ordered his troops to leave it alone.

The Vimy Monument is, perhaps, Canada's best-known memorial, at least to Canadians, but most Canadians will never see it. It soars high above the heights of Vimy Ridge, commemorating all of Canada's fallen in the First World War. Around its base are carved the names of

11,285 Canadians who were killed on French soil and have no known graves. They are the missing.

While the monument is impressive in size and scope, it doesn't shout Victory! Instead, it quietly mourns Canada's losses.

The Canada Bereft statue, also known as Mother Canada, faces northeast over the Douai Plain at Vimy. The figure of a young woman in mourning symbolizes Canada grieving for her lost soldiers. The statue was carved from a single 30-ton piece of stone.
Patricia Chernesky photo

The monument is the artwork of Walter Allward, one of our most famous sculptors. He began in 1925 and completed his work 11 years later, at a cost of $1.5 million. Time and weather took its toll on the monument, which was restored in the early part of the 21st century.

The twin pylons of the monument soar 27 metres (90 feet) above the ground or 110 metres (360 feet) above the Douai Plain below the ridge. There are 20 figures in all around the monument, but the most significant is that of a cloaked and hooded woman, her eyes cast down, facing the east, symbolizing a young nation mourning her lost sons. Thousands of tons of a special concrete, reinforced with steel, were poured to build the base, while the towers were made of a durable limestone imported from Croatia. The work had to be done with care because the landscape was littered with unexploded munitions.

**Orland making notes on the Vimy Monument
with the Canada Bereft statue in the background.
Sylvia French photo**

The 250-acre parcel of land around the monument was ceded to Canada by France to be used in perpetuity as a battlefield park. Trenches, shell craters, and tunnels have been preserved to show Canadians today what you fellows were facing. On-site tour guides are well-informed Canadian university students who have been specially selected to tell the story of Vimy to visitors.

Only when you climb the heights of Vimy do you appreciate the strategic importance of the ridge. You didn't make it to the top, so I'll tell you what you would have seen.

The approach from the southwest, which is the direction from which the four Canadian divisions were attacking, is a relatively easy ascent, were it not for machine-gun fire and shells. The steep drop of the ridge is on the northeast side, behind the German defences. The ridge provides a commanding view of the French fields to the southwest, and Douai Plain with its coalmines and industrial sites to the northeast. The Germans captured the ridge in October 1914 and successfully resisted efforts by the British and French to dislodge them. The Canadian attack of April 9-12, 1917 was much better planned and prepared, relying on previous experiences, improved information, and even photographs of German emplacements taken from the air. It followed a week-long continuous bombardment of shellfire to soften up the German defences. The Germans called it the Week of Suffering as they huddled to evade more than a million shells that rained down on them. In the actual attack itself, a "creeping barrage" of shellfire moved slowly ahead of the attacking forces to keep the Germans underground and in their shelters.

A wreath placed at the Belleville cenotaph by Orland and
Sylvia French in honour of Oscar French and Leonard McConnell.
Pte. McConnell was a cousin of Sylvia's mother; he died at
Passchendaele, and his name is carved on the Menin Gate in
Ypres as a soldier who was never recovered from the battlefield.
Orland French photo

Your role was to assist in the taking of the town of Thelus, on the
southwestern flank of the ridge. This was achieved on the morning of
April 10, but you were killed on the first morning, April 9. The Germans
held out on a high point nicknamed "The Pimple" until April 12,
when the 10th Canadian Brigade overran them. The Canadian Corps
lost 3,598 dead and 7,004 wounded in the Vimy attack; the German
casualties are unknown but they also gave up 4,000 men who became
prisoners of war. Given that hundreds of thousands of Allied soldiers
had already died in earlier futile efforts to take the ridge, the Canadian

losses seemed acceptably low. Still, the death toll represented almost six per cent of the 66,000 we lost in the war.

Your thankful nephew,
Orland

AN INCIDENT AT VIMY

Dear Uncle Oscar:

Further to my previous letter about the Vimy Monument, I want to tell you about a funny thing that happened when I reached the top of Vimy Ridge. A German shot me. That's right, a hundred years after the battle, Germans are firing Canon's at Canadians on Vimy Ridge. Hard to believe, isn't it? Okay, I will concede that he shot me with a camera. Even though the camera is called a Canon, it is not a cannon the fires shells. It takes pictures. And he wasn't a hostile German in uniform, but a very friendly fellow from Berlin who was, like me, a tourist on Vimy Ridge. In fact, he had lived for a time in Montreal.

His name was Peter, and he was interested in my project to write letters to you. Now that I had been shot by a German, I explained to him, I would have to write another letter explaining how and why. He thought that was very clever and funny. When I got home, he sent me some reminiscences from people on the "other side" who were shooting at you and dropping shells on your trenches.

He wrote, "One of my uncles, Jakob Kohnen, a relatively tough guy, was a machine-gunner at the Somme. He said he always hoped or prayed that the assaults would not be in his sector to spare him using his gun on people he did neither know nor could hate." The Battle of the Somme was a terrible killing field. It astounds me to think that the British forces could lose, in one day on July 1, 1916, 57,000 men. Seventeen thousand dead and 40,000 wounded. Never mind the

17,000 dead; how do you treat 40,000 wounded? How could you plan a battle so badly that you would lose 57,000 men in one day?

You must have realized that the machine gun was a marvelously efficient killing machine. I don't know what your role was, since a machine gun could require up to eight men to supply and operate. But if you were on the trigger, and maybe you would take turns, it must have required nerves of steel to mow down men you didn't know, killing and maiming them and destroying life. Of course, it was kill or be killed, and if you allowed them to reach your position, you would be a dead man yourself. Sorry. Of course you are, anyway. I remember reading about a Turkish commander at Gallipoli, where Australians were being cut down by the hundreds, standing up and shouting in English, "Go back! Go back! You haven't got a chance." He was appalled by the slaughter caused by his own guns. Of course, the Aussies didn't listen, and they were massacred.

Peter from Berlin, who became an e-penpal, corresponding through the Internet, sat down with me while his friend Klaus took our picture. It didn't seem at all unusual in the 21st century to sit on the steps of the Vimy Monument with a citizen of a former enemy (twice) and reminisce about a long-ago war. At that point, I had not yet found your grave, and so you had not become as real to me as you were a few hours later when we were putting flags and poppies on your grave and propping up your photo against the headstone.

**Three German tourists and me (right) share wartime
Stories on the steps of the Vimy Monument
Sylvia French photo**

I will tell you some other stories passed on by Peter. He said, "In Bavaria, where I lived several years near Wuerzburg, First World War veterans talked sometimes about the time at the Somme near Arras and Vimy and that they felt very lucky to have survived."

Of course, Germans fell by the thousands, just as the Allies did. Peter tells of how the toll of war impacted the women in Germany: "My father, Albert Kerber, a high-school teacher, born in 1907, experienced as a boy scene he claimed he could never forget. His father (my other grandfather) was station master at Zeitz and later at Hildburghausen in Thueringen. My father saw how, at the beginning of war, the trains left with relatives waving goodbye. As the war dragged on, mothers and wives collapsed in grief when the train with their beloved ones pulled out of the station toward the front. My father said that the worst part was that all this (was anticipated) and that medics had already been waiting with stretchers to transport specially stricken women to hospital."

The women knew that many, like you, would not return. Their sons and husbands and fathers might be gone forever. It was for many of them the last time they would see their loved ones.

In our grieving of war, sometimes it is difficult to remember that there were two sides suffering. This was made starkly clear to us when we visited the German cemetery at Neuville-Saint Vaast near Vimy, where 44,833 bodies are buried, collected after the war from battlefield burials and small cemeteries in the area.

Your nephew,
Orland

A PERMANENT PATCH OF GRASS

Nine Elms Military Cemetery
France

BURIAL REPORT

UNIT	6th Bde. Can. Machine Gun Co.
REGIMENTAL NUMBER	408445
RANK	Private
NAME	FRENCH, O.
DATE AND NATURE OF CASUALTY	9-4-17 Killed in action.
WHERE BURIED	Nine Elms Military Cemetery, Thelus, France, 3 miles N. of Arras
NUMBER OF GRAVE	Plot 4, Row D, Grave 15
MARKING OF GRAVE	A temporary wooden memorial with all particulars of the deceased inscribed thereon has been erected to his memory.

Extracted from Burial Reports, Directorate of Records, Ottawa, July 8, 1921

Panoramic view of Nine Elms Military Cemetery near Thelus, the village
where Pte. Oscar French was killed. A plaque in the cemetery reads:
"Thelus was taken by the Canadian Corps on 9 April 1917, the opening
day of the Battle of Vimy Ridge. This cemetery, which was named
after an elm copse, contains the graves of 155 British, 529 Canadian,
and 54 French soldiers who fell in the capture of the Ridge and during
subsequent fighting."
Patricia Chernesky photo

Dear Uncle Oscar:

Well, I went to France and found your little patch of grass in Nine
Elms Military Cemetery. I must say, it is kept very neat and tidy, as is
every Canadian military cemetery in France, thanks to the diligence
of the Commonwealth War Graves Commission.

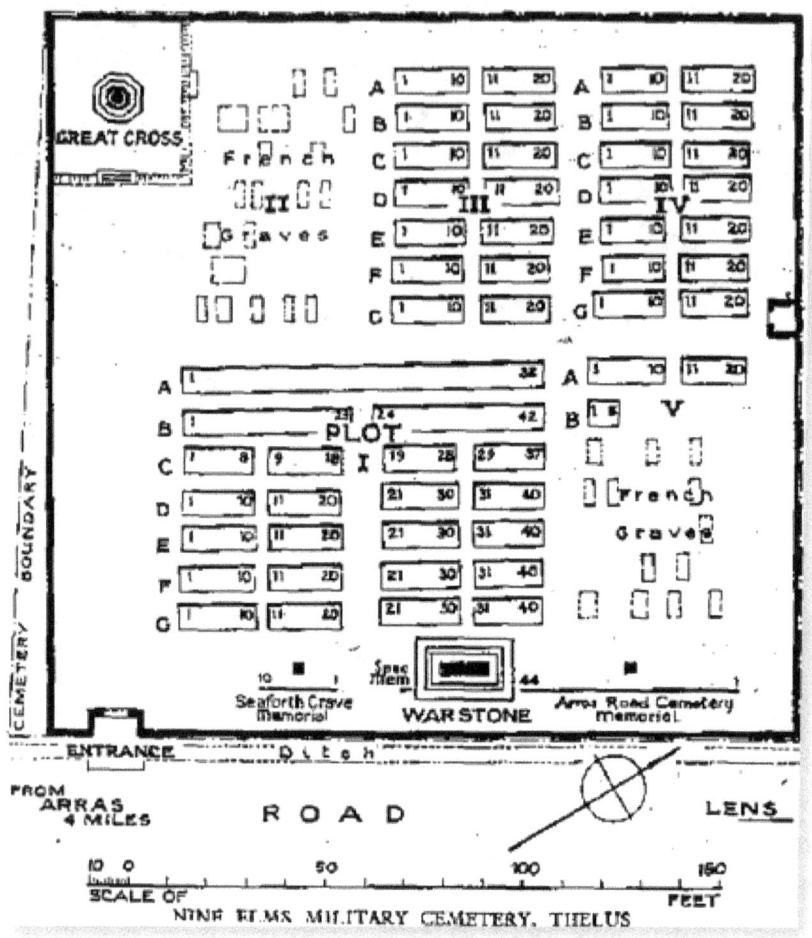

Map of Nine Elms Military Cemetery issued to Pte. French's family. Uncle Oscar is in Plot IV, Row D, grave 15, in the northwest corner. French family archives

You're not easy to find, sandwiched as you are between a turnip field and an expressway. Without a detailed map, a satellite photograph of the area, and particular instructions from a Canadian expert who has visited the cemetery, we might not have found you. You're at the end of a narrow curving lane that hightails its way across a field, snakes its way around another Commonwealth cemetery, and deadends at Nine

Elms. We found it a few miles north of Arras, off the road between Neuville-St. Vaast and Thelus, the village you were trying to liberate when you were killed.

Orland French and his sister Patricia Chernesky, nephew and niece of Pte. Oscar French, at his graveside.
Sylvia French photo

But there we were, on a cool and overcast Sunday in October, looking for Plot 4, Row D, Grave 15 in the Nine Elms Military Cemetery. And there you were, right where the map said you were. I might have spotted your grave from a Google overhead satellite shot except that you are buried under a tree that obscured the view. Our party was four: my wife Sylvia and myself and my sister Pat Chernesky and her husband Richard. Pat and I are children of Elmer, as you might have surmised, the little brother of whom you spoke so fondly in your letters. I must say, it was slightly disconcerting for me to find a gravestone bearing the name "O. French". That could be me, too.

Four of the family visiting Oscar's grave. Front: Orland French and his sister, Patricia Chernesky. Back: Richard Chernesky and Sylvia French. Patricia Chernesky photo

I hope we didn't disturb you with our little graveside ceremony. We placed some modern Canadian flags, a poppy which has become a symbol of remembrance for the dead of world wars, and a photograph of you in your uniform. There was even an appropriate sound of gunfire, unexpectedly provided by French bird hunters in the adjacent field.

Richard Chernesky warily watches local hunters in a turnip field next to
Nine Elms Military Cemetery, while Orland takes notes.
Patricia Chernesky photo

We sang a couple of verses from "O God, Our Help in Ages Past."
The second verse seemed particularly appropriate:

Time, like an ever-rolling stream
Bears all its sons away;
They fly forgotten, as a dream
Dies at the opening day.

Between 1914 and 1918, time turned from a stream into a boiling,
churning floodtide bearing away millions of sons and daughters in the
horrors of the First World War.

Richard also sang you a song, "What a Wonderful World," a
poignant tribute made famous by jazz singer Louis Armstrong that was
used with great emotional irony in a film called *Good Morning, Vietnam*.

Against a mélange of horrible inflictions on the civilian population of Vietnam, Armstrong crooned these words:

I see trees of green, red roses, too,
I see them bloom, for me and you.
And I think to myself,
'What a wonderful world...'

I was moved to tears in the movie, and I was choking up in Nine Elms Cemetery when Richard sang it over your grave. And then he said softly, "It is a wonderful world. Thanks guys."

We have so many to thank. The numbers of soldiers lost by both sides in the First World War are absolutely astounding. The large cemeteries are breathtaking in their scope, so let me concentrate on your little cemetery. Military cemeteries are scattered all over the combat areas of northern France, both from the First and Second World Wars (yes, sons of the fathers killed in WWI went out and got killed in WWII). Nine Elms is one of the smaller cemeteries.

Orland French taking notes at Nine Elms Military Cemetery.
Sylvia French photo

I'm wondering what the land was like when you were laid to rest. It's flat and smooth now, but wherever it has been preserved as it was in 1918, as around the Vimy Monument, it is pocked with shell holes, mine craters, and trench passageways. Your little cemetery occupies 3,355 square metres of France enclosed by a low brick wall. It lies beside the main road from Arras to Lens, on which thousands of vehicles a day, more than you could ever imagine, whiz by.

**Orland French planting flags on his Uncle Oscar's grave.
Sylvia French photo**

Although you died on April 9, 1917, I suspect you were not buried here until sometime later. On your burial records, there is a reference to "exhumation", so I am guessing you were buried twice, at least. The first would have been a hasty burial after the battle, the second more permanent. Burials were made in the first three rows of Plot 1 in the spring and early summer of 1917. The rest of the cemetery was made after the armistice by the concentration of bodies from 499 temporary British and French graves from the nearby battlefields of Neuville-St.

Vaast. This was a common practice. As you would see, if you could view the cemetery, your headstone is next to that of Joseph Defayette, an infantryman who died in the same shell explosion that killed you.

Some bodies were placed in available caverns. Near Nine Elms, for instance, is the Zivy Crater Cemetery where the bodies of 53 soldiers, five unidentified, are buried in a mine crater with an appropriate round monument on top. You must have been aware that some of your buddies went out into the battlefield and were never seen again. They have been commemorated in special places. The names of the missing at Vimy are carved into the base of the Vimy Monument. At Ypres in Belgium, where there was an overwhelming loss of human life, we found the name of Pte. Leonard McConnell, a cousin of Sylvia's mother. He was one of 55,000 lost and missing soldiers whose names are carved into the Menin Gate.

While we approached your grave in a tentative and slightly reverential mood at first, we soon became more relaxed and appreciative of our surroundings and your place in the world. We wondered if it was possible that we were the first of your immediate family to visit your grave. I had not heard of others. But in the soil immediately in front of your gravestone, we found a little plastic Canadian flag lapel pin, possibly purposely placed there by a family member. There is a registry book for visitors to sign, and the very last person who signed it before us was a man from whom I had bought a guidebook in Canada. He visits war cemeteries frequently and had been at Nine Elms just a week earlier.

Before we left Arras and the Vimy area, we passed Nine Elms on the highway several times. We became quite casual about it, shouting out "Hello Oscar" every time we went by the cemetery. I was reminded of your description of shouting out the train window whenever you went through a town in Quebec on your way to Halifax. But we were much more respectful and less rowdy. Maybe you heard us, nevertheless.

Your grateful nephew,
Orland

P.S. You have been well remembered elsewhere. Your passing is recorded on the family headstone in the graveyard at Waverley United Church, your name is on both the Waverley War Memorial and the War Memorial in Midland, Ontario, and the town of Midland named a lane after you.

Satellite image of Nine Elms Military Cemetery, courtesy of Google Earth. Oscar's grave is in the upper left part of the cemetery, under the trees. The highway on the right runs from Arras to Lens.

Satellite image of Vimy Ridge, courtesy of Google Earth. The Vimy Monument is north of the wooded area. Nine Elms Military Cemetery is near the bottom of the picture.

Gravestone of Pte. Oscar French at Nine Elms Military Cemetery. The inscription reads. "408445 Private O. French Can. Machine Gun Corps 9th April 1917". Orland French photo

Orland and Sylvia French at Oscar's grave.
Patricia Chernesky photo

Fog lends a haunting feeling to a German cemetery at Neuville-Saint-
Vaast, near Vimy Ridge. Over 40,000 German soldier are buried here,
four to a grave marker. The graves includes those of 129 Jewish soldier
who died fighting for Germany.
Sylvia French photo

Oscar French and Joseph Defayette
were killed by the same shell on April 9, 1917.
Orland French photo

MEDALLIONS AND OTHER HARDWARE

THE MEMORABILIA of war include a few pieces of memorial hardware tucked away in a drawer for safekeeping. This can include the large medallion issued in the name of a dead soldier, any medals he or she might have collected, a hat badge, and a Silver Cross for the grieving mother or wife.

Bronze medallion issued to family of every soldier killed in action. Each has the soldier's name on it. These are still known to collectors as a "dead man's penny."
French family archives

Every mother or widow (next of kin) of a soldier who
died in battle received the Memorial Cross, more
popularly known as the Silver Cross. The round medallion
is Pte. French's identification tag, nicknamed "dog tag."
French family archives

Hat badge of the Canadian Machine Gun Corps.
Frank O'Connor collection

MEMORIES OF VIMY

April 9, 2012
Belleville, Ontario

Dear Uncle Oscar:

This was actually my first letter to you. The idea of responding to your letters jelled in my head as I attended a Vimy memorial service in the town of Trenton, which we know now as Quinte West. It's just a few miles west of here. You probably wouldn't be familiar with it, although you passed through it by train on your way to Halifax.

In your day, Trenton was a little port town at the head of the Bay of Quinte, where the Trent River empties into Lake Ontario. It had no military significance, although today it is the home of one of Canada's largest and most important air centres, known as Canadian Forces Base Trenton. The base was established in the 1930s. From here, troops and supplies are dispatched by air to centres of conflict and civil emergencies all over the world. For instance, at this writing, Canada has sent a relief mission from Trenton to a typhoon disaster in the Philippines.

You might wonder, looking up at those fragile cloth-and-stick kites you call aeroplanes, how this is possible. We do that with huge planes such as the Globemaster transport craft, which when fully loaded, with a payload of 170,900 pounds, can weigh more than half a million pounds. It can cruise nearly five miles up for 2,800 miles! The plane is 174 feet long with a wingspan of 170 feet and a cargo compartment 88 feet in length. You could put a whole squadron of your little biplanes in the hold.

But, back to the Vimy service. Today is Easter Monday, 95 years to the day that you were blasted into Kingdom Come on Vimy Ridge. The service was held at 11 a.m., which, except for the time difference between France and Trenton, was about the time of day your comrades were forcing their way up the ridge through German fire. I don't know whether you were alive or dead at that point. Today was cold and blustery, about eight degrees Celsius, although not as cold as the snowy weather you faced on that Easter Monday at Vimy.

Not many towns commemorate the Battle of Vimy. It's not as well known to the public as Remembrance Day in November. They do in Ottawa, of course, and Governor General David Johnston was in France today attending a special ceremony at the Canadian war memorial at Vimy Ridge. For the ceremony in Trenton, only 15 or so civilians turned out to watch. About three dozen veterans participated, and a handful of cadets showed up as well. We have no more veterans of the First World War, as the last died in 2010. I expect that as we draw closer to the 100th anniversary on Vimy in 2017, commemorations will become more common.

While it was a sombre occasion, you would have enjoyed a lighter moment. The wind off the bay was chilling all of us as the parade of dignitaries arose to speak, one after the other. We looked forward to hot coffee. Finally the master of ceremonies said, "If you can stand the wind, we'll hear a few words from Mayor John Williams." Then he said, "Oh, I should correct that," but Mayor Williams cut in, "You got it right." It's the kind of thing the mayor himself would have said.

There was actually a man in genuine First World War army dress, right down to the puttees and canteen. Douglas Lawrence, who has no military rank since he was never in the army, is what is known as a re-enactor. These are people who dress in authentic military uniforms to replay battles and other military actions at different periods in history. Re-enactments of the War of 1812, involving "troops" from both sides, are very popular. Mr. Lawrence has been re-enacting a First World War soldier since 1970 and participated in ceremonies at Vimy in 1992, on the 75th anniversary of the battle.

Today's ceremony was organized by Branch 110 of the Royal Canadian Legion, a veterans' association formed in 1925 as the Canadian Legion of the British Empire Services League. From that beginning, today the Legion claims more than 340,000 members in 1,500 branches. Fortunately, Branch 110 with its hot coffee, sandwiches, and well-stocked bar was right next-door. We were glad to get out of the blustery cold and sit down to lunch in the warmth, even though the windy mayor came to join us.

While inside, I struck up a conversation with Jackie Nezezon, who had also lost an uncle at Vimy. He was Private James Caldwell from Bonarlaw, a little Waverley-sized community north of Trenton. He also died on April 9, 1917 and is buried near you in Nine Elms Military Cemetery.

Your nephew,
Orland

THE REMEMBRANCE SEASON

Belleville, Ontario
Nov. 11, 2014

Dear Uncle Oscar:

The Remembrance Season is over and I am glad of it. I feel much like I do on Boxing Day, when the relentless pre-Christmas bombardment of seasonal celebration is over and the advertisers have declared a ceasefire. In this case, the heavy bombardment of media reminiscences, like a creeping barrage leading the way to Remembrance Day, have ceased when we reached the targeted commemorative moment of 11 a.m. on November 11. That was the official moment of signing of the armistice that ended the war that snuffed out the lives of you and sixteen million others.

Remembrance Day used to be just that, a day set aside so we won't forget what you fellows did. Ceremonies are in the morning of November 11, and at 11 a.m., a bugler sounds Last Post, followed by two minutes of silence, followed by Reveille. You may know it as Rouse. Work out the timing, and you will find that the signing of the armistice is marked at the 11th hour of the 11th day of the 11th month of the year. It wasn't a holiday; if you weren't at a cenotaph, you paused in whatever you were doing at 11 a.m., then moved on with your business. Remembrance Day was originally known as Armistice Day and was officially declared as such by King George V in November 1919.

We no longer call it Armistice Day because a hundred years and what seems like a hundred wars have passed since. Remembrance Day encompasses the Second World War, the Korean War, the Afghanistan War, and numerous peacekeeping actions around the world in between. Locations like Croatia, Cyprus, Middle East, Suez, Rwanda; probably places you have never heard of because the world map keeps changing.

Now the Day has become the Season. The onset of the season begins with the flowering of the blood-red poppy on prominent lapels. Usually these are on politicians, or people appearing on television, signaling that the period of remembrance is upon us. The first poppies appear after Halloween on October 31 (itself a commercialized season). We have divided our year into seasons; the onslaught of Christmas lights and advertising will not appear until after November 11.

The wearing of the poppy has become *de rigeur* and has spawned controversy over whether it demonstrates remembrance of the fallen (you) or is actually a celebration of war and the military machines which will produce more war dead (like you).

Why the poppy? You can thank Canadian physician Lieutenant Colonel John McCrae for that. He wrote this poem on May 3 after the death of a friend and fellow soldier:

In Flanders Fields, the poppies blow,
Between the crosses, row on row,
That mark our place; and in the sky
The larks, still bravely singing, fly
Scarce heard amid the guns below.

We are the Dead. Short days ago
We lived, felt dawn, saw sunset glow,

Loved and were loved, and now we lie
In Flanders fields.

Take up our quarrel with the foe:
To you from failing hands we throw
The torch; be yours to hold it high.
If ye break faith with us who die
We shall not sleep, though poppies grow
In Flanders fields.

McCrae was persuaded to have it published. He tried *The Spectator* in London, only to be rejected, then sent it to *Punch,* which published it on December 8, 1915. McCrae achieved a rank of high standing as a consulting physician, but he contracted pneumonia, developed cerebral meningitis, and died in hospital on January 28, 1918. Since the poem was published more than a year before you died, you may well have been aware of it.

The popularity of the lapel-pin poppy was first promulgated by The American Legion, and then taken up by the British Legion and other legion organizations around the world, including Canada. The Legions sell tens of thousands of poppies before every Remembrance Day, also known as Veterans Day in the United States. Boxes of paper or plastic poppies appear everywhere, and you drop a donation into the box and take a poppy. Inevitably some of the boxes are stolen, leading to tear-besotted news stories about what an evil crime this is and an insult to our fallen soldiers. In our community this year, a couple of boxes were stolen by two unfortunate individuals who apparently had experience in stealing poppy boxes in previous years. They were more to be pitied than punished.

Sorry, Uncle, I have been distracted from my ruminations on the Remembrance Season. This year, the Remembrance Season was intensified by two events. First, this year marked the 100th anniversary of the beginning of the First World War. We have so many wars to commemorate; 2014 was also the 75th anniversary of the beginning of the Second World War, and in 2012 we marked the beginning of the War of 1812. Which commemoration, it seems, despite being fanned by funds from the federal government, fizzled out, like the real war itself. The second thing that happened was the killing of two Canadian soldiers in Canada in a set of bizarre actions that were ostensibly unrelated but still connected by the fact that the perpetrators were pro-Islamic fanatics. One in his car ran down a soldier in a parking lot in Quebec and killed him; the other gunned down an honour guard at the War Memorial in Ottawa, then forced his way into the Parliament Buildings where he was shot dead by the Sergeant at Arms of the House of Commons. (Our ceremonial officials are not to be trifled with.)

It was a most spectacular day, all caught on film and distributed around the world. It sparked an intense outcry of support for our military. Crowds at the cenotaphs only days later were swollen from previous attendances. We suddenly woke up. We were shocked into realizing that the conventional war has been supplanted by wars of terrorism. In few conflicts today do people put on a recognizable uniform, line up facing each other, and start shooting. Our enemies can be anyone among us, building bombs, carrying guns, killing enlisted soldiers and civilians alike as they seek justice for some cause or other. The war has come to us; the only difference between the two dead soldiers and any one of us was that they were wearing a uniform and were targeted as a symbol of the state.

I'm writing this now, a few days after the cessation of Remembrance Season. I confess to once having been rather indifferent to the Day. But since moving to Belleville, I have become much more attuned to the dedication of, and the sacrifices made, by the men and women who plant the flag of Canada's military endeavours overseas.

In Belleville, we live next to Canadian Forces Base Trenton. This is where our foreign military exploits are honed from the broad policy of engagement made in Ottawa into the sharp stick of execution. Politicians in Ottawa decide where people like you are to be deployed; the men and women at the base are the ones who actually climb into the jet aircraft that we see thundering into the night sky to some unknown fate in some foreign land. And when some come back in boxes, carried home to their families in funeral corteges, the cost of participation in foreign conflict becomes apparent.

Coming as it does in mid-November, Remembrance Day is often a sombre, grey, chilly affair. Last year, I returned from the Remembrance Day service down at the Cenotaph chilled to the bone. It was windy and rainy and cold today, and even a goose-down jacket couldn't keep out the November chill. Some soup and coffee kind of warmed me up. Standing out in the rain for an hour and a half really took its toll on me.

I can almost hear you laughing. Standing out in the cold and rain for 90 minutes! After what you guys went through, days and days of rain and rats and cold and sleet and mud up to your knees, that must sound like a walk in the park, with the promise of a warm house and soup and coffee and maybe something stronger after the ordeal. Well, we're a soft lot in the 21st century.

And how do we mark this day? Well, if you are self-employed and working in what we call the private sector, you keep on working. If you are fortunate enough to be on the public payroll, or working in a bank, you get the day off to do what you will. There is a growing movement to make Remembrance Day a statutory holiday. It already is in seven provinces, but not in Ontario and not nationally. Proponents say remembrance of you fellows is important enough to merit a whole day off; opponents say taking a couple of minutes at 11 a.m. more than makes the point.

Of course, those who are working rarely even notice the 11 a.m. observance. Nor would many more people make their way to the Cenotaph if it were a national holiday. The next issue would be whether the day off should be on the actual November 11 or annexed to the closest weekend so we can make something out of it. Of course, if you remember November, you will recall that it is not a good month to do anything much on a weekend. Too cold to go to the beach or hike in the hills, no snow to go skiing, too rainy to do much outside. In other words, not much of a season for a recreational holiday.

Anyway, one of the arguments for having a holiday is that this is what our guys gave their lives for. I can't imagine you ever said you'd lay down your life so future generations of Canadians could have a holiday, but it sounds better in retrospect.

Remembrance Day continues to be a major milestone every year, as ongoing military struggles continue to add fuel to the memories of those who died in battle. And so I think of you, someone I never knew in person, a hundred years after you gave up your life for Canada.

Rest in peace forever in France.

Your nephew,
Orland

OTHER CORRESPONDENCE AND ARTICLES

The following letter was contained in the box with Oscar's letters. It is unsigned and is possibly missing the last page. It appears to be a hand-written letter of encouragement prepared for men about to go overseas. The note may have accompanied a gift of money given to Uncle Oscar by the community as he prepared to depart; possibly the money he used to buy the watch with a five-year warranty.

Waverley, Ont. Oct. 23, 1915

To Mr. Oscar French: –

In her time of distress "Mother England" called on her sons across the "Big Pond" and right royally have her sons responded to her call.

From Australia, New Zealand, from India and from Canada has gone for the answer, "We are coming, Mother England, a hundred thousand strong."

Throughout the whole of the Dominion of Canada our sturdy boys rallied and are still rallying to uphold the honour and integrity of this your Great British Empire. Our boys have left their homes, they have left their loved ones, they have put aside their cherished ambitions and have undergone successfully the trials of a vigorous training, in order, if it is necessary, to lay down their life for the cause that is just and true.

Many of our young men have gone to the firing line and gave their last drop of blood in defense of the noble struggle of our worthy motherland.

You are now about to depart from our Fair Dominion to enter into that inferno of shot and shell in which your companions have already so valiantly upheld the name and fame of Canada. Many more will follow your noble lead, proud to stand shoulder to shoulder and hurl back the invading Teuton. In a few short weeks, you will be face to face with your "Duty." You will be among strange peoples; you will see strange sights, you will encounter many difficulties; you will reap rewards, but remember in your darkest hours and your greatest rewards we will be with you – if not in flesh, then in spirit. And if our prayers and our blessings will lend you arm strength and carry you safely through to the end, they are yours from the bottom of our souls.

Mr. French we are proud to have you in the ranks along with our other sons fighting for our homes and our Grand British Constitutions, and prouder still will we be when we shake your hand and welcome you safely back to the land of your birth and the village of your boyhood.

On behalf of your many friends who will await your return after the war is over, I wish you the greatest of Good Luck and if you believe in good luck charms I endow you with four leaf clovers, horseshoes, and rabbits feet by the score.

Mere words cannot fully express our feelings so I wish you once again a safe return and ask you to accept this small token as a remembrance of the many pleasant hours you have spent in Waverley.

(no signature)

TWO FRIENDS LOST IN ACTION

Uncle Oscar often referred to friends of his who had also signed up, wondering what had become of them. Here are two references:

Niagara-on-the-Lake, June 13, 1915

Billie Quinlan and George Reynolds left with the reinforcements last Wednesday and I guess they are well on their way across the ocean by now.

France Nov 27th, 1916

I haven't had any word from George Reynolds since I seen him more than two months ago but hope his wound is not serious and he is getting along alright.

As it turned out, George Reynolds suffered the same fate as Oscar. He died on April 9, 1917. The *Elmvale Lance* of May 10, 1917, reported:

> *On Monday, a message from Ottawa was brought*
> *to Mr. John Reynolds, Waverley, that his son, Lance*
> *Corporal George Reynolds, was killed in action on*
> *April 9th. A memorial service will be held in Waverley*
> *Orange Hall on Sunday, May 13th.*

Oscar's death notice was contained in the same issue of the Lance, in somewhat more flowery language. The style depended on the village correspondent who filed the report:

Once more a Waverley boy has gone to never return. Oscar, son of Mr. and Mrs. Sam French, was shot in action on Easter Monday, somewhere in France. Oscar was the third of our boys to fall upon the battlefield fight for his King and Country. These boys forsook home and friends and went away with courage to fight the foe, not knowing whether they would ever return. A memorial service was conducted in the Orange Hall Sunday afternoon. A very large assembly gathered to show respect to the parents as well as the slain. The call will come to each of us. Are we ready? Are there not young people as well as old to-day whose ears are deaf to the call of the Master? Would that all could listen to the Saviour's call when repeated by some friend or minister. To the heart-stricken parents, family and friends their well-wishers extend to them through The Lance *heartfelt sympathy in their hour of sorrow.*

LISTED TOGETHER FOREVER

THE CENOTAPH in Waverley, Ontario, also known as the Waverley Soldiers' Memorial, lists the names of local men who died in the First World War. It commemorates soldiers from the townships of Tay, Medonte, Tiny, and Flos. The names below appear in the order they are listed on the monument. Some of them were friends of Uncle Oscar.

TAY

William Quinlan

Oscar French

J. Chas. Montgomery

W. Wesley Neilly

Alvin Jones

Harry Rummney

Marshal Ney

Norman Vincent

Ernest Clapp

James Linton

Norman Russell

William Kennedy

Frank C. McNabb

Frank Kitchener

Alfred Clark

James Johnston

John N. Carter

Norman Swartman

James Currier

John Bell

Ronald Wright

Archibald McDonald

Andrew W. Durnford

Earl Ralston

James Langley

Wallace H. Burns

MEDONTE

Fred Reynolds

George Reynolds

Ambrose V. Archer

John Grigg

Wesley Campbell

Herbert Duddy

William Farragher

Fred Higgins

Cleveland Mount

Douglas Kitchen

Russell Middleton

Mervin Nash

Fred Rumford

Robert Raaflaub

Charles Orr

George Nelles

Hilton Williamson

Howard Tudhope

William Tigen

Edward Innes

Con. Buckley

W. Johnston Leslie

TINY

Lorne Bell

Colonel Bell

Jos. H. Blackstock

Wm. H. Braithwade

William A. Foster

Earnest N. Moore

Peter Lacroix

Howard Kemp

George Dusome

Harry Ellery

Albert Sterritt

Arthur Bailey

Percy Arnold

FLOS

Walter L. Middleton	Thomas J. Forsythe
Oliver S. Gilbert	William S. Ritchie
Howard Bell	L. W. Rolfe
C. Verner Train	Walter French
Ernest Donaldson	Wm. H. Carruthers
Oscar Kerr	Patrick Mitchel
David W. Kerr	George Gore
James Drysdale	Joseph Smith
Alfred Davis	George W. Vansickle
Richard McFadden	James Paterson
A. Roy Shipcott	M. Grant Lawson
Wm. C. Humphries	
Alex Polson	
Leonard Ralph	
George VanBuren	
Morley Snider	

This message is inscribed at the top of the Medonte stone:

"This monument was erected by the Ladies Patriotic League of Waverley and voluntary public subscription – A.D. 1920 In memory of those who gave their lives during the Great War in Europe 1914-1918"

Each stone is also inscribed at the top:
"Who dies for freedom lives."

And at the bottom:
"And their name shall live forever."

Some names on the Waverley Memorial also appear on the Midland (Tay), Elmvale (Flos), and Penetanguishene (Tiny) cenotaphs.

Waverley Soldiers' Memorial in Waverley, Ontario.
Names of soldiers killed in the First World War are
engraved on the sides of the central monument. The four
outer obelisks were added after the Second World War.
Photo courtesy Tay Heritage

Monument at Waverley Soldiers' Memorial for Tay Township.
Pte. Oscar French is listed second from the top.
Orland French photo

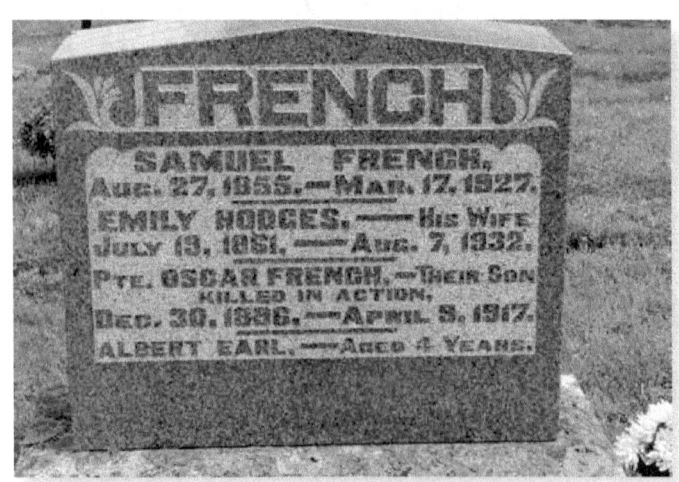

Family headstone in the cemetery of Waverley
United Church, Waverley, Ontario.
Orland French photo

Entry to French Lane in the Town of Midland, Ontario.
The lane was commemorated in the name of Pte. Oscar French.
Orland French photo

OFFICIAL SYMPATHIES FROM OTTAWA

The following letter was received by Uncle Oscar's father, Samuel French, from the minister of militia and defence for Canada:

Minister's Office, Ottawa, June 16th, 1917
Personal

Dear Mr. French —

I desire to express to you my very sincere sympathy in the recent decease of your son #408445 Pte. Oscar French, who in sacrificing his life at the front in action with the enemy, has rendered the highest services of a worthy citizen.

The heavy loss which you and the Nation have sustained would indeed be depressing were it not redeemed by the knowledge that the brave comrade for whom we mourn performed his duties fearlessly as well as became a good soldier and gave his life for the great cause of Human Liberty and the defence of the Empire.

Again extending to you in your bereavement my condolence and heartfelt sympathy,

I am

Yours faithfully
A.E. Kemp
Minister of Militia and Defence for Canada

SETTLING THE ESTATE

Subsequently, Uncle Oscar's mother received the following letter from Ottawa, dated October 30, 1917.

From – The Officer i/c Estates, Militia Headquarters, Ottawa, Ont.
PTE. O. FRENCH, NO. 408445, 2nd C.D.F.G Coy.

Madam: –

With reference to the estate of your late son, the soldier named in the margin, I have the honour, by direction, to inform you that I am this day dispatching to you, packet No. F-735, containing the only article of personal effects recovered, and would request that you be good enough to acknowledge receipt of same on the enclosed invoice.
    I have the honour to be, Madam, your obedient servant,

G. Morley (signature)
Lieut. For Office i/c Estates

(I don't know what was in the packet. Probably his I.D. tag)

• • • • •

The following letter was issued from Ottawa:

Ottawa, May 27th, 1919
From – The Adjutant General, Canadian Militia

To –
Samuel French, Esq., Waverley Ontario
408445 Private Oscar French
Canadian Expeditionary Force

Sir –
I beg to enclose herewith, official certificate of death in respect of the marginally noted soldier.

W.W. Stinson
For Director of Records
For a/Adjutant General

THE 37TH BATTALION (NORTHERN ONTARIO), CEF

PTE. OSCAR FRENCH was recruited by the 37th Battalion in the spring of 1915. The battalion recruited men from northern Ontario – Waverley must have been deemed to have been in northern Ontario – and mobilized at Niagara Falls. It was authorized on November 7, 1914 and embarked for Britain a little more than a year later, on November 27, 1915. Throughout the rainy and cold winter of 1915-1916, the men trained in Britain for battle in France. The 37th supplied reinforcements to the Canadian Corps already in the field, replacing the dead and wounded as they were carried away from the Front. In July 1916, shortly after Oscar was transferred to France, its remaining personnel were absorbed by the 39th Battalion. This battalion was disbanded on May 21, 1917. I have a long horizontal photo of rows of soldiers of the 37th Battalion assembled on a field at Niagara – presumably Uncle Oscar is in there somewhere, but I've never played Where's Waldo to find him.

SHORT-FORM LETTERS

SOLDIERS COULD SEND quick messages home using pre-printed field post cards. They were able to check off the applicable messages or draw a line through the parts that didn't apply. While these quickie short forms weren't as friendly as hand-written letters, at least they informed families of the soldier's condition and that he was still alive. The text on the cards read as follows:

Front –

The address only to be written on this side. If anything else is added the post card will be destroyed.

Back –

Nothing is to be written on this side except the date and signature of the sender. Sentences not required will be erased. If anything else is added the post card will be destroyed.

I am quite well.

I have been admitted into hospital (sick, wounded) and am going on well and hope to be discharged soon.

I am being sent down to the base.

I have received your (letter dated_____, telegram dated
_____, parcel dated _____)

Letter follows at first opportunity.
I have received no letter from you (lately, for a long time).
Signature only_____

WAR DIARY
OR INTELLIGENCE SUMMARY

6th Canadian Machine-Gun Company, April 1-9, 1917

Place	Date/Hr	Summary of Events and Information
Coy Hdqrs Neuville St. Vaast	**April** 1	Weather fine but cloudy. Crews cleaning guns and filling belts, also carrying up ammunition 90000 rounds. Repairs to dugouts and trenches damaged by shell fire. 11000 rounds fired on targets located at A12 a 6.7 to A11 a 9.9½, Balloon Avenue CT, A6 b 6.½ to A10 b 6.3., A5 c 4½.8 to A5 c 5.4.
	2	Weather cold with heavy wind. Heavy snow fall towards night. Crews cleaning guns filling belts and carrying up ammunition 90000 rounds. Repairs to dugouts and trenches damaged by shell fire. Building anti-aircraft positions near V8 position. 11000 rounds fired on targets located at A12 a 6.7 to A11 a 9.9½, BALLOON AVE CT, A6 b 6.½ to A10 b 6.3., A5 c 4½.8 to A5 c 5.4. and A12 a 9½.9¾ to A12 c 4½.9½.
	3	Weather fine with wind. Crews cleaning guns and filling belts. Carrying up ammunition 14000 rounds. Repairs to dugouts and trenches damaged by shellfire. 7000 rounds fired on targets located as follows: Squares A5b A6c and A11b.
Neuville St Vaast	4	Weather fine. Crews cleaning guns and filling belts. Repairs to dugouts and trenches damaged by shell-fire. The Company was relieved during the night 4/5th April by the 4th and 5th Cdn M.G. Coys. [O.O. No 51 attached] No 4 Coy relieving in Thelus Rt. Sub-Sector and No 5 Coy relieving in the Thelus left sub-sector. Relief was complete at 1.30 a.m. April 5th when Company moved to hut billets in Mount St. Eloy. The Company went into line for the tour of duty at full strength and had five casualties all shrapnel wounds.
Mt St Eloy	5	Weather fine and very clear. Company resting. Thorough examination of guns, equipment and spare parts.
	6	Weather dull and cloudy with heavy rain showers. Company resting and preparing for coming operation
	7	Weather fine but cold and cloudy with heavy wind. Company resting and preparing for coming operation.

	8	Weather cloudy with wind and showers. Company moved into the line to join in attack on Vimy Ridge as follows. [O.O. No 52 attached] Nos. 1 and 2 Sections under Lts Waddington and Stonehewer moved independently across country and took up Barrage Positions along RHINE TRENCH. These guns formed complete Battery with Lt WADDINGTON as Battery Commander. They were in position with guns laid at 12 midnight night 8/9th. Nos. 3 and 4 Sections under command of Lts HARDIMAN and WILLIAMS were attached to the 27th and 29th Bns respectively. These sections joined the Battalions at Mt St Eloy at 8.30 p.m. and moved into assembly positions with them. The OC and 2nd in Command moved to Bde Hdqrs in Zivy Cave early in the evening
Zivy Cave	9	Major Eastham O.C. visited all the battery positions of his group, that is 2 batteries consisting 8 guns M.M.G. Bde 8 guns 6th Cdn M.G. Coy and 8 guns 13th M.G. Coy (British), at 2.30 a.m. and found everyone in place and guns correctly laid. At Zero hour these guns opened fire in accordance with Corps Instructions and continued firing until Zero + 75 when they ceased fire and proceeded to new position in the vicinity of Thelus from which they were to cover the advance of the 6th Cdn Inf Bde. Lt Waddington's guns passed safely through the barrage and were dug in with guns laid by 9 a.m. No casualties occurred while moving but shortly afterward No 2 Section had Ptes French and Defayette killed and 4 men wounded by shell fire while later in the day Ptes Lee and Relph were caught in fumes from gas shells and slightly gassed. Upon the 6th Cdn Inf Bde obtaining their objective these batteries ceased fire and laid their guns on S.O.S. line in accordance with Corps Instructions. No 3 Section under Lt. Hardiman advanced about 8.30 a.m. in Rear of "D" Company 29th Bn. 2 gun temas under Lt. Tucker on the right of D Coy and 2 gun teams under Lt. Hardiman on left flank. The teams advanced through consolidation lines until enemies wire was reached at B1 c 7.4. From this point Lt. Hardiman with two guns took up position covering advance of D Coy to the Bois de Ville. Whilst these covered advance Lt Tucker with two guns entered the wood, dug in and got into action firing heavily upon enemies artillery with good results until ammunition began to run short when men were sent back to carry up supply. As soon as D Coy had dug in Lt Hardiman and guns moved into the Bois des Ville on the left of the two first guns. Owing to the fact that D Coy 29th Bn had 8 Lewis guns in the wood and that the field of fire in the wood was poor these 4 guns were withdrawn 150 yards from the wood which gave them a much greater field of fire. No 4 Section advanced under Lt Williams in rear of D Coy 27th Bn. The final objective was reached without casualties. Two guns being placed in unfinished German Trench in front of 2nd line of wire on crest of slope and one gun on each flank of 27th Bn. Weather was stormy with snow, rain and wind.

FURTHER REPORTS FROM VIMY

News report, **Midland Free Press,** *April 25, 1917*

Canadians Fought Five Days Subsisting on "Iron Rations"

British Headquarters in France, April 15 (1917) – It is one of the petty perversities of the great world war that some of the most Homeric fighting on Vimy Ridge should have been about a place rejoicing in the name of "The Pimple." The *Associated Press* correspondent met some worn and muddy Canadians returning from beyond "The Pimple" yesterday afternoon. Among them were many Nova Scotians. They had been fighting from Sunday night until Friday night, and declared they had enjoyed every minute of it.

Some of the Canadians had subsisted on "iron rations" for five days, and had practically no water for three days. But they never thought of turning back for food or drink until their task was completed. They swung along with the dog-tired, but satisfied, gait of men returned from a successful day's hunting expedition.

Elmvale Lance, *April 12, 1917*

All Canadians in Vimy Fight

London Cable – "From a reliable source," says the *London Standard,* "we hear that the whole four Canadian divisions went over Vimy. The capture of this key position … is purely the reward of having skillful preparation by the leaders, back by incomparable troops."

Pte. Harold C. Allen, to his mother, Jennie Allen of Toronto, April 17, 1917. Printed in the Elmvale Lance, *May 17, 1917*

Greatest and Grandest Undertaking

You will have read all about the glorious actions of the Canadians in the newspapers. April 9th was a great day, and we were successful beyond all expectations. Of course we had casualties but nothing in comparison with what was done. It was the greatest and grandest undertaking in which we have ever been engaged. I can tell you I was glad to be alive that day and to go over Vimy Ridge with the boys. I hope to be home soon and then I can tell you personally about it. I suppose all you want to know is that I am safe and unharmed.

Letter from Pte. Alfred McWatters at Hertford, England. Printed in the Elmvale L, *May 24, 1917*

Captured 10,000 Huns

The Canadians made a great name for themselves lately when they won a great battle in France and took over 10,000 prisoners. They captured Vimy Ridge, one of the strongest fortifications the Huns had.

The English papers don't give the Canadians the whole credit as they are likely to say "the British". Nevertheless, the Canadians did the work and made a name for themselves this time if they never did before, and with casualties too.

Midland Free Press, *April 26, 1917*

Canadians Captured German Field Pieces

Prisoners who were attached to the German batteries complain that so many German guns were lost because of a shortage of artillery horses. They say that the British were up and over their pieces before they could be hauled down to safety. On the Vimy Ridge alone the storming Canadians took four 8-inch howitzers, nine of the famous 5.9 guns, the most mobile and useful piece in the German battery, and 23 other pieces.

Elmvale Lance, *May 3, 1917*

Vimy Trophies for Dominion to be Exhibited at Various Fall Fairs

Canadian Headquarters in France – A varied assortment of Vimy trophies, machine gun, mortars and field guns, are being prepared to be shipped out to Canada. These will be features of the fall fairs. From the dugouts of Vimy Ridge and from prisoners taken there were obtained many objects, diaries and other documents, indicating the efficiency of our preparatory artillery fire as well as the accuracy of our information on which it was based.

(Two captured German machine guns were allotted to the Cenotaph in Waverley. These were in place until at least the 1950s, and then mysteriously disappeared.)

Canon Frederick G. Scott, C.M.G., D.S.O., senior chaplain, First Canadian Infantry Division, Canadian Expeditionary Force, 1914-1919. From his memoirs, The Great War As I Saw It:

Victory on the Dot

In spite of the numbers of wounded and dying men which I had seen, the victory was such a complete and splendid one that April 9th, 1917 was one of the happiest days in my life, and when I started out from the signallers' dugout on my way back to Ecoivres, and passed the hill where I had seen the opening of the great drama in the early morning, my heart was full of thankfulness to Almighty God for his blessing on our arms. I arrived at my room in the Chateau at about half-past two a.m., filled with dreams of victory and glory, and awoke well and fit in the morning, more than ever proud of the grand old First Division which, as General Horne told us later, had made a new record in British war annals by taking every objective on the scheduled dot of the clock.

LETTER FROM WILL FARAGHER

On January 6, 1918, Uncle Oscar's mother received a letter from France from Pte. Will Faragher, a friend of Oscar and the family.

Mrs. French, Dear Friend:

I received your most welcome letter some time ago and I was very glad to hear from you for I am always glad to get the good old Waverley news. I was very sorry to hear Howard Bell had been killed. I didn't know he was in the army. I saw Luke Adamson and Ernie Dundas last fall but I haven't seen or heard from them since. I sure think Waverley has done its bit in this war for the size of it but the majority of the poor boys have been killed. I was wounded on Nov. 2nd and was in the hospital for nearly two months but I am alright again and I hope to rejoin my battalion soon again. Out of 70 men who came over in the draft there are only two of us left and we have both been wounded but not very seriously I am glad to say.

I don't know if I will ever get to see Oscar's grave any more for we are on a different front from where the poor boy was killed but you can trust me if I ever get a chance I will go and fix it up for we were more like brothers than friends for I had chummed with him steady for about ten years. I had him up to our house for tea the last night he was in Canada before he left for overseas.

Well I guess I will close for now with best regards to all the folks.

I remain Yours Sincerely
Pte. Will Faragher

William Edward Faragher was killed on August 27, 1918. His name is one of 88 listed on the four memorial stones at the Waverley Cenotaph (spelled as Farragher).

LETTER FROM UNCLE VERNE

In the box of letters from Uncle Oscar, I also found a letter from Verne, Oscar's brother. Note the difference in writing style. The Halifax Explosion occurred Dec. 6, 1917. Verne survived the war. He and his wife Carrie farmed near Carrot River, Saskatchewan.

Dec. 30th, 1917

Dear Mother,

Will try and write a few lines today have been a little long in writing this time I got the parcel you sent yesterday the jar of ground plums got broke the towel soaked up most of the juice of them it didn't hurt the cake much thanks very much and thank Dad for the tobacco. We can't get Canadian tobacco over here what they make in this country is a lot stronger and about three times as dear. I had five days pass at Christmas was down to Frittenden to Uncle Ben Hodges it's a far nicer country down there than around here and the people seem more like Canadians there is three of the girls at home with your uncle and aunt one of them is married her husband is in France I just seen one of the Foremans cousin Allice. I was lucky to get a pass there wasn't many got a pass. We have been having fairly good weather lately a little cold sometimes but not much rain I suppose you's will be getting some cold weather over there now I wonder what kind of a winter they are having out West this winter I haven't heard from May for some time now. The mail don't seem to be coming very regular lately I think there must of been some got blown up at Halifax. Well Mother it is nearly supper time so will make this letter short and get it posted today hoping you's are all well with love from

Verne

PART TWO: LETTERS FROM THE
WAR

This section contains transcripts of letters written during the First World War by Pte. Oscar French to his mother Mrs. Samuel French of Waverley, Ontario. She was the grandmother of author Orland French, nephew of Oscar. None of Oscar's letters was addressed or written to his father.

PTE. OSCAR FRENCH'S
LETTERS TO HOME

The following letters were written by my uncle, Private Oscar French, between the time of his enlistment in the spring of 1915 until April 8, 1917, the day before he died on Vimy Ridge. Although the language is straightforward and clear, and his handwriting was exceptionally legible, there are some lapses in grammar and spelling which have been faithfully represented here. Almost all are to his mother, my grandmother, but a few to his siblings have been included. My letters of response in the first part of this book are based on Uncle Oscar's comments and observations in these letters.

FIVE-YEAR GUARANTEE

Partial letter written from Exhibition Camp in Toronto

Undated, probably spring 1915

(We engaged in) a sham fight but we drove them back and took several prisoners and three of their bicycles. In the afternoon they tried to cut off our field kitchens but we wouldn't stand for that and we had another brush with them. It is a great day to-day. I think I will go out to Annie's on the car as soon as church parade is over. I can be away from then until 9.30 tonight. I got a wristwatch with that money I was given. It is not a very fancy one but I got a five-year guarantee with it and it has been running fine so far. Well mother I will have to go on church parade now so will close and write soon again.

> Yours with love
> Oscar
> Pte. O. French
> Machine Gun Section
> 37th Battalion
> Exhibition Camp
> Toronto
> No. 408257

FIRST TIME AT THE FALLS

June 13, 1915
Niagara-on-the-Lake

Dear Mother –

Received your welcome letter the first of the week and will now try and write you a few lines. Was very much surprised and pleased to see Owen, Jennie and Annie. I had given up hope of them coming when I met them Tuesday morning. I got a pass for the rest of the day and went to the Falls. I was not allowed to go on the boat so went down on the car. It was half-past four when I got down there and as they had to leave at half-past five did not have very long to spend with them there. I enjoyed my trip very much however. It was the first time that I had seen the Falls. Billie Quinlan and George Reynolds left with the reinforcements last Wednesday and I guess they are well on their way across the ocean by now. I hated to see some of our fellows going and the rest of us staying behind. We had a big review parade yesterday. The 36th, 37th and 35th Battalions were reviewed by the headquarters staff. I heard some talk of the 36th leaving here next Saturday. We haven't much idea when the 37th will leave. We were to a church parade this morning and it was very hot. We have to stand all the time.

That must have been some garden party at the Scarlett's. Would of liked to of been up but will try and go up next week for two or three days. Was over to the Y.M.C.A., last night and two fellows gave an exhibition of fencing and bayonet fighting then there was a three round boxing bout. They have singing and moving pictures over there nearly every night. Well mother you said in your letter that you would of liked for me to of been at home to-day as it would be your last Sunday in the old home but as I had one pass this week I could not get another. Quite a few of the fellows went up to-day but I will have to take my turn next week. I was inoculated on Thursday for the first time and I certainly knew it the next morning. They jab a needle into you just above the heart and that night we were a pretty looking bunch of mutts going around with one shoulder stuck away up in the air and the other one sagging down near the ground. We didn't have anything to do the next day which was one consolation. We get another dose next week on the other side and another one after that on the arm. They will not go near as hard with us as the first one did. Anybody who refused inoculation was placed in detention and given the alternative of taking it or paying for their release. It is the best thing that can be done with a bunch of men as typhoid is dangerous during this hot weather. They make us keep our tents good and clean and tidy. It has been very hot here this last week and has been threatening to rain to-day but hasn't come as yet. We were issued with light suits and straw hats the other day so it is much nicer drilling now. Has there been much rain up your way lately? I see by the papers that there hasn't been much rain in the West. I wrote to the folks out there but haven't received an answer as yet. Well it will soon be haying and harvest time again. I guess dad and Owen will be busy at the hoe crop as this is the time that the weeds like to grow. Is Roy still working at Penetang. I think Laura said in her letter that he was down to Scarlett's the night of the garden party playing ball. You were saying that Owen and Jennie were having a reception when they came back. Write and tell me about it. I sent you a couple of snap shots in my last letter but they were not very good. Will try and have some photos for you the next time I write. Well I guess I will have to close for this time. With love

from Oscar
Write soon

ROUTE MARCH TO QUEENSTON

Niagara Military Camp
A Company
37th Battalion C.E.F.
Aug. 22, 1915

Dear Mother –

Well Mother it is very wet here to-night so will try and write you a few lines. I was very sorry to hear that the crops have turned out so poorly, there was such good prospects when I was up home last. It has been very wet down here for this last month rain about every other day. Yesterday we were going to have a big review by the Duke of Connaught but it rained so hard that they had to put it off. There was a big Red Cross fete down at the Queen's Royal in the afternoon and at night. A number from the 35th and 37th battalions went down and did physical drill. We did physical drill with rifles and the band played for us. Our searjeant (sic) major told us that we did well. We had free tickets for the concert at night but it was raining so did not bother going. Well I guess our battalion will be going to the exhibition for a day or two. It was in the paper today that the 37th and 35th were going over. There is to be a big march past on military day before the Duke of Connaught. I think that is on Sept. 2. I see by the papers that the 35th, 37th, 38th, 74th, 75th, 76th and 94th battalions are going to Toronto for the winter. There is to be another reinforcement draft to be picked out before long I think. Toronto would be a good place to winter but I would like to get to England. I guess if McClinton goes with the next draft, I will go but if he don't I expect he will send the recruits that came into our platoon last week. Billie is well liked down here and seems to get his men in shape much faster than most of the other officers. We had another route march to Queenston on Friday. There were five battalions in all which made about four thousand men. It was over a mile between the head company and the rear. Our battalion has certainly got some band. They're downplaying at the big Red Cross fete most of Friday and Sat.

I would of liked to of been up home when Ruby and Annie was there. Have you had any word from the West lately. I see that they are expecting a record crop out there this year. That is one consolation since the Ontario crops were so poor. There was thousands of dollars worth of damage done to the fruit and canning industry down here. The cherry crop turned out pretty fair I think and the peach crop is not so bad. It has been very cold at nights. I was over on sick horse picquet (picket) on Wed. night watching the sick horses and was glad to have my greatcoat on. That will make it bad for garden stuff like tomatoes.

The German submarines have been very active this last week. I wonder if the sinking of the *Arabic* will have any effect in drawing the United States into the war. I guess the Yankees will satisfy themselves by sending a few more friendly notes. I see there were two Americans drowned on the *Arabic*. Well mother I was thinking of signing over about twenty dollars a month. They will send it home every month out of my wages and after we get moving around I won't have a very good place to keep it. It may come in useful and if you don't use it all dad can put it into the bank in his name and draw

it for me when I come back. Well I guess I will close now hoping you are all well. I remain

Yours with love

Oscar

Write soon

GOING HOME TO SEE ERNE

Partial letter, probably written in September 1915
Niagara-on-the-lake

The cooks are having quite a time to get the meals it has been so wet and such a high wind. Both of our big mess tents were blown down last night and we had to carry our grub down to our own tents to eat so we would be out of the rain. The tailor's tent was also blown down and all the stuff in it got a good soaking.

Well mother I hope you are none the worse for your trip to Dundas. I wished you could of come across to the camp while you were down. If Erne is up home about the 1st of October, I will likely see him as I am applying for a pass to get up home then. We are expecting another trip to Parry Sound in two or three weeks so will have plenty of traveling for awhile. We expected to go to Parry Sound from Bracebridge yesterday but they had some bother about the expenses, so we didn't get going. It certainly costs somebody some money when a bunch of about fifty goes away like that. I hope Uncle Steve is able to get around again. It will soon be Elmvale fair time again. I think I heard that it was on the third and fourth of next month so may be home then. Well mother will close now with love from

Oscar
Write soon.

I LOST MY CAP FROM THE TRAIN

Niagara
Sept. 26, 1915

Dear Mother –

Received your welcome letter the first of the week and since then have been to Bracebridge and back again. Instead of leaving on Monday as was intended we didn't go until Wednesday. We left here on the first boat Wed. morning and got to Bracebridge about six o'clock that night. We had two hours to spend in Toronto before our train left so had a look around and got my dinner in Eaton's. I lost my cap out of the train window somewhere between Bradford and Alandale and didn't get it until Friday morning. A section man found it and they sent it on up. We were in Bracebridge Thursday and Friday and came back yesterday. We got into camp about eight o'clock last night. We had a pretty fair time. We boarded at one of the hotels and I was only out to drill the last afternoon we were there as I ... (*rest of letter missing*)

TWENTY-FIVE DOLLARS EVERY MONTH

Niagara Camp
Oct. 9th, 1915

Dear Mother –

Received your welcome letter yesterday and was pleased to hear from you again. Was also pleased to get Erne's letter. Will he be going home before next Sat. I may be up then as our passes will start soon. Was glad to hear you liked that picture. It certainly is a good one. You certainly would have some trouble picking me out. Our section was right in the rear beside the band. Erne was saying that he had a great time at Elmvale fair with Dora.

Well mother we are going to have another trip tomorrow. The machine gun section is going to Burlington for the day. I guess tomorrow is Thanksgiving Day. We had special church services this morning. Owen was asking me in his letter if I could not get up for a couple of weeks hunting. I certainly would of liked to have gone but such a thing as a week's pass is out of the question for us. It has been pretty cold down here at nights for the last week or two, but they have been issuing us lots of socks and underwear. We were inspected by the Duke of Connaught here on Thursday. It was a great day and there were ten battalions of infantry and three batteries of artillery which took part in the march past. We had another route march last Friday but not as long as the one we had the week before. I had a new pair of boots issued to me the other day and I think they are a great improvement on the pairs we had. We are also allowed to use dubbin or grease on them and they are much softer and keep the wet out much better than when we had to use polish. You were asking me about lending you some money now. After this month I had signed over twenty-five dollars a month to you. The paymaster sends you a check every month and I get the rest. The last two months pay I let the paymaster put in the British War Loan for me. If you would like it right away mother, I can get it but if it would suit you as well will send you twenty-five dollars in each of the next three months pay. Will be up soon I hope I see you then. I remain yours lovingly.

Oscar
Write soon

FIRST PRIZE GUN ASSEMBLY

Niagara Camp
Oct. 13th, 1915

Dear Mother –

Will try and write a few lines now as we were dismissed early to-day. It has been very warm here to-day, much different from the weather we have been having. We had a muster parade first thing this morning and then a kit inspection. We get a lot of inspections every little while now to see if we have lost anything or not. If we lose anything that they have issued to us we are charged up for it. I had everything except my big knife. I got three handkerchiefs, a towel and two pair of socks the other day. They were sent from Barrie to the fellows who had been there last winter. I am pretty well of(f) for socks now as I have six or seven pair.

We had a nice trip to Burlington on Monday. We left here about eight o'clock on the streetcar for St. Catharines and took the train from there to Burlington. It was dinnertime when we got to the fair grounds. We did a little drill and signaling and then four-gun teams were picked out and we had a competition to see which team could set up the gun the fastest. The team I was in won first prize, setting up the gun in twenty-eight and a half seconds. When we were coming back that night the train stopped for half an hour in Hamilton but we were not allowed to leave the car so we sung and made all the noise we could. The train was pretty well crowded and some civilians came into our car but we made so much noise that I guess they were more than glad to see us get off at St. Catharine's.

Well mother it won't be long now before the camp here will be broken up. Some of the battalions are going to start on their six-day march to Toronto next Monday. The 35th battalion is getting ready to go overseas in a week or two. We don't hear much about where we are going to winter. Is Uncle Steve getting around now. Billie Parker must be having quite a time of it sitting up at nights now watching his store. Somebody around there must want a chance to see the Waverley fire brigade in action. Well mother will close now as it is about dinner time and I am never behind then. Hope to be up soon.

Yours lovingly
Oscar

IN THE MOVING PICTURES

Exhibition Camp Toronto
Nov. 4th, 1915

Dear Mother –

Just a few lines to let you know I am well and am getting along fine. I like the camp here fine but would rather sleep in the tents than in the barracks. It has been raining nearly all day so we haven't been doing much. I was downtown this morning and got some of my teeth filled. I was to the army doctors in Niagara several times to get them fixed but they didn't give me much satisfaction so I thought I had better get them fixed up before I lost them. I was up before our lieutenant the other day for being a day over my pass and got one day's C.B. and lost two days pay. We had a big concert last night in the building where we are quartered and a lunch to finish with. I got up to see Annie last Sunday. Silas was home then but he said he was going up to Newmarket with his machine this week. Their house will be good and cosy when they get it fixed up. Silas said he hadn't time to get it fixed up right just now as he wanted to get at the drilling before it got too late. I was down to the Strand theatre the other night to see our battalion in the moving pictures. It was pretty good. It showed us just as we were coming into the city and while we were eating our dinner and then just as we came into the exhibition gates. The artillery got in from Niagara to-day just at noon when it was raining hard. There are two or three battalions to come in yet but they are all on their way. We were lucky to get moved just when we did before it got wet. We didn't have any rain all the time we were on our way.

I suppose Owen and Dad will be busy with the turnips now or have thy got them in. Is Goldie in at Fred's yet and how is Uncle Steve getting along. Will close now with best love from

Oscar

FIVE HUNDRED SHOTS PER MINUTE

Toronto Exhibition
Nov. 19th, 1915

Dear Mother –

Received your welcome letter this week and will try and write you a few lines now. This has been a very unpleasant day here, raining most of the time so we haven't been doing very much drilling but we had a lecture on machine guns this afternoon and did some signalling. This morning I was learning to run a machine we have for filling machine gun cartridge belts. A belt holds two hundred and fifty cartridges and we have a machine that fills a belt a minute. The machine gun is capable of firing two belts of cartridges that is five hundred shots per minute but wouldn't keep it up long as it would soon get red hot and then the shells would jam.

We haven't got any more word about when we are going to leave as yet but will let you know as soon as we do. I hear that the 58th battalion are leaving tonight. They have been busy packing up all week. I seen in the paper the other day that Luke Adamson and E. Dundas had enlisted. I guess they will be in that new battalion they are raising of men all from Simcoe. I was wondering where they will be stationed for the winter as a full battalion went from Niagara to take up winter quarters in Barrie, Collingwood and Orillia. These are about the only places in Simcoe that are able to winter many men.

You were saying that Alma Hodges was in Grace Hospital here. I didn't know whether she was a nurse there or is she sick. I haven't gone up there yet but perhaps will go up Sat. afternoon as we don't do much drilling then. I answered Erne's letter the other day.

We were supposed to have gone out to Long Branch this morning to do some shooting but as it was pretty wet we did not go. We intended going out to-day and stay there all night and come back tomorrow so we would have had to of carried our blankets and our other equipment, so I was just as well pleased it rained. It is about ten miles out to the ranges. Billie Faragher was down here last Sunday. He said that he had joined the stretcher bearers.

I was sorry that Goldie did not get that address copied out that night as Mrs. Quinlan was saying while I was down there that she would have liked to have it but I will copy it and send it to you and you can give it to them. I had a letter from May the other day and she said they had a bumper of a crop this year. She said Will's wheat run about forty-five bushels to the acre and they threshed over five thousand bushels. She said he was having a time of it getting out as he had only got three loads out in three weeks. Well mother will have to close now. Write soon again.

Yours with best love.
Oscar

THE WORK OF A SINGLE GERMAN SPY

Exhibition Camp Toronto
(undated)

Dear Mother –

Received your welcome letter to-night and will answer to-night as I am not going out. I guess it will be my last chance of writing in Toronto as we expect to take the train for Halifax to-morrow night at seven o'clock. We didn't expect to leave until Thursday morning but the colonel told us to-day it was thought best to take the train at night so we wouldn't have such confusion getting around at three or four o'clock in the morning like the 58th did. I guess we won't get to Halifax until Saturday at least and we may be there a few days. I think that our battalion will be sailing on the *Lapland* but am not sure.

I suppose mother you heard about the big powder factory up near Parry Sound being blown up yesterday. We got the news here last night and the 74th and 75th battalions received orders to be ready to go up there but they did not go as there were plenty of soldiers much nearer than Toronto. I don't know as sending soldiers up there would be much good as it likely was the work of a single German spy. It seems funny that more of the Germans in Canada who are having just the same privileges as British shouldn't be in the pen. I told you in my letter last night Mother that we were to have an oyster supper to-night I think but it has been cancelled as most of the fellows were anxious to get downtown and see their friends to-night. I wasn't much disappointed as I haven't got much love for oysters anyway. I was kind of surprised to hear that Stan and Davey were going to enlist. I should think that Dave would hardly pass the examination. You must have had more snow up there than we have had here. We had hardly had enough snow to whiten the ground but it has been pretty cold lately. I guess it is just as well for us that we are going to England for the winter as the building we are in would be pretty cold through the winter. We expect to be in huts or tents in England with a stove for each hut and then only about a dozen men are together which is much better than for a thousand to be crowded in one barracks all together. I would like very much to be at home for Christmas Mother but will have to try and get a pass while in England and go and have a jolly good feed of English beef and plum pudding. I suppose you haven't received my check yet of my pay of November. You will likely get it at the end of the month. Well Mother I will likely get another chance to write to you at Halifax and will write as soon as we reach England and give you my address and let you know how I made the voyage. Us fellows are having bets whether we will get seasick or not. Well I guess I will have to close now. Will write to you whenever I get a chance and please don't worry Mother if sometimes my letters don't come regular as sometimes, we don't get much chance for writing. Tell Goldie I will answer her letter soon as possible. Your loving son

Oscar

READY FOR THE TRAIN TO HALIFAX

Toronto Exhibition
Nov. 24th, 1915

Dear Mother –

Will try and write you a few lines now as we haven't got only but a few hours before we take the train. We had a parade just after dinner in our full equipment just to see that everything was ready and we have been dismissed until half-past four but are not allowed to leave the exhibition grounds. We expect to take the train at 7:30 to-night instead of in the morning. We certainly have a fine day for our departure from Toronto and there are a lot of visitors in to see us off. Our old major who was with us this summer and was transferred to another battalion about a month ago was up to see us off at noon while we were at dinner. The boys nearly cheered the roof off when he was through speaking. We certainly thought a lot of him and are very sorry he is not going with us. I wish I could send you a picture of myself with our full equipment on. It certainly looks to be a load when we have it all on but we don't notice it heavy as it is all fastened to a harness that fits over our shoulders and is connected with the belt.

Well mother I guess I will have some new experiences when we reach England learning to count our money in pounds shillings and pence and learn to look interested and not laugh when a Cockney is talking to me. All the boys are keen to get away and have been singing and yelling all day.

Well mother will have to make this short as it is near the time for falling in. Remember me to all and tell Uncle Steve I will try and write to him when we get settled down on the other side. Will write a letter or card at Halifax if I have time.

Your loving son,
Oscar

YELLING FROM THE TRAIN WINDOWS

Nov. 26th, 1915
11 A.M.

Dear Mother –

Well mother will try and scratch you a few lines now but it is pretty hard to write as the train keeps rocking. We boarded the train in Toronto about half past eleven on Wed. night but did not leave until about 6:30 the next morning. I have enjoyed the trip fine so far. We reached Montreal about six o'clock last night and stopped there about an hour to get water and coal but we were not out of our cars. We are now just about the Quebec and New Brunswick border and expect to reach Halifax early tomorrow morning. We passed through Levis, a town just across the river from Quebec about midnight last night and our first stop this morning was at a town named Riviere du Loup. The fellows had lots of fun with the Frenchmen there making fun of their town. The country is very rough here. There is very near enough snow here for sleighing and the windows on our car were coated with frost last night. Our train just passed another French town called Rimouski now. Every town we pass we stick our heads out of the window and yell till we can't see. Our section were lucked to get a car up near the engine as we are right behind the dining-car and get our meals first. Our car is well heated too; several fellows from back in the end cars said they were so cold last night that they couldn't sleep. A news agent came into the train this morning selling boxes that were filled up with different truck. Some of the fellows bought a box from him and got a lot of trash that was no good and most of it was made in Austria or Germany. That made them mad and they were going to pitch the guy out.

12 A.M.

Just passed through another French town named St. Luce. The fellows are starting to go in for dinner now.

Just have stopped at a town name Mont Joli. We were here for about half an hour and got off the train for a few minutes and snowballed each other. We have fun with the French trying to make them understand us.

7 A.M. Nov. 27, 1915

Well mother we had to get up at five o'clock this morning and get packed up as we expect to get to Halifax soon. We travelled the fastest last night that we have since we started. It is very wet and foggy where we are now. We passed through Moncton in New Brunswick early this morning. I don't know whether we will board our boat to-day or not. It certainly is fine sleeping on the car. We had to put our watches an hour ahead when we got to New Brunswick as their time is different than ours.

Well mother we have to start and get our packs on now so will have to close for this time. I don't know whether I will get another chance to write until we get to the other side but if I do I will. Will close now with love.

Oscar

CROSSING THE ATLANTIC ON THE *LAPLAND*

Bramshott Camp
Liphook, Hants, England
(undated)

Dear Father and Mother –

I will now try and write a few lines as it has been my first chance to do so since we left Halifax. Well we made the voyage safely and are now in Bramshott Camp in Hantshire. We had a splendid voyage across the Atlantic, the weather being fine and no German submarines appeared. I wasn't seasick either, so I guess I didn't do so bad for my first voyage.

We reached Halifax on Saturday Nov. 27 at noon and went aboard the liner *Lapland* soon after we arrived. The *Lapland* pulled away from the wharf about six o'clock that night and you should have heard the cheering, it nearly deafened me. We remained in Halifax harbour over Saturday night and set sail the next morning soon after daybreak. It rained during most of our first day's voyage. It was four days before we saw a boat of any kind. We had nothing to do on the voyage except get our places picked out for each man in case of emergency. It wasn't necessary to take any very great precautions until we got into the danger zone, that is right around the shores. On Saturday night December 4th we slept on deck beside our rafts and lifeboats with our life belts beside us. Luckily no German submarine got scent of us as we were not protected by a warship or escort of any kind. We didn't get much sleep either as it rained off and on during the night. We reached Plymouth harbour yesterday morning about half-past eight. We didn't get off the boat however until about 3:30 in the afternoon. The *Lapland* was too big to get into the dock so we were taken off in little tenders. We were put on the train as soon as we reached the dock. Well mother my first sight of England was certainly a grand one as I don't think I ever saw a more beautiful place than the harbour of Plymouth. The fields are quite green now and the high cliffs along the shore are covered with a reddish moss. The towns here look quaint to us and in the towns the streets are very narrow and the houses are much more closer together than in Canadian towns. The fields in the country are laid out in all sorts of queer shapes and they are generally fenced with hedges. And you should see the trains and railways here. I had to laugh at the engines. Some were painted red and green and they looked so small. The coaches are much different to ours. They are divided up into little compartments that will seat about eight persons comfortably. We were unlucky enough to have to travel most of our journey from Plymouth here after dark so we couldn't see much but what I have seen of England I like fine. When we got to Exeter, our first stop from Plymouth, we all got free tea and buns from the mayoress of Exeter with a card in each package of buns. We reached our destination a place named Lipshook about half-past one this morning and then marched about two miles to camp.

The camp here is much different from what we had at Niagara. We are in huts here instead of tents and there is almost a perfect city of them. They are laid out in streets and blocks as in a town. I heard that there are about thirty thousand troops in this camp alone and there are big armies in training in camps all around us.

The buildings or huts we are in hold about fifty men. We have got pretty good grub here for our first meals. We had some swell barley soup and stewed beef with potatoes and green peas for dinner. We don't eat all together like we did at Niagara either but a couple of men are sent from each hut and they go to the camp kitchen and draw provisions for all the men in the hut. This is much handier than the old method when about two hundred men lined up for their meals and if you happened to be the end of the line you usually had to wait a half an hour before you got anything to eat.

There is no town very close to us here but we are only about forty miles from London and about the same from Portsmouth. I think I will try and get up to London for Christmas or New Years. One of the boys in our section asked me to go up to Scotland at New Years with him. His home is in a town in the south of Scotland.

We got a great reception in all the towns we came through last night. The old men and women and kids came out on the streets and yelled to beat the band and our guys sure made some noise too. I was talking to one of the boys in the 35th Battalion here this morning and he said that he didn't think that the Canadians here would ever reach the front. He said that he had been up to Aldershot and there is a great army of British troops camped there and they have been in training all summer. They will go to the front first and that is not likely to be until next spring. I guess we will be camped here for quite a time anyway.

Say mother was there a report in the Canadian newspapers that the *Lapland* had been torpedoed and all the troops lost. We heard when we got here that a report had spread in Canada that she had been sunk. A few days after we left Halifax the wireless telegrapher picked up messages asking for our whereabouts, but he was under orders to send no messages whatsoever. They might have thought at Halifax that not being able to get an answer from her, that she was sunk. I suppose it was all a story but I was thinking of you, if you had heard a report that she was sunk.

I am very sorry that I shall not be with you this Xmas. Write and let me know if Erne, Verne or May came home this winter. Tell Goldie and Dora to write whenever they can as I certainly like to get letters from home. I was wondering how Dad would like to work one of the farms here. They certainly look queer. One thing we got is lots of rain. At present it is coming down to beat the Dutch. Except for the rain and mud I think we are in for a pretty good winter.

Well mother I will write quite often and let you know how I am. Tell Owen I will write to him as soon as I can. Will close now with the best of love.

Oscar
Address: Pte. O. French
M.G.S. 37th Batt.
Bramshott Camp
Lipshook
Hants
England

SEEING LONDON AND ALL THAT

Bramshott Camp
Lipshook, Hants, Eng.
Dec. 16th, 1915

Dear Mother –

Just a few lines to let you know I got back to camp again from my pass to London and had a fine time. I came back last night on the night train. I got a letter last night that you addressed to the Toronto camp but we had left before it got there so it was sent on here.

London certainly is a fine city. While I was there I was to the British Museum, the Zoological Gardens and the Tower of London. We spent all day Monday going through the British Museum and then didn't nearly see all. A guide took us around and showed us through the libraries. We saw the letter Captain Scott wrote just before he died after reaching the South Pole a few years ago. The mummies were the first I had ever seen.

On Tuesday we went to the Zoological Gardens and it was dark before we had gone all through them. I don't think there is any country in the world that they haven't got some kind of animal or bird from. Some of the snakes were over twenty feet long and the mud turtles were as big as wash-tubs but they smelt so bad I couldn't stay with them long. Tell Goldie they have an old sea-lion there that beats the one in Riverdale Park all to smithereens.

The last day we were in London we went to the Tower of London that used to be the King's palace and a state prison. We were through the Bloody Tower where the two young princes were murdered way back in the time of Richard II and seen the narrow stone stairs where their bodies were found many years after they were murdered. The portcullis or gate that is raised and lowered and which was made at the time of William the Conqueror nearly one thousand years ago is still there. We were through the armoury and seen the old arms and armour that they used to use. One of these suits of armour worn by Henry VIII weighs about one hundred pounds and then his horse is covered with armour also. The first cannon that were used look to be about as dangerous for the man who is firing it as the man he is firing at and the old flintlock pistols are about the size of a small rifle. We were across the court-yard where the scaffold stood that Anne Boleyn wife of Henry VIII and Lady Jane Grey and many others were executed. The guard showed us the window where Lady Jane Grey sat and watched her husband being beheaded and a few hours later she was taken out and beheaded herself.

The best we have seen in the tower was the crown jewels. I intended getting a picture of them but didn't but will if I go back again. They have one big glass cage, about the size of an ordinary room, filled with crowns, scepters, maces and many other pieces of jewelry all of solid gold and studded with diamonds. One wine fountain alone cost about fifteen thousand dollars and was given to Charles II by the council of Plymouth. There are four or five salt cellars of solid gold about one foot high and the same around. I guess it would make most of us a pretty classy salt dish. I got a guide for the Tower of London before I went in and will send it to you.

I had quite a time finding my way around the city as the streets are about as crooked as the Penetang road but there is no fear of getting lost as long as there is a London cop around. They use the Canadian boys pretty good over here. I don't know whether we will get a pass at

Christmas or not but if we do I am going back to the place we stopped at in London. It is only a board and lodging house but they certainly used us fellows good while there.

It has been raining here as usual to-day and the mud is getting pretty bad. We expect to move to another hut to-morrow and it will be much better than the place we are now in. I suppose it will be after Christmas when you get this letter mother so write and let me know how you enjoyed yourself and who were with you this year. I suppose they will be having a Christmas tree at Waverley this year. Will close for this time with best love and wishes for a Merry Xmas and Happy New Year to all.

Oscar

A BIRTHDAY LETTER

Bramshott Camp Dec. 30th, 1915

Dear Mother –

Well Mother as this is my birthday I will try and write you a few lines to let you know I am getting along fine and am well hoping you are all the same. It still is very wet here yet and most of the boys have had colds from wet feet but I have been pretty lucky. I have a slight cold now but nothing worth mentioning. I got weighed last night and I guess the English climate is doing me good as I weigh about ten pounds more than I did when in Toronto. I weigh 155 pounds now. We were inspected this morning by General Steele and General Lord Brooks who is in command of the camp here. We had a route march on Tuesday around the country and through several little villages. The country here is very strange to us but it is very pretty. There are half a dozen villages within an hours walk of the camp here.

I suppose you have read in the Canadian papers about that French Canadian lieutenant who murdered a sarjeant (sic) here three weeks ago. He has been tried now and the jury returned a verdict of willful murder. The sarjeant gave him over a thousand dollars of Canadian money to get changed into English money in London. When the lieutenant came back he got the sarjeant at the house he was stopping at and murdered him. They found his body in a stable at the back of the house wrapped in blankets and bound up with wire. There were over forty wounds on the body. The lieutenant was suspected and arrested.

We tried to get another pass for New Years but I guess we won't get them but if they are as good to us then as they were on Christmas I won't mind.

What are they doing for sport around Waverley this winter. Has anybody started up a rink there. I haven't seen any ice or snow this winter yet but we get all the rain we want. Everything is as green as in summer here now. We didn't have to go far to get holly to decorate our hut up for Xmas as it is very common around here. How is Grandpa this winter. I have intended writing to him but have kept putting it off. Elmer won't have far to go to school this winter. Give the farthing and three penny piece for his bank. Well Mother I will close now hoping you are all well. I remain yours with love,

Oscar
Write soon.

THREE PENCE FOR AN EGG

Bramshott Camp Dec. 20th, 1915

Dear Mother –

I will try and write a few lines to-night and let you know that I am getting along fine hoping you are the same. We have been doing our first real drilling to-day as it was fine and forgot to rain. I don't expect to get a pass for Christmas but may get one on New Year's. I would just as soon not go on pass on Christmas anyway as we expect to have a holiday here and they are putting up extra chuck.

I don't see how working men live over here on the wages they get. I heard that things were about half the price here that they were in Canada but I think if anything they are a littler dearer. They pay three pennies or six cents here for an egg. It is pretty hard to get butter but they sell some kind of dope called… (rest of letter missing)

SEND ME SOME CANADIAN NEWSPAPERS

Bramshott Camp
Jan. 3rd, 1916

Dear Mother –

Will try again and write you a few lines now as we have just come off parade for to-day and I have nothing to do now until supper. This has been a beautiful day here just like a spring day in Canada and I think it is about the first day since we have been here that the sun has shone and it has not rained. I can hardly believe it is January as I suppose in Canada now it will be below zero most of the time. We haven't had any return mail from Canada yet but I heard that there is a large Canadian mail in but it has not been sorted yet.

We are having a much easier time here than we had in Niagara. The hours for drill are much shorter and we have had no very long route marches yet but when we go on a march we have to take our full equipment that is take our blankets, great coat, mess tin, water bottle and haversack. Our meals have improved a lot and we have a much handier system of getting them than we were used to. There is one big mess room for all the men and on Sunday they have their church parade there.

We had a pretty quiet day on New Year's. I couldn't get a pass so had to content myself here. They don't make very much of New Year's day here but it certainly is a high day in Scotland. A couple of Scotsmen in our section were very much disappointed because they could not get a pass home. Our officer has gone away so we are without an officer at present. One of our boys got a letter from Canada to-day and he was showing us a slip of paper cut from a Canadian newspaper which gave an account of the time our battalion left Toronto and what a fine battalion it was. Of course, we don't take much stock of that as every battalion that leaves Canada gets a great write up in the papers. I am going to send you some English papers. I can't get used to them or read them like I read the Toronto papers. I wish you would send me a bunch of papers once in a while.

I suppose Roy is still working at the planing mill in Midland. If Verne is at home this winter tell him to write and if he isn't let me know and I will write to him. Well Mother this is all I have to say now. Hoping you are all well I remain yours lovingly,

Oscar

DEATH OF A GRANDFATHER

Bramshott Camp Jan. 17

Dear Mother –

Just a line to let you know that we are getting along well and have no complaints. I received letters from Owen, May and Goldie yesterday and was surprised to hear that May and Verne had come home. Owen said in his letter that you and father had gone to Dundas as Grandpa was very low but that they had got word later that he had passed away. I was so sorry that I did not see him before we left Canada. Just wrote him a letter the other day saying that I had intended going over last summer ...

(rest of letter is missing)

COLT MACHINE GUN SCHOOL

Shorncliffe, Feb. 3rd/16

Dear Mother –

Just a line to let you know that we have moved from Bramshott and at present are at the Colt Machine Gun School here. We didn't know just when we were coming down but at half-past one on Tuesday morning, we were called up to get ready to go to Shornecliffe (sic) early in the morning. We got here early in the afternoon and we are now quartered in a fine brick barracks. We expect to get our kits in a few days. Some more of the boys from our battalion are coming down in a few days. The camp here is much better than the one at Bramshott and there is no mud.

I got another letter the other day from your aunt who lives at Frittenden in Kent, the same county that we are in. She asked me to try and get to see them if I could get a pass. We will most likely get a pass after we have completed our course at the school here.

I suppose May and Verne are still with you yet or have they gone back to the West. I got a letter from Roy the other day and he said he had been laid up with the grippe for a couple of weeks and the children had been sick also. Agnes must have had quite a time if they were all sick at once.

Shorncliffe is quite a pretty little town and there is a large town called Folkestone a few minutes ride from here. Well Mother I guess this letter will be pretty short as I have some work to do now. Hoping you are all well I remain.

Yours with love
Oscar

ZEPPELINS CAUSING A SCARE

(Letter to sister Dora)
Napier Barracks Shorncliffe

Feb. 17th, 1916

Dear Dora –

I got yours and Goldie's letter the other day and I was certainly glad to hear from you. I am always glad to get letters from home and hear how you all are. I suppose you are having quite a time this winter getting your skating free and having all the boys taking you for a skate. Is Dalton at Waverley this winter to take you down home? We have been having a very easy but tiresome time of it for these last two weeks as we have been quarantined in our barracks on account of one of the boys taking the measles. We will soon be out now I think. This is a fine little place down here, much better than the one up at Bramshott where we were at first. We are quite close to the sea and go down along the shore every day for an hours walk. I suppose when you get this letter Verne and May will have gone West again or getting ready to go. Did Annie come up with Verne and Goldie when they came home.

The Zeppelins are causing quite a scare over here now. All the cities and towns are as black as a pack of black cats after night. We have to put blankets up over our windows as soon as the lights are turned on. I haven't had any more passes since were up at London and haven't much hopes of getting one for some time. Has Goldie been stopping back with Owen this winter. How is Rhoda getting along. Well Dora I must close now. Write as often as you can. Tell Goldie that I will write to her soon.

Yours with love
Oscar
Pte. O. French No. 408445
Machine Gun Detail
37ᵗʰ Battalion C.E.F.
Napier Barracks
Shorncliffe, Kent

LOOKING FOR A PHOTOGRAPH

Napier Barracks
Shornecliff
Feb. 11th 1916

Dear Mother –

Received your letter of the 13th of last month yesterday and was very pleased to hear from you again. We hadn't received any mail for over a week as it had been delayed in being sent from Bramshott down here. I also received another letter from Bessie Hodges. She asked me to send her my photograph. I haven't any good ones with me but will try and get some taken as soon as we are out of quarantine. We have been quarantined nearly a week now but expect to be out soon. We have been having fine sunshiny days for the last week but it is raining to-day. They have been taking us out for exercise… *(rest of letter missing)*

RUSSAN VICTORIES OVER THE TURKS

Napier Barracks
Shornecliffe (sic)
Feb. 21ˢᵗ 1916

Dear Mother –

Received the papers that were sent to-day and was pleased to get a Canadian Newspaper to read again. We are still in quarantine yet. We were to have been out to-day only they had no stuff to fumigate our barracks so we were delayed in getting out. We are beginning to feel as though we would like to get out and start drilling again. It snowed a few flakes here to-day, the first we have seen since coming to England. I got a letter from Dora day before yesterday and she said you were having a hard time to keep your snow in Canada this winter.

I suppose you have been reading of the great Russian victories over the Turks. It will help a lot to relieve the British forces in Mesopotamia. If the war ends this year, as a lot of people here think it will, the new battalions they are recruiting now will hardly see active service. Dora was saying that Elijah and Art French had enlisted. I think they will have some time making a soldier out of Arthur. Well Mother I guess this letter will have to be pretty short as we haven't much news to tell having been shut in so long. Write soon. I remain

Yours lovingly
Oscar

ANOTHER SIMCOE BATTALION

Napier Barracks
Shornecliffe (sic)
Feb. 25th, 1916

Dear Mother –

Well Mother we have got out of our quarantine at last after nearly three weeks of it. They let us out on Wednesday after we had cleaned and scrubbed and fumigated our barracks. We have been having a little of the weather we have been used to having in Canada as it snowed two or three inches the day before yesterday and it is quite cold to-day. This is the first snow we have had this winter. I was over to Folkestone on Wednesday night and everybody was out on the street snowballing. They have snow so seldom here that they seem to think it is great fun. I was through the Museum they have over there and although it is not very large they have some very interesting curiosities in it.

I got a long letter from Tine the other day. She was speaking of some disease Will Smith had but said that she guessed that you had told me about it but you hadn't said anything about it to me. I hope it is not serious. I hear that they have started to raise another Simcoe battalion so there must be lots of men available yet. I am fatigue man for our hut to-day, that is I have to go and get our meals at the cookhouse and sweep the floor and keep the place tidy. Yesterday we had a short examination on the Colt machine gun. I don't know how we made out. They blindfolded us and then timed us to see how long each one of us took in taking a gun apart and putting it together again. They gave us five minutes to do it in but you can be certain that there wasn't many to do it in that time.

Is Rhoda getting along alright. Did Annie come up with Verne and Goldie when they came home. I hope you have got over your sickness that you had after you came from Dundas. Well I must close now. Remember me to all. Hoping you are all well I remain

Yours with Love
Oscar

GETTING MY TEETH FIXED

Risborough Barracks
Shorncliffe
Monday, March 6th

Dear Mother –

As we have been so busy this last week, I haven't had much time to write but will try and write a few lines now. We left Napier Barracks and were attached to the 32nd battalion on March 1st. We were issued with two uniforms and boots the same day and was up all-night doing patrol duty. We carried our rifles and equipment and each man had 25 rounds of ammunition. We were divided up in groups and each group had to patrol one of the roads around the camp. Last week they caught a German spy in a Canadian uniform. He tried to get away but was shot in the leg and was caught. After we had been up all night, we drilled the next day and were warned for patrol that night but luckily did not have to go out. Last night most of our section were out on piquet (picket) over in Folkeston. We were in before twelve, so it was all right. This morning I was on a fatigue party drawing rations from the camp stores for the 32nd. We brought over more than 450 loaves of bread and four quarters of beef besides bacon, sugar and tea. This is the battalion rations for a day.

I have been up to the dentist every day since we came down here and he is not through with me yet. I was over to a dentist in Folkestone and he started to fill one of my teeth but as there is a dentist here in the battalion I thought I had better let him fix it up and it would cost me nothing. One of the fillings I had put in at Toronto came out last night and I went over and had him fix it.

I didn't get this finished at noon so will make a try to finish it now. I have been busy this afternoon helping to load some empty boxes on the transport wagons and putting them on the train down at the station. It has got quite cold again and snowed some this afternoon. Most of our boys have to go out in piquet again to-night but I don't think my name is down to go out. We are still quartered in barracks yet which is one good piece of luck as tents wouldn't quite suit my fancy these cold nights.

Well Mother I suppose you will soon be getting some warm days now. I suppose Owen and Dad will be busy wood cutting now. Is May and Verne still with you yet. Tell them to write whenever they can as sometimes I have quite a time to keep all my letters answered up. Tell Goldie I got her letter and will write as soon as possible.

I remain
Yours lovingly
Oscar
Pte. O. French No. 408445
Machine Gun Draft 37th Batt.
32nd Batt C. E. F.
Risborough Barracks
Shorncliffe, Kent

ROSS RIFLE
BETTER THAN LEE-ENFIELD

Risborough Barracks
Shorncliffe
March 13th, 1916

Dear Mother –

Just a line to let you know I am alive and well and hoping you are
the same. I haven't had any word from Canada for two weeks now as
the Canadian mail has been held up in London to be fumigated as a
disease had broken out on the boat it came over on. Everybody is sore
because they are not getting any mail and some of the boys have been
expecting parcels for the last two months. We have just got in from the
ranges and had our dinner. We were up at five o'clock this morning
and had our breakfast and were ready to leave for the ranges which are
about five miles away at six o'clock. We got back at half-past one and
had a good hot dinner. We fired five rounds apiece on the 100, 200,
300 and 400 yard ranges. Some of us have the Ross rifle and some the
Lee-Enfield. I have a Ross and believe it is the better of the two. The
Lee-Enfield that they are using now is very much shorter than the Ross
but the bayonet is very long. I was issued with a British uniform and
it is pretty big for me. I don't like it as well as the Canadian uniforms,
the cloth is much poorer.

The boots they have given us are about as heavy as a ton of lead
and the soles are covered with steel plates and hob nails so that when

we are walking along the streets we make a noise like a whole regiment but they keep the water out which is the main thing. We expect to put two or three weeks in at the machine gun school when we have finished our shooting. Measles are still quite common around the camp, there was a hut quarantined right by ours the other day. The whole battalion may be quarantined if they keep on spreading. We have been having some very fine warm weather these last few days. There has been some very heavy snowstorms in the north of England lately. Quite a few trains have been blocked. I did not get this finished last night so will make another start to-night. We were out at the ranges again this morning but it was so foggy we could not see the targets so came back again without doing any firing but will go out again tomorrow. The dentist has been having quite a time in filling one of my teeth. After he had been working with it about a week he filled it one morning but the filling came out that night. I suppose your snow will be all gone when (you) get this and Owen and Dad will soon be working on the land. Hope you have been keeping well through the winter. Well Mother I must close now. Hoping to hear from you soon I remain

Yours lovingly

FUMIGATING BLANKETS

Risborough Barracks
Shorncliffe
March 25th, 1916

Dear Mother –

As I expect to be busy tomorrow I will try and write a few lines to-night and let you know that I received the socks and parcels alright yesterday. The socks will certainly come in handy this wet weather. We have been very busy all this week, having been down to Folkestone on picquet (picket) two nights and on guard once. I was on picquet (picket) last night and the night before. We have to go down to Folkestone about six o'clock and walk the streets till ten and if anybody gets cutting up, we have to run him up to the guard house. The sargeant (sic) told us to-night that we would all be on fatigue work to-morrow, Sunday. This morning I was helping to fumigate some blankets. If anyone gets lousy they have to have all their clothes and blankets fumigated and have a bath themselves.

(balance of letter missing)

MARCH PAST BEFORE SAM HUGHES

Risborough Barracks
Shorncliffe
April 2, 1916

Dear Mother –

Will try and write a few lines now and let you know that I am getting along alright. This is a fine warm day here, it makes me think of the fine spring days you usually have in Canada at this time. We have been practicing these last few days for a big review to be held tomorrow and a march past before Sam Hughes. I heard that the King and Lord Kitchener and some others would be here to inspect us on Friday. We have a swell parade ground here for inspections and march pasts. We haven't started at the machine gun school yet but may do so this week. We have been doing night picquet (picket) at Folkestone for this last two weeks. Each man has to do a picquet (picket) about every third or fourth night.

I don't know what is the matter with the mail but some of us haven't got any for about two weeks now. We have been changed around so much this last month or so that I guess (it) causes some delay. I suppose May and Verne will now be in the West again. Well Mother I see in this mornings paper that they got a Zeppelin that came over here on a raid last night. It was shot down at the mouth of the Thames and it surrendered to a British patrol boat. I heard that there was another one brought down but I am not sure. There was about sixty people killed and injured in the raid over here. As it is a very fine day to-day there will likely be some German sea planes over. They generally like to make a raid over here on Sunday. I had a narrow escape from being quarantined again last week. We have to change from the hut that we were in into another. I went into one hut but later changed over again into another and the first hut I was in was quarantined in the next day. I was thanking my lucky stars as I don't know what I would do if I was quarantined for another three weeks now. Our boys of the 37th are scattered all around the barracks now and some are under quarantine. One hut that some of our boys are in was under quarantine for about three weeks and they were going to get out the next day but another one of them took the measles that night and they were put in for another three weeks. Did Rhoda go back to Midland again. I have been intending to write to her but haven't seemed to find the time. I guess Owen and Dad will soon be busy seeding. Well Mother I must close now and try to write more next time. Hoping you are all well I remain

Your loving son
Oscar
Pte. O. French No. 408445
Machine Gun Detail of the 37th Batt.
Machine Gun Base
13th Reserve Brigade Risborough Barracks
Shorncliffe, Kent
England

HIRED HELP SCARCE IN CANADA

Risborough Barracks
Shorncliffe
April 19th, 1916

Dear Mother –

Just a line or so to-night to let you know that everything is all O.K. with me and have nothing to complain about. We are having more spring weather over here now so it is hard for a person to stay in the barracks when we are through of our drill. I put in for a pass for the Easter weekend but it was turned down as nearly everyone put in for one and only ten per cent could go. I would like very much to go up and see your aunt and uncle. A couple of our fellows beat it up to London without a pass after breaking out of quarantine but they got ten days apiece in the can as they call it when they came back. Well next Sunday will be Easter and I guess I will spend it in camp. We are getting a holiday on Friday so we are told but often what we are told don't turn out to be right so I am not expecting to have a big celebration or get fed up like we were at Xmas. We expect to start at the school on Monday or Tuesday. Yesterday I was out with a gang making machine gun emplacements in some trenches out at the aerodrome which is about two mile from here. There are quite a few aerodromes for aeroplanes around the camp but they are well guarded and no one is allowed around them.

We were out this afternoon getting some pictures taken of the officers and men of the Machine Gun Base. I don't know whether the guy that took them will be around selling them or not. If he does I will get a couple. There are about two hundred machine gunners at the base here now. I guess that hired help will be pretty scarce in Canada this summer. Owen said in his letter that Jack Adamson had hired for 45$ a month besides a house, cow and hens. I hear that they are granting a furlough to soldiers during the seeding season the same as they did last summer at harvest time. Well Mother I must make this letter short now. Hoping you are all well I remain

Yours Lovingly
Oscar
Pte. O. French No. 408445
Machine Gun Base
13th Reserve Brigade
Risborough Barracks
Shorncliffe Kent

BEAUTIFUL EASTER SUNDAY

Risborough Barracks
Shorncliffe
April 23rd, 1916

Dear Mother –

As this is Easter Sunday I will try and write a few lines as I guess it is the first Easter that I have been away from home. I received your welcome letter of April 2nd yesterday and also received one from Dora to-day. I suppose that you are not sorry that the long winter is over again. I guess that all the farmers will be busy with the seeding when you get this letter. We have had a very beautiful day to-day, sun was shining and nice and warm. We had our church parade this morning and were also on a church parade on Good Friday morning. There is a large gymnasium at Napier Barracks that is now used as a church. We had a holiday on Good Friday and we are also having a half holiday tomorrow. I didn't fare so very well for eggs to-day, had a couple. They are pretty nearly as good as gold here, four cents apiece, something different from the price they generally are at this time in Canada. Dora told me in her letter of Fred Elliot's death. It certainly was a big surprise. I was also very much surprised to hear that Dave Quinlan had enlisted and that Fred Adamson was moving out to work the farm. What is Mrs. Quinlan going to do. It will certainly be a trial for her I should think with Dave enlisting after Billie and Davey had gone. You were saying that you were going to send another box. Thanks very much. Never worry about sending me socks for some time ... *(rest of letter missing)*

GETTING SWEATY ON ROUTE MARCHES

Risborough Barracks Shorncliffe
June 3rd, 1916

Dear Mother –

I received your very welcome letter of May 16th yesterday and was very pleased to hear from you again and also to get Dora's letter. I don't know whether this letter will go on this weeks mail or not but if it doesn't you will have to forgive me for not writing sooner. We have been pretty busy this last week doing route marches and sometimes we go out at night. Well we are still in the same place here yet but we may move out at any time now. There is a story going around that we are going to be sent as a machine gun company to the 4th Division. Our officer inspected all of our equipment this morning and we were fitted out with anything that we required. We are having grand weather now, hasn't rained for a couple of weeks and sunshine every day. They have been giving us a route march nearly every day for the last week or so and we carry our full equipment. It certainly brings the sweat out when the day is very warm … *(rest of letter missing)*

LORD KITCHENER LOST

Risboro' Barracks
Shorncliffe
June 12th, 1916

Dear Mother –

Just a line to let you know I am in the best of health hoping that you are all the same. Well I am still in England yet but for how long I cannot say. Fifteen of the boys from this base left here last Friday for France and there are still about a hundred of us left that are now ready to go. I see the Canadians have been doing some pretty stiff fighting this last week. There were long pieces in to-days paper about the great fight they had made at Ypres. Well it looks as if things have begun to brighten up a little. The Russians have certainly made a great start if they only keep it up. We have been having some wet weather this last few days, rained nearly all day to-day but we were out for a route march this morning. The side roads that we marched on were pretty muddy but most of the roads here are paved.

I got a letter from Roy last week and he said that they were forming a great camp near Barrie this summer at a place called Angus Plains and they expected that they would have about forty thousand men there training. They certainly must have been getting some men last winter. He said they were pretty busy in the shop now making frames that were to be used at the new camp. I suppose Dad and Owen have finished their seeding and hoe crops by now. I hope the wet spring that you have had will not affect the outcome of the crops. Owen said that the fall wheat was looking good. The nights are pretty cold here, one night I thought there was quite a frost but I don't think that it effected the garden stuff any. Some of the potatoes I have seen were nearly out in blossom and cabbages and other garden stuff look to be about a months growth (ahead) to what they are in Canada at this time.

Wasn't that a corker about Lord Kitchener being lost. Nobody would believe it until they had seen a paper. They are having quite a time to determine on a man to take his place. I don't think that they will get anyone any better. I was wondering how George and Billie are making out. I wrote to Davey and got Bill's address but forgot to copy it off before I destroyed the letter. I don't think I told you that we are now living in the married quarters that the married men of the British army used to live in. There are fifty different houses all built together in two rows and there is an upstairs to each house. We had twelve men in the one I am in, seven sleeping upstairs and five down. Two of the fellows sleeping downstairs (left) so now there is only three of us. Well Mother I must close now so this will get tonights mail. Remember me to all. I now remain

Yours Lovingly,
Oscar

HEADING FOR FRANCE

Risboro' Barracks
Shorncliffe
Monday June 19th, 1916

Dear Mother –

Just a line in reply to your very welcome letter which I received a few days ago. I haven't very much time to-night but will try and scribble you a few lines. Well Mother I guess the next address I will have will be in France as I expect to leave to-night or early in the morning. There is a draft of over forty of us leaving. There are four of my old chums along with myself going to the 6th Brigade and the others are going to the 2nd, 3rd and 4th Brigades. We had no idea when we were going until yesterday just after church parade when we had a medical inspection to see if all were fit. We have been busy ever since getting our kit packed and fitted out and have been inspected by staff officers several times. Last week we had a course on the Lewis Machine gun for a few days but our draft was called before we were through. Anyway I like the Colt gun better than the Lewis ... *(rest of letter missing)*

STILL HEADING FOR FRANCE

6th Brigade
June 24th, 1916

Dear Mother –

Just a line this afternoon to let you know that I am quite well. I wrote you a letter a few days ago and said that I expected to leave for France the next morning but it happened that we did not get away but will be leaving to-morrow morning along with the draft of about three hundred and fifty infantrymen and forty machine gunners. We even moved from Risboro Barracks on Wednesday and have been staying in tents with the 30th Reserve Battalion until we leave. We have just been waiting with all our kit ready these last three or four days and have had no drill to do. There has been quite a lot of rain here this week but the mud has not been bad. Some of the farmers have already started haying around here. I suppose that is what everybody will be busy at around home when you get this letter.

Well I have had quite a stay in England now, nearly seven months and I am not sorry that we are going across the channel. Nearly all of the old 37th battalion boys are now in the trenches and I would like to have my turn. I got a letter from Tina the other day and also one from Roland Allin and yesterday I got a big package of newspapers from May. When you write again let me know if there has been any casualties of any of the boys from around home who are now in the trenches. We were confined to our barracks last night and to-day and we found it kind of tedious staying in. We were up to the quartermasters this morning and were issued with new rifles and bayonets. Well Mother I am sorry that I hadn't a chance to write a longer letter but will write as soon as possible again. I have now only ten minutes till lights out. Remember me to everybody. I now remain

Yours lovingly
Oscar
Will give you my address as soon as I find out what it is.

RAINING IN FRANCE

Somewhere in France
June 26th, 1916

Dear Mother –

Well Mother you see that I have reached France at last. I landed early this morning and had a nice little march up to our quarters. We are in tents for to-night and don't know when we will get a move from this camp. I had an uneventful voyage across the channel. We left Shorncliffe early on Sunday morning and did not get aboard our boat until four o'clock in the afternoon. It has been raining all day to-day so I am sticking to my tent tonight. I was up to the Y.M.C.A. for a short while and seen one of the boys that I drilled with in Barrie, he came over with the second draft of our battalion last summer. He had been back to the hospital few days with a slight shrapnel wound in the knee. He said that he had seen George Reynolds and several other of the boys who came over in our first draft.

I did not get this letter posted last night so will add a little now. I have been sent out to the training camp all day to-day and we just got back in time for supper. It rained all morning but it cleared up and the sun began to shine this afternoon. We are not allowed to leave the camp here without a pass so have not been down to any of the villages around here yet. We have quite a time trying to make the French shopkeepers understand when we want to buy anything. The country around here is more like Ontario than England was. Say Mother when

271

you write again I wish you would send me a handkerchief as I was unable to get mine out of the laundry when we left Shorncliffe. I will have to make this letter short now but will write again as soon as possible. Hoping that you are all well. I now remain

Yours lovingly
Oscar

HARRY IS ALL BROKEN-HEARTED

Somewhere in France
July 7th, 1916

Dear Mother –

Just a line to let you know that I received yours and Dora's very welcome letter dated June 5th and was very pleased to hear from home again. I only got it on last night's mail so you see it had been a month in coming over. Well I am getting along fine over here so far. I was sorry to hear of Joe Simpson being laid up. I got a letter from Tina when in England and she was telling me about him. I got a letter from Aunt Lizzie some time ago but have not answered it yet. Rhoda certainly must be having a hard time of it just getting over one sickness and getting into another. Tell her that I will try and get her letter answered some time. I haven't got any letters from the West for some time but got a large bundle of papers from May just before leaving England. She sent me a lot of Orillia papers and Elmvale Lances and a Western paper. Roy sends me papers every now and then and I certainly like to get them. The Waverley ball team certainly done well for their first game of the season to get that ten dollars. They must have had quite a time at the garden party.

I was certainly surprised to hear that Ethel Scarlet and Mr. Ardell were married. I suppose poor Harry is all broken-hearted now.

Well we are having some pretty fine weather here now and I hope it keeps up. Well I can't tell you anything more so will have to close. Hoping that you are all well I remain

With best of love
Oscar

THE 12TH OF JULY WALK

Somewhere in France
July 11th, 1916

Dear Mother –

I received your welcome letter of June 11th along with Aunt Goldie's a couple of days ago and was very pleased to hear from you again. I was sorry to hear that Rhoda has not improved any. I guess you wouldn't be sorry to get Aunt Goldie's help for a few days. Well I am still well and getting along alright out here so far. I suppose Goldie is with Owen and Jennie this summer again. Tell Dora to keep on writing to me if I don't write to her very often as I like to get her letters. I suppose that you will all be taking in the 12th of July walk this year. Write and let me know where they held it. I suppose Roy is getting plenty of work this summer at the planing mill. I suppose Annie will be with you for a visit sometime this summer. Well I can't give you any news here so I guess that you will have to do all the writing. Write again soon and let me know how you all are. I now remain

Yours with love
Oscar

BILLIE MISSING, GEORGE WOUNDED

Somewhere in France
July 19th, 1916

Dear Mother –

Just a line or so to let you know that I received your letter dated the 26th of June and was pleased to hear from you again. I was very sorry to hear about poor Rhoda, hope that she will get around again soon. You were telling me about Billie being missing. I do hope that he will turn up all right. One of the boys told me about him just after I came over and about George being wounded in the hand. I think I mentioned it in one of my letters to you. I got a long letter from Annie the other night but she did not mention going up home this summer. By her letter Silas must be having pretty good success with his well driller this summer. She said that he had got one flow at Newmarket at 300 feet.

Well I am getting along fine over here and am feeling fine. We have been having some grand weather this last few day but it is pretty cold at nights. I have just come in from watching a baseball match. I suppose the two Simcoe battalions will be training at the new Camp Borden this summer. I was glad to hear that Joe Simpson was some better. I guess Dad and Owen will be busy with the harvest when you get this letter. I was glad to hear that the crops were so fine. Who has Jim McFadden got to help him this summer? I guess labour is pretty scarce now after so many enlisting. I don't know whether you will be able to read this writing or not as I have a poor pencil. Must close now. Hoping to hear from you soon I remain

Yours lovingly
Oscar

ETHEL SCARLETT MARRIED THE SCHOOL TEACHER

Somewhere in France
July 30th 1916

Dear Mother –

Just a few lines to let you know that I am quite well and getting along first class. I haven't had any letter from you for two weeks now, so I have been wondering if some of my letters have gone astray. We have been having some very fine weather but lately it has been pretty warm but would rather have it that way than cold and wet. You said that you would write and let me know if you got any more word of Billie Quinlan. Let me know where Davey is too if you know. I guess they would be at Borden Camp. I haven't had any word from the West for some time now. I suppose everybody will be busy harvesting now. Did Aunt Annie find a buyer for the threshing mill. I haven't had any word of how Rhoda was getting along since your last letter. Hope that she will soon get better. I was certainly surprised to hear that Ethel Scarlett had married Ardell the schoolteacher. You said that he had come right through to France. What was he in that he could get right over here. I suppose Annie will be paying you a visit sometime this summer. The last word that I had from Roy he was very busy at the mill. Tell Dora not to forget and write whenever she can if I don't answer as often as I should. Did you and Dad take a holiday. Well Mother it is pretty hard for me writing letters over here so I will send field cards quite often. Hoping to hear from you soon I will now close.

Yours lovingly
Oscar

TOO BAD ABOUT BILLIE QUINLAN

Somewhere in France
August 8th, 1916

Dear Mother –

I received both of your letters dated the 13th and 17th of July a couple of nights ago and was very pleased to hear from you again. Thanks very much for the handkerchief that you sent me. I was also very glad to get Goldie's and Dora's letters. Well at present I am quite well and getting along first class. I got a letter from Roy last night and a couple of Annie about a week ago. She said that you sent her my address in France. Roy says that both work and wages are much better than what they had been. He said he would have liked to have gone out West during the harvest but could not get away very well. It has been two months or better since I have had any word from the West. That was certainly too bad about Billie Quinlan after he had come through safe out here for about a year. I have been trying to look up George whenever I get a chance but his battalion is generally in the line when we go out. We are having some splendid weather now, very warm in the day but the nights are rather cold. I like it much better here than I did the time we were in the training camps.

I got a letter from Davey Quinlan a few days ago and he said that he expected that his battalion to leave for England shortly.

Dora was saying in her letter that Joe McWatters and Frank Turl had had a scrap. I guess it would sure be some exhibition. Give Aunt

Annie my thanks for the handkerchiefs she is sending me. I will have to close now. Hoping you are all well I remain

Yours with love
Oscar

ALL TOO BUSY MAKING COIN

Somewhere in France
August 13th, 1916

Dear Sister –

(Probably Annie, who was married to Silas, mentioned in letter. Not Goldie or Dora who are also mentioned. Letter in envelope addressed to Mrs. Samuel French, his mother.)

I received your letters dated July 3rd and 16th both on the same day about a week ago and was very pleased to hear from you again. The one that you had addressed to England must have been delayed for quite a while over there. I have been having a couple of days rest lately with an inflamed corn. It swelled up so that I couldn't get my boot on so went down to the hospital and had it lanced. I am at the rest camp now until it gets better. We certainly are having some swell weather since I have been over here, sunshine nearly every day and just warm enough to be comfortable but gets rather damp and cold at nights. I got a couple of letters from home a few days ago and Mother was telling me about Billie Quinlan being killed. In the first report his mother received he was reported as missing. It certainly was too bad after he had been out here so long and came through alright. George Reynolds had a wound in the hand but did not get to England with it and is back with his battalion now.

Mother was telling me in her letter that there wasn't much hope of Rhoda lasting much longer as the doctor says that she has cancer in the stomach. She had gone down to Orillia with Aunt Sarah the last that I had heard of her. You didn't say anything in your letter about going up home for awhile this summer. It would be too bad if Ted and Elmer didn't get together for a few days play and a couple of scraps. Mother was saying that Alden had been staying with them for a few days. Has Erne sent you a picture of his wife yet? I hardly ever hear from him now, in fact I haven't had a letter from the West for about three months. I guess they are all too busy making coin to write to their poor relations. I was wondering if Erne would be coming down East this winter with his bride as he would have Verne there to look after the place. If he does come, I certainly would like to be home too. Well we are doing our best at present to get what is left of Belgium done up in the sandbags and are making pretty good headway. Silas must be having pretty good luck with his machine this summer. Three hundred feet is pretty deep to go for water, isn't it? I got a letter from both Goldie and Dora this week… *(rest of letter missing)*

SAM HUGHES WAS HERE

Somewhere in France
August 19th, 1916

Dear Mother –

I received your very welcome letter of July 31st a day or so ago and was very pleased to hear from you again. I haven't got the box yet that you posted on the same day but parcels are generally a week or so longer than letters in reaching us. I was very surprised and sorry to hear of Mr. Campbell's death. It certainly must have been an awful shock to the family as he dropped off so sudden.

Well, we are having a little spell of wet weather now but at present we are not up in the trenches to enjoy it. Yesterday Sam Hughes was here and inspected the 6th Brigade. The King was over here last week but I don't think he visited the Canadian front. I got a letter from Verne a day or so ago, the first I have had from him for a long time. He says the crops are pretty good out there this year, Well Mother I must hand this letter in now or it will not go to-day. Will write and let you know as soon as I receive the box. Hoping you are all well I remain

Yours with love
Oscar

FRENCH FARMERS GROW FINE CROPS

Somewhere in France
Sept. 1ˢᵗ, 1916

Dear Mother –

Just a line to let you know that I am quite well and getting along alright. I received the box you sent me and your letter dated August 5th on the same day about a week ago but have been so busy since that I didn't get a chance to write a letter. I certainly enjoyed the good things you sent me especially the fruit cake. Those shirts came in alright as we had turned in our undershirts and the top shirts are kind of rough. Well everything has been alright this last while. We have been having some pretty heavy rains lately, the first we have had of any account for two months. Most of the French farmers have their grain cut and in stooks now. They certainly grow some fine crops. At present we are quartered at a farm.

I suppose you have finished the harvest by now at home. Did Roy go West this fall. I had a letter from Verne and one from May a few days ago and Verne said that Roy was thinking of going out for a few months in the fall. I had a small parcel from Bessie Hodges a couple of weeks ago and a letter. She said that she would send me some newspapers but haven't received any yet. She hadn't been feeling well and had been home for a time. Is anyone running the threshing mill for Aunt Annie this fall or has she sold it. I suppose Elmer has started school again by now. Tell him to write me a letter some time when you do. I get letters from Annie quite often, sometimes one every week. Well Mother I can't write long letters over here so will close now. Hoping you are all well I remain.

Yours with love
Oscar

Thank Dora for the cigars and tell her that I will write as soon as possible.

THIS IS SURE SOME LIFE OVER HERE

Somewhere in France
Sept. 8th, 1916

Dear Dora:

I received yours and Goldie's letters to-day along with one from Laura and as it has been so long since I have written to you I will try and do so now. You were speaking of the very hot weather that you were having. Well it certainly is not unpleasantly warm over here to-day, just cold enough to make you want to hop around and keep on the move. I want to try and see George Reynolds to-day as I hear that the battalion he is in is quite near us. That certainly was too bad about Billie. One of the boys down at the base told me that he was killed when we landed in France but when I heard from home he was reported as missing. Have the battalions that Davey and Luke are in sailed for England yet. I had a letter from Davey just before they left Barrie for Camp Borden and he spoke as though they would be leaving soon but I see that they have had a months furlough since then. Is Stan Drinkill around Waverley this summer. I heard that he was working for Tudhope but I guess he would be helping his father through the harvest.

How long a visit did Annie have with you this summer. Laura said that she wanted her to go down with her when she went home but didn't think that she could get away. Well Dora this is sure some life over here but I like it better than in the training camps in England. I read Ardell's letter that was published in the *Lance* that Mother sent in the parcel. If you get any good magazines I wish you would send me some or some *Saturday Evening Posts*. Tell Mother and Goldie that I will write as soon as possible. I will have to close now but don't forget to write whenever you can. I remain.

Yours with love
Oscar

I guess you have some time making out the writing I do but can't write at all with lead pencil.

GEORGE WAS LOOKING FINE

Somewhere in France
Sept. 17th, 1916

Dear Mother –

Just a line or so to-night before I turn in to let you know that I am quite well hoping that you are all the same. At present we are out for a rest. On our last trip up we had quite an exciting time of it for awhile but most of our boys are back again alright. We are having swell weather at present. No rain and just warm enough to be comfortable. I had a letter from Erne the other night, the first I have heard from him in a long time. Did I tell you in my last letter that I had seen George Reynolds and some more of the boys from around Elmvale. George was looking fine. Have you done your threshing this fall yet. I heard that Alf Brown was running the threshing mill around there this fall. Did Roy go West for the harvest. Erne said in his letter that he had been wanting Dad to go out with him. Well Mother my paper is done so will have to close. Write whenever you can and give me all the news from home. I now remain

Yours lovingly
Oscar

OUT OF THE LINE
FOR A FEW DAYS REST

France, Sept. 23rd, 1916
6th Canadian M.G.Co.
Second Division C.E.F.

Dear Mother –

As I have nothing to do just now I will write a few lines in reply to your welcome letter of Sept. 1st which I received a few days ago. I got a letter from Annie and Aunt Annie to-day. Well the summer and good weather have about left us now and we have been getting quite a lot of rain lately although it has been very fine to-day. Our brigade has been out of the line for a few days rest. The last time we were in one of the boys who came with me to France from our old battalion was slightly wounded and is in the hospital now.

This summer seems to have gone very fast to me. It seems only a few days ago since I landed in France but it is just three months now. Xmas will be here before we know it. Owen said in his letter that Vern or some one from the West would be likely to come down sometime this fall or winter. Well Mother I will have to make this short now as it is too dark to see. Hoping you are all well I remain

Yours with love
Oscar

A YEAR SINCE MY LAST PASS HOME

France Oct. 6th, 1916

Dear Mother –

Just a few lines in reply to your welcome letter of Sept. 13th to let you know that I am quite well as yet. Our company has done another turn in the line and just now we are back in rest billets. We have been getting quite a lot of rain this last couple of weeks, rained most of the time the last time that we were in so wasn't very comfortable. We have been lucky this last while as regard to casualties. I got a letter from Annie and May to-night. May said that their crops had not filled out as good as last year but wheat was a better price. She had not been over to see Erne or Verne this summer, said that it was a long drive and it was pretty hard to get away in the summer months. Well I guess the best of our weather is over now. We hardly had any rain throughout July and August but have been getting more lately. Dora said in her letter that the battalion Davey Quinlan was in may not come over until spring. They are certainly having a long training since they joined. It is just about a year since I had my last pass home now. I think it was about the last of October when I was home last fall. I suppose Elmer is going to school now. Tell Aunt Annie that I got her letter all right and will write as soon as possible.

Well Mother I must close now. Write soon and let me know how you all are. I now remain

Yours with love
Oscar

SEND ME A PAIR OF LONG BOOTS

France Oct. 18ᵗʰ, 1916

Dear Mother –

Just a line or so this afternoon to let you know that I am quite well and getting along first rate. We are in the line again at present but it has been pretty quiet to–day. The weather has got quite a lot colder recently but we haven't been having much rain. To-day has just been like an October day in Canada, a little sun now and then but always cold enough for an overcoat. I suppose all the farmers around home will be very busy now with the root crop and the fall ploughing.

Say Mother I got a letter from Laura the other day and one from Tina and heard of the new arrival at Owens. I have been expecting a letter from home lately but it may come in to-nights mail as we got none last night. I suppose Owen will have his time occupied this winter. I suppose Goldie is still with Owen. Well it is not very far off Xmas now, time passes so very fast. Say Mother if it is not too much trouble and you get a chance to buy them would you send me a pair of long boots. I don't know what they will cost or what it will take to send them but whatever it is I will make it right. I guess Dad would pick me out a pair sometime when he is in Midland. Size eight would be best so that I can wear a couple of pair of socks and get them with good high legs. What kind of a fair did they have in Elmvale this fall. Laura said that Dora had been in for both days so I guess she will be able to tell me all about it. Tell Aunt Annie that I will write as soon as possible and was very pleased to get her letter. I must close now. I remain.

Yours lovingly
Oscar

A SNAPSHOT FROM WINNIE

France Oct. 31st, 1916

Dear Mother –

Just a few lines to-night to let you know I received your and Dora's welcome letters dated October 13th and was very pleased to hear from you again. We have been having some rainy and very uncomfortable weather this last week or so but we have to expect all that at this time of year. We had some quite frosty nights a couple of weeks ago, there was ice on the water lying around in holes, half an inch thick. We have a fine dug-out at present in which to sleep.

I was much surprised to get a letter from Winnie Hodges the other night, I guess Dora had sent her my address. She sent me a snap-shot of herself.

I suppose the boys from around home who are in the 157th battalion will be in England now. Tina said in her letter that the battalion Dave Quinlan is in would winter in Orillia.

Well Mother you will have to excuse my short letters as it is pretty hard to write long ones when everything from here is censored. I have not received the boots but I guess I will get them soon. Will close now. Hoping you are all well I remain

Yours lovingly
Oscar

REGULAR BATHS
AND A CHANGE OF UNDERWEAR

Machine Gun Coy.
6th Brigade Can. Inf.
B.E.F. France November 6th, 1916

Dear Mother –

I will try and write a few lines to-night as the time is going pretty slow. We are out of the line again and back in our billets for a short while. We have a pretty good place to stop in when we are out here. We are in an old house that has been fixed up and bunks put in and there is a couple of fireplaces, so we are able to have a fire when it is cold and wet. We have been issued with our winter clothes, got a leather jacket to-day and it is well lined so ought to be pretty warm. We are able to get a bath quite regular now and that is certainly a great help. Every time we get a bath we get a change of underwear, shirt, towel and socks. I got a bit lousy last summer, sleeping in so many different places but I have got rid of them now. I had a letter from Davey Quinlan last night and was surprised to hear he was in England. I supposed the battalion old Dave is in will be stopping in Canada over winter. Dave's battalion is at Willey Camp England which is only a short distance from Bramshott Camp. Davey was saying in his letter that he heard George Reynolds had been wounded. I haven't seen him since the middle of September and have not heard anything of him. If he was wounded I hope he got to England and is getting along alright. He has had a long time of it out here. A few of our boys have got passes to England this last month or so but I don't expect to get one this winter. Most of us have not drawn for leave yet so I will know better when we have.

Well I suppose when this letter reaches you the preparations for Xmas will be well under way. Dora was saying that you expected Erne and his wife or Verne would be down this winter. I had a big bundle of papers and magazines from May a short time ago. I have not got the ones that you sent me as yet but papers and parcels are generally much longer in coming than letters. I guess Owen and Dad will be busy with the fall ploughing now. I suppose by the price of wheat this fall Erne will soon be quitting farming and going to live the easy life. Well Mother I must close now and get to bed. Hoping you are all well I remain

Yours lovingly
Oscar

A LETTER FROM LITTLE BROTHER ELMER

France Nov 27th, 1916
Dear Mother –

Just a few lines in reply to your welcome letter dated November 8th which I received last night and was so pleased to hear from you again and to get Elmer's letter also. Well I am feeling first rate now myself hoping you are all the same. We had quite a heavy rain yesterday and getting around in the mud to-day is like trying to learn how to roller skate it is so slippery. I was out for rations to-night and coming in after dark I had two or three nice headers. The fellow who was with me thought that was great fun but I got the laugh back on him when he took a dive into a shell hole which was filled with water. I am writing this in my bunk and am a little cramped so you will have to excuse poor writing and make the best you can of it. I was glad to hear that the boots were on the road. I guess I will soon be getting them now. I am sorry if I put Dad or you too much trouble in getting them. I will write and let you know as soon as they come and how they fit. Thanks very much for the parcel you are sending, it certainly is a treat to get some good things from home. Has Owen had any more word from Bill Faragher. I had a letter from Davey Quinlan and Luke Adamson the other day and they were inquiring about him. I wrote to Bill soon after we came to England but have had no word from him so I guess my letter couldn't have reached him. Luke said that they expected to be over here before very long. I haven't had any word from George

Reynolds since I seen him more than two months ago but hope his wound is not serious and he is getting along alright.

How does Laura like living down in Elmvale. I must write to her as soon as I can. I suppose Roy and family will be with you for Xmas. I had a letter from Annie a few days ago. Well Mother I must close now. Hoping you are all well I remain

Yours lovingly
Oscar
On the back of one of the pages of this letter was a list:
Nov 27 Orders by Colonel Webb
1 tin milk
1 tin cherries
½ pound coffee 1 tin milk
1 box of oats
1 fr candles No. 9s
candies toffee
sugar 1 lb

A VISIT FROM BILL FARAGHER

France December 6th, 1916

Dear Mother –

I will now get busy and write you a few lines as it has been some time since I wrote my last letter but I have been handicapped by a sick spell this last few days and I am now doing time in the hospital. I caught a cold and I got so I couldn't eat so I am now on the shelf for awhile resting up. I am sorry not to be able to get out and get some little card or something to send you by Xmas time. I did not get the boots or parcel before I came here but they generally take two or three weeks longer in coming than a letter. A day or so before I came to the hospital Billy Faragher dropped in on me and I sure was surprised to see him. He is in the 20th Battalion. Bill said that he wrote to me several times when I was in England but I didn't get one of his letters. I guess my address changed so many times over there that some of my mail went astray. Bill is just as tall as I am now but neither of us seem to get much fatter. *(Rest of letter missing.)*

A FINE PAIR OF SOCKS

France Dec. 13th, 1916

Dear Mother –

Just a few lines to-night to let you know that I am all OK again and am back to my company again after my little stay in the hospital. I received your very welcome letter dated Nov. 27th to-night and was very pleased to hear from you again. I also had a letter from Dora and received a parcel from Tina and Aunt Lizzie to-night. The parcel was sent a few days before you sent my boots so I guess that they will be along soon now. It generally takes a parcel about two or three weeks longer than a letter in coming. Well I suppose that you will be getting winter in proper style over there now. We haven't been having very much cold weather yet but have been getting lots of rain and that means lots of mud. I got a fine pair of socks in the parcel Tena sent me and with the ones that you sent will be pretty well fixed. I suppose Roy and family will be down with you for Xmas. Dora did not say in her letter if Annie was going up for Xmas or not. I suppose the skating rink will be in full swing now. I guess Mrs. Parker and Dave Quinlan will be greatly missed there this winter.

   (Rest of letter missing.)

LAID UP WITH THE FLU

The following letter was mailed in an envelope marked on the front "On Active Service". A note printed on the envelope read: *"Correspondence in this envelope need not be censored Regimentally. The Contents are liable to examination at the Base. The following Certificate must be signed by the writer: I certify on my honour that the contents of this envelope refer to nothing but private and family matters. Signature: Oscar French"*

France December 19th, 1916

Dear Dora:

I got your letter dated Nov. 15th the other night and was very pleased to hear from you again. Well how did you enjoy your visit down with Annie. Pretty good I guess but I guess you were not sorry to get back home again unless you made a mash on one of them Thornhill boys. How is times around Waverley this winter. There can't be very many young fellows left around there now. I got the parcel mother sent the other night and enjoyed the cake and other things fine. The boots haven't came yet but I guess that they have been delayed some place. I had four or five days in the hospital with influenza and came back a week ago. I felt pretty tough for a couple of days but I was glad to get back again. I got a letter from Winnie a couple of weeks ago, she sure is a great kid. I suppose Goldie is staying with Owen and Jennie yet, she wrote me a letter and told me about the day they went down to Camp Borden.

What kind of a time did you have this Xmas? That seems a funny question as Xmas has not come yet but I guess it will be well over when this reaches you. Was Roy and the family down this year. Mother said in her letter that she did not expect anyone from the West home this year. I'll bet that you are having winter in the good old style now. We haven't had any weather to say real cold yet, get a little frost now and then. Well Dora I will have to make this short. Don't forget to write soon and give me all the news. With love to all I remain

Your loving brother,
Oscar

BLOWING LIKE CATS AND DOGS

France Dec. 23rd, 1916

Dear Mother –

I received your welcome letter dated December 5th this morning and was very pleased to hear from you again and that you were all well. I also got a letter from each (of) Annie and May. I got the parcel you sent me about a week ago and it certainly went fine. I enjoyed the cake immensely. I don't know what has become of the boots as they have not arrived yet but probably they have been delayed some place, it is strange how we get some parcels so promptly and others take so long. We are getting all kinds of weather now, some days it rains and the next it snows and to-day it is blowing like cats and dogs with a little rain mixed in now and then. Well Christmas will be in a couple of days and I guess I will be back in billets then. We have pretty good billets just now and are quite handy to a good bath house where we get a change of clothing quite often. That certainly helps a lot. Last summer we had quite a time with "the soldiers pets" as we often had to go so long without a bath or a change of clothes.

I was amused when I read May's letter. She was telling me about the latest from over at Erne's and she heard that it was twins but didn't believe it. She was saying that there was quite a few little nephews of mine that I have never seen. Erne will be having some time now that he is a daddy and all the trouble he will have trying to run that Ford. By what I hear prices of all foodstuffs in Canada are nearly double to what they were before the war. May said in her letter that wheat was nearly two dollars a bushel in Winnipeg and Annie said that they had paid as high as $1.90 a bag for potatoes and 25¢ a pound for lard. Farmers ought to be enjoying prosperity but I suppose with wages for hired help so high it will take a lot of their profits.

I suppose you are now having winter in the good old style and all the young people around Waverley will be busy skating again. I suppose they have some sort of a rink. I think Dora said that Ike was going to run one. I was glad to hear that George Reynolds's wounds were not serious and that he is all better again. I had a letter from Billie Johnston yesterday and he is over here now in the first battalion. He didn't say whether any more of the boys from around home were out here yet. I must close now. With best love and wishes to all I now remain

Your loving son
Oscar

FINALLY GOT THE BOOTS FROM HOME

France Dec. 31st, 1916

Dear Mother –

Just a few lines to-night to let you know that I am quite well and hope that you are all the same. Well I received the boots a couple of days ago and like them fine, have been wearing them these last few days and they are just the rig for the mud. I can wear a couple of pair of socks in them quite comfortably and will get a pair of in-soles the first chance I get. I have been faring pretty well these last few days. I got the boots and a parcel from May and Annie the same night and last night I got a parcel from Roy so you see that I certainly have not been forgotten. Roy sent me an air pillow that I can blow up and sleep on at night and pack away in my pack during the day, it is just the rig out here. May sent me one of the parcels that Eaton's packs up and it had a lot of useful little articles in it. Annie sent me a fine little cake and I enjoyed it fine. Say Mother you asked me in your letter if I would like any more Oxo cubes. Never mind sending any more as I only use it sometimes when we are in the trenches and I have what you sent me and a box from May.

Well we had our Xmas dinner the day before yesterday and fared pretty well. We have been having some pretty heavy rains this last few days I suppose that is quite different from the weather that you will be having now. What is Owen doing to exercise his horses this winter. I suppose that there is no bush work now. Is Dad keeping a horse out home now. Well Mother I must close for this time. Hoping you are all well I remain.

Your loving son
Oscar.

SANTA CLAUS GOT AROUND THE TRENCHES

France Jan. 11th, 1917

Dear Mother –

Just a few lines to-night to let you know that I am quite well and am getting along first class. I received your letter dated December 18th the other night and was so very pleased to hear from you again. I hope that you and Dad are not suffering from the cold weather this winter but I suppose the severest part of that is to come. Maybe you will be taking that long talked of trip out West next spring, it certainly would be fine for you and Dad both to go. Well I am doing another turn in the trenches at present but may go out soon. The weather has been rather rotten just lately but I am getting now so it is a great disappointment to me if it doesn't rain at least once a day. Well I suppose you all by now have recovered from the Xmas festivities. Tell Elmer that Santa Claus got around the trenches this year as well as at home, we got Xmas stockings filled up with stuff. I think they were sent over by the Daughters of the Empire. Holidays come rather fast for me at this time of year, Xmas, my birthday and New Years all in the same week. I am going to try and send get some pictures of myself some of these days. I think there is a place near here where they take small snap shots. I wonder if you would know me when we get all rigged out in goatskin coat, equipment and steel helmet. It certainly will seem funny to me again when we get back and start wearing civvies after being in uniform so long. I have been in khaki just about two years now. The time has gone fast especially since coming to France. I had a small parcel the other day from Bessie Hodges and a short letter, the first that I have heard from her for a long time. She has left Southampton now and is staying at home. I certainly will be disappointed if I do not get leave to go and see them before going back to Canada. In her letter Winnie said that Ed Norton tried to look them up but for some reason did not get to the right place. Roy is sending me the *Free Press* for the coming year and it is so good to get a home paper out here. I got one to-night. There was a letter in it written by Captain Finlayson from Bramshott Camp and a list of the names of the boys of "D" Company, 157th battalion.

I haven't had a line from Owen now for a long time and I wonder if you couldn't jog his memory and see whether he or I wrote last but I suppose he has all he can do this winter. Well Mother this must do for this time. Hoping that you are all well and with best love to all I remain.

Your loving son
Oscar

REAL CANADIAN WINTER WEATHER

France, January 21ˢᵗ, 1916 *(The envelope was postmarked 1917, so Uncle Oscar seems to have forgotten that the year had changed.)*

Dear Mother –

I received your welcome letter dated Dec. 26ᵗʰ a few days ago and was very pleased to hear from you again also to get Goldie's letter. That was strange that you got no letter from me for two weeks as I think I write at least once a week but I suppose that a letter goes astray some time(s), We have been having some real Canadian winter weather these last few days, the ground is covered with snow now and it is quite cold. We are having a few days rest out of the trenches just at present and we are pretty well off as regards our billets. I came across one of the Tennant boys that used to live around Waverley, he came over in the same battalion that Luke was in and is in the same battalion as Bill Johnson out here. I tried to find Bill but didn't see him.

When you write again put my address #408445 Pte. O. French 6th Canadian Machine Gun Company B.E.F. France. I had a letter from Verne to-day, he said that they were having some real cold weather now. He expected to go out to Empress for his Xmas dinner. That was certainly too bad about Mrs. Biddome. Well Mother you will have to wait for longer letters until after the war but I will write soon again. Hoping you are all well I remain

Yours Lovingly
Oscar

IN HOSPITAL WITH BRONCHITIS

France Mar. 10th, 1916 (1917)

Dear Mother –

I am very much afraid that you will be thinking that I am getting very neglectful as regards writing as it has been some time since I wrote last but I have been feeling rather tough this last week or so. I was admitted into the field hospital nearly two weeks ago with bronchitis but expect to be out soon now. There was three or four days that I was feeling pretty blue but I am just about all O.K. again now. The weather is much warmer now that when I wrote last and is shaping around something like spring. Of course we get a daily shower of rain or several showers with a little snow mixed in once in awhile but I am quite naturalized to that sort of stuff now. I guess when this letter reaches you that the snow will be all gone over there for another year.

I haven't had any mail since coming to the hospital so expect that there will be quite a lot for me when I get back to my company. I guess that I will get your parcel when I get back also. I got the one that the Waverley Patriotic League sent me and it sure was fine. I got another one from Laura about this same night filled up with everything good. Well Mother I guess I will have to close now. I suppose Elmer will soon be getting a few holidays now. It won't be long before spring work on the land will begin. With kind love to all I remain

Your loving son
Oscar

XMAS CAKE WAS CERTAINLY GOOD

France Mar. 20th, 1916

Dear Mother –

I will write a few lines to-night and let you know that I am all O.K. again and back with the company. I had a few days in the rest camp after I came out of hospital. The day that I got back I received your very welcome parcel and enjoyed the eats fine. The apples had kept first class and that piece of your Xmas cake was certainly good. A little bit of good stuff like that sure goes good out here. Those socks that you sent will come in quite useful as we are getting quite enough rain and mud to satisfy us just at present. However it will not be very long now before summer is here and we will be getting some fine weather. I don't know what is the matter with the mail coming from Canada now as I haven't had a letter from you for over a month and have only had your parcel and a letter from Verne and Tina since before I went to the hospital and that is a month ago. Most of the boys are saying that they haven't been getting any so I guess some of these fine days we will be getting a bunch of it.

I suppose that Dad and Owen will soon be working on the land again now. The winter wheat over here is up fine and green now. I guess hired help will be harder than ever to get this summer. Well Mother I guess I will have to close now. Hoping to hear from you soon I remain.

Your loving son
Oscar

MAIL HAS BEEN VERY IRREGULAR

France March 29th, 1917
(Rec. Toronto April 27)

Dear Mother –

Just a few lines in reply to your very welcome letter dated Feb. 10th which I received a few days ago and was very pleased to hear from you again and also to get Dora's letter. Mail has been very irregular in coming lately. I don't know whether you are getting my mail regularly or not, hope so anyway. Lately we have been having some pretty good weather but it has been raining the greater part of to-day. I will not be sorry when the dry weather comes. We have just got our rations and the mail in for to-day. I got a letter from Owen written on March 8th. Prices for most food stuffs seems to be very high, he said that he had sold some of his potatoes for three dollars per bag and at one time they were four and a half to five dollars in Toronto. I was very sorry to hear that May had been laid up with rheumatism. I hope that she is fully better by now. Well I will have to close for this time. Tell Dora that I will answer her letter as soon as possible. Hoping that you are all well I remain

Your loving son
Oscar

I AM QUITE WELL,
HOPING YOU ARE ALL THE SAME

France April 8th, 1917

Dear Mother –

Just a few lines to-day to let you know that I am quite well, hoping that you are all the same. I received the parcel containing the socks and under clothing and was very pleased to get them. Give my best thanks to Miss Scarlett for the socks. That cake you sent had kept fine and moist and so did the ginger cakes. I guess it was too warm for the apples as they were about half rotten but I was very glad to get them at that. We are having a swell day here to-day, the sun is shining and it is warm as summer. It is certainly a very welcome change after having so much rain and mud. I guess that you will not be sorry that spring has come again after the cold winter that you have had.

I suppose that the soldiers who are in Canada this spring will be getting a month or so on furlough while the seeding lasts. I guess that hired help will be scarcer than ever this summer.

Well Mother I am in rather a poor place for writing now but will write soon again. With best love to all I remain

Your loving son
Oscar

Private Oscar French never wrote his mother another letter. He was killed at Vimy Ridge the next day, April 9, 1917. This letter was postmarked as received at Waverley on April 28, 1917, 19 days after his death.

Memorial Book, page 240, showing Oscar's name. *The First World War Book of Remembrance* **is located in the Peace Tower on Parliament Hill.**

IN MEMORIAM

· PTE. OSCAR FRENCH

6TH BRIGADE, MACHINE GUN SECTION, C.E.F., FRANCE

KILLED IN ACTION
ON APRIL 9TH, 1917
AGED 20 YEARS, 3 MONTHS AND 10 DAYS

**An In Memoriam card, front and back, found in a family photo album.
French family archives**

Oscar French kept in touch with his numerous sisters and brothers, as well as his mother. In the summer of 1915, he sent his brother Verne a postcard at his home near Holbeck, Saskatchewan. This the text. The postmark appears to read Field Post Office No. 1, Niagara, 1915

August 2. The date is not clear, but Oscar was at Niagara-on-the-Lake through the summer and fall of 1915. The postcard was discovered in a family album. The postcard picture portrays Oscar in full uniform. It appears to be a studio shot.

"Dear Bro –

"Just a card to let you know I am getting along O.K. I am still at Niagara and expect to be here another month at least. Haven't been up home since the first of July but expect to go soon. Will write a letter soon. Your bro, Oscar."

BIBLIOGRAPHY: LETTERS TO VIMY

Atlas of the European Conflict; Rand McNally & Company, Chicago, 1914

Barris, Ted; *Victory at Vimy*, Thomas Allen Publishers, Toronto, 2007

Barton, Peter with Banning, Jeremy; *Vimy Ridge and Arras,* Dundurn Press, Toronto, 2010

Climo, Percy L.; *Let Us Remember, Lively Letters from World War One*, self-published, Cobourg, Ontario, 1990

Dancocks, Daniel; *Gallant Canadians, The Story of the Tenth Canadian Infantry Battalion 1914-1919*, Calgary Highlanders Regimental Funds Foundation, Calgary, 1990

Dawson, L.; *A History of Canadian Forces Postal Services*, self-published, 1992

Dyer, Gwynne; *Canada in the Great Power Game*, Random House Canada, Toronto, 2014

Evans, Martin Marix; *Victory on the Western Front*, Arcturus Publishing Limited, London, 2013

First World War Centenary Edition, Legion Magazine, Kanata, Ontario

Forty, Simon; *Mapping the First World War – Battlefields of the Great Conflict from Above*, Anova Books Ltd., London, 2013

Goodspeed, Lt.-Col. D.J., editor; *The Armed Forces of Canada 1867-1967*, Queen's Printer, Ottawa, 1967

Granatstein, J.L. and Morton, Desmond; *Marching to Armageddon*, Lester & Orpen Dennys Limited, Toronto, 1989

Granatstein, J.L.; *The Greatest Victory*, Oxford University Press, Don Mills, Canada, 2014

Hannon, Leslie F.; *Canada at War*, The Canadian Illustrated Library, McClelland and Stewart Limited, Toronto, 1968

Hunt, C.W., *Dancing in the Sky*, Dundurn Press, 2009

Hunter, Andrew E.; *A History of Simcoe County*, Simcoe County Council, 1909, reprinted by Mackinaw Productions, Oshawa, 1998

Macdonald, Lyn; *They Called It Passchendaele*, Penguin Books, 1978

Macfarlane, David; *The Danger Tree: War and the Search for a Family's Past*, Macfarlane, Walter & Ross, 1991

O'Shea, Stephen; *Back to the Front*, Douglas and McIntyre, Vancouver/Toronto, 1996

Our Canada, Wartime Memories from the Great War to Modern Times, October/November 2014, The Reader's Digest Magazines, Montreal, QC

Scott, Canon Frederick G.; *The Great War as I Saw It*, CEF Books, Ottawa, 1999, first published 1922

Shaw, Susan Evans; *Canadians at War – A Guide to Battlefields of World War I*, Goose Lane Editions, Fredericton, New Brunswick, 2011

Sheffield, Gary; *The First World War in 100 Objects*, Sevenoaks, a division of the Carlton Publishing Group, London, England, 2013

The Ontario Readers Fourth Book, authorized by The Minister of Education for Ontario, The T. Eaton Co. Limited, Toronto, 1925

The War Graves of the British Empire, Thelus Military Cemetery, Nine Elms Military Cemetery, Thelus, France; compiled and published by order of the Imperial War Graves Commission, London, 1928

Vance, Col. Donald J.; *Remembering the Men of North Hastings Killed in the Great War*, Wallbridge House Publishing, Belleville, Ontario, 2007

Vance, Col. Donald J.; *The Dead of the 75th Battalion*, Wallbridge House Publishing, Belleville, Ontario, 2004

Also numerous sources from the Internet

INDEX

Montreal Canadiens, 63, 64

moving pictures, 215, 225

Mrs. Samuel French, V, 11, 211, 281

N

Nancy, 60

National Hockey Association, 63

National Hockey League, 63, 65

Nellie McClung, 108, 111

New Democratic Party, 111

New Zealand, 48, 133, 147, 148, 184

New Zealand Tunnelling Company, 147

Newsy Lalonde, 65

Niagara Camp, 4, 5, 33, 221, 223

Niagara Military Camp, 26, 29, 34, 217

Niagara-on-the-Lake, 8, 21, 186, 215, 313

Nicholas II, 49, 55

Nine Elms Military Cemetery, IV, 9, 144, 160, 161, 162, 163, 165, 166, 169, 170, 177, 317

Nottawasaga River, 60

November 11, 141, 142, 143, 178, 179, 183

O

O God, Our Help in Ages Past, IV, 165

O. French, 8, 164, 170, 214, 238, 250, 256, 261, 263, 306

Oliver Grigg, 63

one dollar a day, 29

Ontario, 4, 6, 8, 9, 11, 19, 23, 39, 41, 48, 54, 58, 59, 63, 73, 87, 95, 97, 98, 133, 169, 175, 178, 182, 188, 191, 192, 193, 196, 197, 211, 218, 271, 315, 317

Orangemen, 41

Orland Clare, 11, 99

Orland French, 1, 4, 6, 8, 10, 12, 14, 18, 20, 22, 24, 28, 30, 32, 36, 40, 42, 44, 46, 48, 50, 52, 54, 56, 58, 60, 64, 68, 72, 76, 80, 82, 88, 90, 92, 94, 96, 98, 100, 102, 104, 106, 110, 113, 114, 116, 118, 120, 122, 124, 126, 128, 130, 132, 134, 136, 138, 140, 142, 148, 150, 152, 154, 158, 162, 163, 164, 166, 167, 168, 170, 172, 174, 176, 180, 182, 190, 192, 193, 196, 204, 211, 216, 218, 222, 224, 226, 228, 230, 232, 234, 236, 238, 240, 246, 250, 254, 256, 258, 270, 272, 274, 278, 280, 282,

294, 296, 300, 302, 312, 316

Orr Lake, 18, 19, 61, 73

Oscar, 1, 4, 5, 6, 7, 8, 9, 10, 11, 12, 16, 17, 21, 26, 29, 34, 41, 46, 47, 48, 57, 58, 61, 62, 66, 70, 74, 79, 84, 86, 91, 93, 99, 101, 108, 112, 117, 123, 125, 127, 128, 129, 136, 141, 144, 146, 149, 154, 156, 161, 162, 163, 164, 167, 168, 169, 170, 171, 172,175, 178, 184, 186, 187, 188, 190, 192, 193, 194, 195, 196, 197, 206, 208, 211, 213, 214, 216, 218, 219, 222, 224, 226, 228, 230, 232, 234, 238, 241, 243, 246, 248, 250, 252, 254, 256, 261, 263, 267, 270, 272, 274, 275, 276, 278, 280, 283, 285, 287, 288, 289, 290, 291, 292, 294, 296, 299, 300, 302, 303, 305, 306, 307, 308, 309, 310, 311, 312, 313

Oscar French, 1, 4, 6, 7, 12, 16, 46, 58, 128, 154, 161, 163, 170, 172, 184, 188, 192, 193, 194, 196, 211, 213, 299, 311, 312

Ottawa, 23, 63, 72, 76, 99, 110, 160, 176, 181, 182, 186, 194, 195, 196, 316

Ottomans, 55

outdoor rinks, 63

Owen, 13, 93, 95, 96, 117, 122, 123, 137, 215, 216, 221, 226, 238, 247, 250, 256, 258, 261, 263, 266, 267, 275, 276, 289, 291, 294, 295, 299, 303, 305, 308, 309

P

Parry Sound, 38, 219, 229

Passchendaele, 112, 113, 154, 316

Patricia Chernesky, V, 151, 161, 163, 164, 165, 171

Patricia Louise, 99

Patriotic Ladies of Waverley, 6

paymaster, 222

Pearl Harbour, 28

Penetanguishene Road, 23, 60

Plymouth, 17, 94, 236, 240

poppy, 164, 179, 180

Pretoria, 23, 24, 25

Prince Edward, III

Princess Patricia's Canadian Light Infantry, 3

Prussia, 50, 51

Pte. Oscar French, V, VII, 3, 161, 163, 170, 192, 193, 194, 197, 211, 213,

Simcoe County, XVI, 8, 18, 19, 60, 87, 111, 316

Simcoe Foresters, 84

Sir James Yeo, 58, 59

Sir Wilfrid Laurier, 23, 59

somewhere in France, 9, 70, 78, 91, 93, 101, 124, 187, 271, 273, 275, 276, 277, 279, 281, 283, 284, 286, 288,

songs patriotic, 66

South Africa, 23, 24, 25, 86

Spring Offensive, 142

Stanley Cup, 64

Statute of Westminster, 25

Stephen Harper, 130

Susan Evans Shaw, VI

Sylvia, V, 97, 145, 152, 154, 158, 163, 164, 166, 167, 168, 171

Sylvia French, 152, 154, 158, \ 163, 164, 166, 167, 171

T

The Globe and Mail, III, 72, 73, 97, 99,

The Great War, 11, 26, 34, 96, 118, 121, 149, 190, 204, 316, 317

The Maple Leaf Forever, 45

The Royal North-West Mounted Police, 82

Thelus, 9, 146, 154, 160, 200, 201, 317

The Ottawa Citizen, III, 72, 99

Thomas, 17, 93, 119, 190, 315

Toronto, 16, 19, 34, 38, 41, 57, 59, 63, 64, 65, 70, 72, 73, 98, 127, 131, 138, 203, 214, 217, 220, 224, 225, 227, 229, 231, 233, 239, 242, 246, 256, 309, 315, 316, 317

Toronto Maple Leafs, 64, 65

Toronto Star, 57, 72, 73

Tower of London, 47, 106, 239, 240

Treaty of Versailles, 142

Trenton, 175, 176, 177, 182

Triple Alliance, 48

Triple Entente, 48

Turkey, 56, 74, 75, 77

U

U-boats, 27, 28, 123, 130, 133

Union Jack, 42, 43, 44

Union of Soviet Socialist Republics, 55

United Church, 20, 169, 192

United States, 26, 27, 59, 63, 67, 68, 180, 218

X